Russia, America and the Cold War, 1949–1991

SEMINAR STUDIES   IN HISTORY

Russia, America and the Cold War, 1949–1991

Second edition

MARTIN McCAULEY

PEARSON
Longman

Harlow, England • London • New York • Boston • San Francisco • Toronto
Sydney • Tokyo • Singapore • Hong Kong • Seoul • Taipei • New Delhi
Cape Town • Madrid • Mexico City • Amsterdam • Munich • Paris • Milan

PEARSON EDUCATION LIMITED

Edinburgh Gate
Harlow CM20 2JE
United Kingdom
Tel: +44 (0)1279 623623
Fax: +44 (0)1279 431059
Website: www.pearsoned.co.uk

First edition published in Great Britain in 2004

© Pearson Education Limited 2004

The right of Martin McCauley to be identified as author
of this work has been asserted by him in accordance
with the Copyright, Designs and Patents Act 1988.

ISBN 0 582 78482 4

British Library Cataloguing in Publication Data
A CIP catalogue record for this book can be obtained from the British Library

Library of Congress Cataloging in Publication Data
A CIP catalog record for this book can be obtained from the Library of Congress

10 9 8 7 6 5 4 3 2 1
08 07 06 05 04

Set by 35 in 10/12.5 Sabon Roman
Printed in Malaysia

The Publisher's policy is to use paper manufactured from sustainable forests.

CONTENTS

Introduction to the series   viii
Acknowledgements   ix
Foreword to the second edition   x
Maps   xi
Chronology   xiii

PART ONE: CONTEXT   1

1. INTRODUCTION: THE PROBLEM   3
     Ideas and Beliefs   5
     Security   11
     Culture   17

2. THE COLD WAR IN PERSPECTIVE   23
     Cold War I   24
     Brinkmanship   25
     Détente   26
     Cold War II and the end of the Cold War   27
     Characteristics of the Cold War   28

PART TWO: ANALYSIS   33

3. COLD WAR I: 1949–1953   35
     The Berlin blockade   35
     China   36
     NSC-68   38
     The war in Korea   39

4. TO THE BRINK AND BACK: 1953–1969   43
     The search for a new relationship   43
     Khrushchev takes over   44
     The Geneva summit   46
     The Hungarian Revolution   47
     Asia   47
     The Middle East   49
     Other Third World states   51
     Brinkmanship: Berlin   52
     Brinkmanship: Cuba   56
     The war in Vietnam   58

5.   DÉTENTE: 1969–1979   60
     Forging a new relationship   60
     A new president and a new approach   61
     China changes sides: rapprochement with America   62
     SALT   63
     The German problem defused   64
     The Middle East   64
     The agenda changes as Ford takes over   66
     Africa   67
     The Helsinki Accord   69
     A new president sows confusion   70
     Carter and Brezhnev reach agreement on SALT II but on little else   72

6.   COLD WAR II: 1979–1985   73
     Détente fails to satisfy American aspirations   73
     Carter's mixed record   74
     Disastrous decision making in Moscow: intervention in Afghanistan   75
     Carter, Brzezinski and Cold War II   76
     A new president and a new departure   76
     Andropov and Reagan: missed opportunities   78
     Failure and success for America   80
     The ground is prepared for better relations with Russia   80
     Reagan improves relations with China   81

7.   NEW POLITICAL THINKING AND THE END OF
     THE COLD WAR: 1985–1991   82
     The new political thinking   82
     The Gorbachev–Reagan summits   83
     The Bush–Gorbachev relationship is slow to develop   88
     Gorbachev and Europe: our common home   90
     Germany unites   91
     Gorbachev and eastern Europe   93
     Gorbachev and China   94
     Gorbachev's domestic difficulties cause problems for Bush   94
     The Gulf War leads to joint superpower policy   96
     Gorbachev's problems mount   97
     The last summit   99
     The attempted coup and after   100

     PART THREE: ASSESSMENT   103

8.   THE JUDGEMENT   105
     Introduction   105
     Sources of hostility between the superpowers   109
     Why did America come to guarantee west European security?   110
     Why did Russia and America gradually become systemic rivals?   112
     A hard lesson for the superpowers: empires are liabilities   114
     Is there a link between good government and economic prosperity?   114
     Was the growth of nuclear arsenals inevitable?   116

Why did the Cold War end?   116
America's changing doctrine   117
Was the USA an imperialist power?   118

PART FOUR: DOCUMENTS   119

Glossary   149
Who's Who   162
References and further reading   178
Index   183

INTRODUCTION TO THE SERIES

Such is the pace of historical enquiry in the modern world that there is an ever-widening gap between the specialist article or monograph, incorporating the results of current research, and general surveys, which inevitably become out of date. *Seminar Studies in History* are designed to bridge this gap. The series was founded by Patrick Richardson in 1966 and his aim was to cover major themes in British, European and world history. Between 1980 and 1996 Roger Lockyer continued his work, before handing the editorship over to Clive Emsley and Gordon Martel. Clive Emsley is Professor of History at the Open University, while Gordon Martel is Professor of History at the University of Northern British Columbia, Canada, and Senior Research Fellow at De Montfort University.

All the books are written by experts in their field who are not only familiar with the latest research but have often contributed to it. They are frequently revised, in order to take account of new information and interpretations. They provide a selection of documents to illustrate major themes and provoke discussion, and also a guide to further reading. The aim of *Seminar Studies in History* is to clarify complex issues without over-simplifying them, and to stimulate readers into deepening their knowledge and understanding of major themes and topics.

ACKNOWLEDGEMENTS

We are grateful to the following for permission to reproduce copyright material:

Akademie Verlag GmbH for extracts from *Jahrbuch fur Historische Kommunismusforschung* by Dashichev; Vladimir Bukovsky for extracts from *Judgement in Moscow* by Vladimir Bukovsky © Vladimir Bukovsky; Faber and Faber Ltd and International Creative Management for extracts from *Kennedy v Khrushchev The Crisis Years 1960–1963* by Michel Beschloss; Regnery Publishing Inc for extracts from *Judgement in Moscow* by Vladimir Bukovsky © 1995 Henry Regnery Publishing Inc. All rights reserved; Transworld Publishers and Doubleday, divisions of The Random House Group Limited and The Random House Group Inc for extracts adapted from *Mikhail Gorbachev: Memoirs* by Mikhail Gorbachev published by Doubleday © 1995 Mikhail Gorbachev, English translation © Wolf Jobst Siedler Verlag GmbH, Berlin; Weidenfeld & Nicolson and International Creative Management for extracts from *The White House Years* by Henry Kissinger.

In some instances we have been unable to trace the owners of copyright material, and we would appreciate any information that would enable us to do so.

FOREWORD TO THE SECOND EDITION

Communism was the great challenge to America and its allies in the second half of the twentieth century; terrorism is the challenge of the twenty-first. Communism, represented by the Soviet Union, China, eastern Europe and a host of Third World states, was easily comprehensible. Its ideas and ideals could be traced back to the European Enlightenment in the eighteenth century. It was a secular religion and its goal the kingdom of heaven on earth. Terrorism, by way of contrast, especially the suicide bombers who prefer death to life, is almost incomprehensible. It presents a great intellectual challenge, probably a greater intellectual challenge than the ideas and goals of communism. This book pays more attention to the ideas and beliefs or ideology of Marxism. On reflection, it is clear that the *thinking* of the rulers of the Kremlin was informed by the tenets of Marxism but their actions were those of traditional Russian politicians engaged in expanding their country's influence and security. The role of security is of great significance to a country like Russia, invaded three times by a European power in just over a century: in 1812 by Napoleon; in 1914 by the German kaiser; and in 1941 by Adolf Hitler. Present-day America's sense of insecurity was only in the mind. Its geographical location had ensured that it had never known invasion and occupation. Culture is also a significant factor in international behaviour. One can see Russia's attitude and actions as a continuation of its imperial tradition. Blessed (or cursed) with few natural frontiers, Russia was always on the move. So was America until the French and Spanish had been vanquished. Both America and Russia were universalist powers, believing that they possessed social systems that would benefit from world exposure. The collapse of Russia has left one superpower, America, which now, inebriated with the wine of victory, is more convinced than ever that its society is the model for the rest of the world.

Note: Throughout this book, America and the United States are used interchangeably, as are Russia and the Soviet Union. The country now known as Russia or the Russian Federation is referred to as the Russian Federation in this text. Notation in square brackets (e.g. [*Doc. 5*]) refers readers to the corresponding document in Part Four of the book.

Martin McCauley
May 2003

Territory annexed by USSR
1939-40 and reincorporated
in USSR in 1945

Former German and
Czechoslovak territory annexed
by USSR in 1945

States in which Communist
regimes came to power
between 1945 and 1948

The 'Iron Curtain' in 1955

FINLAND

Vyborg

Jallion

Leningrad

SWEDEN

0   500 mls
0   300 km

ESTONIA

Riga   LATVIA

LITHUANIA

Konigsberg   Kaunas

Vilnius

Minsk

SOVIET

UNION

Stettin

GDR
Since 1949

annexed by
Poland from
Germany

Bialystok

Bremen

Berlin

Pinsk

Bonn

SILESIA

Poznan

Erfurt

Dresden

Warsaw

GFR

Breslau

POLAND

Cracow

Nuremburg

CZECHOSLOVAKIA

Przemysl

Lvov

GALICIA

FRANCE

Munich

Vienna

Uzhgorod

Chernovtsy

BESSARABIA

Kishinyov

SWITZ.

AUSTRIA

Budapest

Jassy

HUNGARY

ROMANIA

Trieste

Belgrade

Bucharest

YUGOSLAVIA

BULGARIA

ITALY

Sofia

Tirane

ALBANIA

GREECE

TURKEY

GFR: German Federal Republic (West Germany)
GDR: German Democratic Republic (East Germany)

Map 1 The Soviet Union in eastern Europe

Map 2 Eastern Europe since communism

CHRONOLOGY

1949

25 January — The Council for Mutual Economic Assistance (Comecon or CMEA) is set up by the Soviet Union, Bulgaria, Hungary, Poland, Romania and Czechoslovakia.

4 April — NATO is set up in Washington.

4 May — Four-power agreement in New York on the ending of the Berlin blockade to be effective on 12 May.

23 May–20 June — Foreign ministers' conference in Paris fails to reach agreement as the Soviet Union rejects the Basic Law (*Grundgesetz*) announced for the three western zones on 23 May.

25 September — Tass reports on the explosion of the first Soviet atomic bomb.

1 October — Soviet note on the German question. The western powers are held solely responsible for the division of Germany after the formation of the Federal Republic of Germany on 20 September 1949.

1–2 October — The Soviet Union is the first state to recognise the People's Republic of China.

7 October — The German Democratic Republic (DDR) is established.

1950

13 January — The Soviet Union ceases to participate in the UN Security Council and UN agencies (until 1 August 1950).

31 January — President Truman announces that the USA is to build a hydrogen bomb.

14 February — The Soviet Union and China conclude a treaty of friendship and mutual assistance for 30 years. Port Arthur and Dairen are to be returned to China by 1952 and a long-term credit is granted China. The Soviet Union is to give up its interest in the Chinese eastern railway (the transfer agreement was signed in Kharbin 31 December 1952).

25 June	The Korean war begins.
27 June	The UN, with the USSR absent, approves the uniting for peace resolution to send troops to Korea.
27–29 June	Exchange of notes between the Soviet Union and the United States on Korea. Moscow protests against the intervention of US troops. On 7 July the UN Security Council, in the absence of the USSR, resolves to send a UN force under American command to Korea.

1951

10 March	The Soviet Union, in notes to the western powers, proposes a peace treaty with Germany.
25 May	British spies, Guy Burgess and Donald Maclean, flee to the Soviet Union.
23 June	The Soviet Union calls for a ceasefire in Korea; on 29 June the UN and on 1 July China agree to talks and these begin on 4 July.
4–8 September	In San Francisco a conference to agree a peace treaty with Japan meets but the Soviet Union, Poland and Czechoslovakia refuse to initial the agreement after the Soviet Union had failed to get its amendments accepted.

1952

10 March	Stalin proposes, in a note to the USA, Britain and France, a peace treaty which would result in a unified, neutral Germany; the west sends a non-committal reply on 25 March.
9 April	Another Soviet note on the proposed German peace treaty; the western powers do not reply until 13 May.
26 May	The Treaty of Bonn is signed by the USA, Britain, France and West Germany, ending the occupation and restoring sovereignty to the Federal Republic of Germany. (Four-power responsibility for Germany remained.) Its implementation depended on the Treaty of Paris.
27 May	The Treaty of Paris is signed by France, West Germany, Italy, Belgium, the Netherlands and Luxembourg, establishing a European Defence Community, with German forces under federal control.

16 September	The Soviet Union agrees to restore Port Arthur and their rights over railways to China.
3 October	Britain successfully explodes its first atomic bomb in the Montebello Islands.
5–14 October	The 19th Congress of the CPSU(B) adopts a new statute. The Politburo is replaced by a Presidium of the CC. The CC secretariat, headed by Malenkov, is expanded to ten members. The term Bolsheviks in the name of the Party is dropped. In future the Party will be called the CPSU.
1 November	The US successfully explodes its first hydrogen bomb in the Marshall Islands.

1953

5 March	Stalin dies from a heart attack suffered on 1 March.
7 March	It is announced that Georgy Malenkov has become Chair of the USSR Council of Ministers with L. P. Beria and V. M. Molotov as First Deputies and N. A. Bulganin and L. M. Kaganovich as Deputies. Molotov becomes Foreign Minister, Beria, Head of an amalgamated Ministry of Interior Affairs and State Security, Bulganin, Minister of War and Mikoyan, Minister of Trade.
14 March	Malenkov chooses to give up leadership of the Communist Party and retain the position of Prime Minister. Khrushchev is the main beneficiary.
17 June	The raising of norms in East Berlin leads to the East Berlin uprising against the communist regime. It is suppressed by the intervention of Soviet forces.
10 July	Arrest of Beria on 26 June is made public. He is expelled from the Party, tried for treason and executed on 23 December 1953 (some sources state that he was dead long before his trial).
8 August	Malenkov launches his new course, placing greater emphasis on consumer goods production. Compulsory deliveries from the private plots are reduced and prices paid for state deliveries from the farms are increased.
20 August	The Soviet Union announces the explosion of a hydrogen bomb (explosion was on 8 August).
13 September	Nikita Khrushchev is elected First Secretary of the CC, CPSU.

1954

25 January–18 February	Conference of the western powers and the Soviet Union in Berlin on Germany, the Austrian state treaty and the problems in Korea and Indochina. No agreement is reached.
19 February	Crimea is transferred from the RSFSR to Ukraine.
1 March	The USA tests the first deliverable hydrogen bomb in the Marshall Islands.
21 April	The Soviet Union joins UNESCO in London. Ukraine and Belorussia join on 12 May 1954.
26 April–21 July	The Indochina Conference in Geneva of the foreign ministers of the Soviet Union, France, Great Britain and the USA agrees on the division of Vietnam along the 17th parallel.
7 May	Dienbienphu falls to the Viet-Minh, the day before the Geneva talks were to discuss Indochina. His defeat heralds the end of French influence in Indochina.
29 September–12 October	Khrushchev's visit to Beijing. The Soviet Union transfers its interests in mixed Soviet–Chinese companies to China. A treaty is signed which recognises China as an equal partner and a key member of the communist movement.

1955

18–24 April	Bandung Conference in Indonesia of Afro-Asian states; condemns racism and colonialism.
14 May	In Warsaw, the Soviet Union and Albania, Bulgaria, Hungary, the GDR, Poland, Romania and Czechoslovakia sign a treaty for the defence of peace and security in Europe for 20 years (known as the Warsaw Pact). After ratification it becomes operative on 5 June 1955.
15 May	The four powers and Austria sign the Austrian state treaty in Vienna which confirms the state frontiers of 1 January 1938 and Austria agrees not to conclude a political or economic union with Germany. Austria is to be a neutral country.
9–13 September	Konrad Adenauer, West German Chancellor, visits Moscow. Diplomatic relations are established and all remaining German prisoners of war and civil personnel will be repatriated (some choose to go to the GDR, e.g. General Paulus).

27 October–16 November	Geneva conference of the foreign ministers of the Soviet Union, the USA, Great Britain and France, which fails to achieve any progress on the German question.
18 November–19 December	Khrushchev and Bulganin visit India, Burma and Afghanistan.

1956

14–25 February	The 20th Party Congress in Moscow. Khrushchev, in a secret speech, pillories Stalin for misuse of power and the cult of personality and demands that the Party return to the principles enunciated by Lenin.
17 April	The Cominform is dissolved and replaced by bilateral agreements between the Soviet Union and the individual states.
18–27 April	Khrushchev and Bulganin pay an official visit to London (the first visit by the Soviet leaders to a leading western state since the war) and meet Queen Elizabeth II and Winston Churchill. Agreement is reached only on cultural and trade ties.
20 June	The first Yugoslav visit to the Soviet Union since 1948 (1–23 June) results in Tito and Bulganin signing a statement declaring that wide-ranging agreement has been reached between the two states.
19 October	Khrushchev, Molotov, Mikoyan and Kaganovich unexpectedly visit Warsaw in response to the rehabilitation of W. Gomulka (15 October). Discussions result in Marshal Rokossovsky being recalled (13 November) to Moscow and a treaty on the stationing of Soviet troops in Poland (17 December).
23 October–11 November	The Hungarian Revolution results in the appointment of Imre Nagy as Prime Minister (24 October), then the intervention of Soviet troops (26 October). Hungary leaves the Warsaw Pact on 1 November. A pro-Soviet Hungarian government under János Kádár is formed (4 November) and is the turning point, followed by the entry of a Soviet tank division (11 November).
31 October	After the attack by Israel against the Suez Canal (29 October), the Soviet Union issues a sharp warning to Israel, France and Great Britain.

5 November	The Soviet Union severs diplomatic relations with Israel and threatens France and Great Britain because of their troop landings in Suez (5 November), not excluding a rocket attack against London and Paris.
23 November	Tito is sharply attacked in *Pravda* and suspected of sympathy for anti-Soviet tendencies in Poland and Hungary. Albania began the attacks on 8 November and they spread to all east European states by the beginning of 1957.
5–22 December	Anglo-French forces withdraw from Suez.

1957

5 January	President Eisenhower, in an address to Congress, commits the USA to oppose communism in the Middle East, called the Eisenhower doctrine. Adopted on 9 March.
18 January	Chou En-lai visits Moscow and objects to the leading role of the Soviet Union in its relations with the people's democracies of eastern Europe and supports their desire for more independence.
19 June	The Presidium of the CC, CPSU votes against Khrushchev by 8 to 3 and demands his resignation. However, Khrushchev argues that the Presidium cannot dismiss him as he was appointed by the CC and demands a CC plenum. At the plenum Khrushchev defeats his opponents, partly due to the support of Marshal Zhukov, who placed military planes at the disposal of Khrushchev's supporters (4 July). Zhukov is elected a member of the Presidium but is dismissed as Minister of Defence and loses his Presidium seat on 26 October.
26 August	The Soviet Union announces the testing of its first intercontinental ballistic missile.
19 September	The USA explodes its first nuclear device underground in Nevada.
4 October	The launch of Sputnik by the Soviet Union begins the era of space travel.
15 October	Secret agreement between the Soviet Union and China which provides Soviet help for the development of Chinese nuclear weapons. The agreement is cancelled by Moscow on 20 June 1959.

3 November	Launch of Sputnik 2 with the dog Laika on board. It is the first time a living creature has been sent into space.
14–16 November	Conference of communist and workers' parties in Moscow on the occasion of the 40th anniversary of the October Revolution. Revisionism is stated to represent the 'chief ideological danger' and all parties are committed to defending the 'achievements of socialism' and 'mutual solidarity of workers as the principle of proletarian internationalism in its new form'. There is a clear desire by ruling Communist Party leaders for equality with the CPSU.
5 December	Launch of the first atomic-powered ice breaker, the *Lenin*, in the world.

1958

27 March	Bulganin resigns as Prime Minister and Khrushchev adds the post of Prime Minister to his leadership of the CPSU. This confirms Khrushchev as a strong national leader.
23 October	The Soviet Union agrees to provide credits to build the Aswan Dam in Egypt (after the USA had declined). This is the first breakthrough for Soviet policy in Africa.
10 November	A new Berlin crisis begins with Khrushchev demanding that the allies leave Berlin.
27 November	First Soviet ultimatum on Berlin. The Soviet Union withdraws from the agreement on the administration of Greater Berlin (12 September 1944), on the Control Council (1 May 1945) and its responsibilities under the 20 September 1955 treaty with the GDR. All the rights and duties in these agreements are transferred to the GDR government. West Berlin should become a demilitarised Free City. Khrushchev demands that Berlin problem be resolved within six months.

1959

2 January	Launch of Lunik, the first Soviet two-stage rocket which passes the moon on 4 January at a distance of 7,500km and becomes the first satellite of the sun.

27 January–5 February	21st extraordinary Congress of the CPSU. Khrushchev announces that the Soviet Union has now achieved full socialism and that the phase of the construction of communism has now begun (classless society, elimination of the differences between urban and rural areas etc.).
20 February–3 March	British Prime Minister Harold Macmillan, in Moscow, advises the Soviet to find a compromise solution to the Berlin problem.
11 May–5 August	The conference of foreign ministers from the Soviet Union, the USA, Great Britain and France fails to make any headway on Germany and the Berlin question.
14 September	The Luna 2 space station lands on the moon (launched on 12 September).
15–27 September	Khrushchev's first visit to the USA. He meets President Eisenhower at Camp David (26–27 September) and withdraws his Berlin ultimatum and this leads to the Camp David spirit emerging.
30 September–1 October	On his way home from the USA, Khrushchev visits Beijing and is given a frosty reception.
1 December	The Soviet Union and 11 other states sign the Antarctic treaty, which bans atomic testing and rocket and military bases there.

1960

10 February–5 March	Khrushchev visits India, Burma and Indonesia.
4–13 February	Mikoyan visits Cuba and promises US$100 million credits and agrees to take 1 million tonnes of Cuban sugar annually for five years.
5 May	Moscow announces the shooting down of the US U2 spy plane, piloted by Gary Powers.
16–17 May	The U2 incident when a US reconnaissance plane was shot down near Sverdlovsk (Ekaterinburg) results in the Paris summit failing when Khrushchev demands that President Eisenhower apologise for the incident.
20–25 June	At the 3rd Congress of the Communist Party of Romania, Khrushchev openly attacks the Communist Party of China.
23 June	Chinese–Soviet polemics intensify as China rejects Khrushchev's view that 'peaceful co-existence with the capitalists' is possible and demands a policy of strength against the capitalist world.

17–19 August	Gary Powers, the American U2 pilot, is sentenced to ten years' imprisonment (he is exchanged for a Soviet spy in 1962).
18 August	The Soviet Union withdraws all its engineers and specialists from China.
19 September–30 October	Khrushchev attends the UN, addresses the General Assembly several times, and thumps his desk during a speech by Macmillan (29 September) and bangs on his desk with a shoe during a speech by the Philippine delegate (12 October).
10 November–1 December	The conference of the 81 communist and workers' parties in Moscow supports the Soviet position adopted at the 21st Party Congress.
7–8 December	Sino-Soviet meeting in Moscow fails to overcome split between the two leading communist parties.

1961

20 January	During his inauguration, President Kennedy states that the USA will 'pay any price, bear any burden, meet any hardship, support any friend, oppose any foe, to ensure the survival and the success of liberty'.
12 April	Yury Gagarin, in Vostok 1, becomes the first person to circle the earth.
17–20 April	The Bay of Pigs invasion by Cuban exiles, backed by the CIA, is a disastrous failure.
27–29 May	Soviet advisers and specialists leave Albania and Soviet submarines quit Valona.
3–4 June	Khrushchev and President John F. Kennedy meet in Vienna. Khrushchev demands the demilitarisation of Berlin.
30 July	The draft of a new Party programme is published in *Pravda* (to replace the 1919 programme). The CPSU has moved from being the avant garde of the working class (dictatorship of the proletariat) to being a 'people's party'. War can be avoided and the transition from capitalism to socialism is inevitable are asserted.
6 August	German Titov, in Vostok 2, becomes the second person in space and returns the following day to earth.
13 August	The building of the Berlin Wall begins.

17–31 October	A 20-year plan is discussed at the 22nd Party Congress and lays down the transition to communism. It adopts a new programme and statute (Party rules) and removes Khrushchev's conservative opponents – Stalin's body is removed from the Lenin–Stalin mausoleum and buried nearby on 1 November – and the Chinese and Albanians are sharply criticised.
10 November	The Soviet Union closes its embassy in Tirana, Albania.

1962

10 February	Moscow and Washington agree to exchange Gary Powers for the Soviet spy, Rudolf Abel.
11–12–15 August	The Soviet cosmonauts Major Nikolaev and Colonel Popovich achieve the first joint space flight in Vostok 3 and Vostok 4.
4 September	President Kennedy warns the Soviet Union not to deploy surface-to-air missiles on Cuba.
25 September–7 January 1963	The Cuban Missile Crisis begins on 30 November 1961 when President Kennedy approves Operation Mongoose to 'help Cuba overthrow the communist regime'. The Soviets place short-range nuclear rockets on Cuba and the Americans discover what is happening on 18 October. On 22 October Kennedy imposes naval blockade of Cuba and between 23 and 28 October Kennedy and Khrushchev exchange letters. Khrushchev agrees to withdraw the missiles and the Americans agree not to invade Cuba and remove Jupiter missiles from Turkey. Khrushchev was humiliated but he saved the peace. The two sides informed U Thant, UN Secretary General, that they had arrived at a peaceful resolution of the conflict.
6 November	The USA states that Soviet nuclear bombers, together with the missiles, must also leave Cuba.
20 November	Khrushchev states bombers will leave Cuba but Castro will not permit US verification. US pledge not to invade Cuba is therefore only formalised in 1970.

1963

27 April–24 May	First visit to the Soviet Union by Castro who declares that Cuba now belongs to the socialist camp.

14 June–14 July	The Communist Party of China forwards an open letter to Moscow accusing the Russians of 'restoring capitalism' and betraying Marxism. The treaty on nuclear weapons of 15 October 1957 is annulled by the Russians and after unsuccessful discussions with the Chinese (5–20 June) Moscow refutes the Chinese accusations in an open letter (14 July).
16 June	Valentina Tereshkova becomes the first woman in space, aboard Vostok 6, and returns to earth on 19 June (there were to be no other women cosmonauts).
5 August	The foreign ministers of the Soviet Union, the USA and Great Britain, in Moscow, sign a treaty on the gradual ending of atomic tests in the atmosphere, in space and under water. Many other states later join. It becomes binding on 10 October 1963. France and China refuse to sign.
22 October	The ruble bloc is created by Comecon members with a clearing bank, the International Bank for Economic Cooperation, becoming responsible, in Moscow. The currency unit is the transferable ruble which has a fine gold content of 0.987412 gram or the same as a ruble. The transferable ruble never existed physically but was an accountancy device.

1964

9–25 May	Khrushchev visits the United Arab Republic to be present at the inauguration of the first part of the Aswan dam (work began on 9 January 1960). Khrushchev makes Nasser a Hero of the Soviet Union. However, towards the end of the year Nasser begins to play Moscow off against Beijing and China extends a loan of US$80 million on 21 December 1964.
12 October	Launch of the first spacecraft Voskhod with three cosmonauts. They return on 13 October.
14 October	Nikita Khrushchev is removed as First Secretary of the CC, CPSU and as Prime Minister at a CC plenum which elects Leonid Brezhnev First Secretary. Aleksei Kosygin becomes Prime Minister. It is agreed that in the future no person will simultaneously be able to be head of both Party and government.

1965

18 March	First walk in space by cosmonaut Aleksei Leonov.
1–5 May	The suggestion for a world communist conference by the Soviet Union on 10 February 1963 never comes about because of Chinese opposition. Instead, a consultative meeting of only 18 parties (among those absent are China, North Vietnam, North Korea, Indonesia, Japan and Romania) undermines Moscow's continued attempts to dominate the world movement. It has to accept partnership relations between communist parties.

1966

10 January	Kosygin helps to bring the Indian–Pakistani conflict to an end and both sides sign an agreement in Tashkent. This is a coup for Soviet influence in Asia and helps to stem the increase in Chinese influence.
29 March–8 April	The 23rd Party Congress removes Khrushchev supporters and there is a partial rehabilitation of Stalin, cultural policy becomes less liberal. The Politburo is reintroduced and Brezhnev becomes General Secretary of the Party (the previous holder of the position was Stalin). The military budget is increased.

1967

27 January	A Soviet–US–British agreement on the peaceful use of space is signed simultaneously in Moscow, Washington and London and becomes effective on 10 October.
21 April	Stalin's daughter, Svetlana Alliluyeva, is granted political asylum in the United States.
23–25 June	President Johnson and Aleksei Kosygin, the Soviet Prime Minister, meet in Glassboro', New Jersey, for a mini-summit.

1968

8 May	The Soviet Union, Poland, East Germany, Hungary and Bulgaria convene in Moscow to discuss the Prague spring, launched by Dubcek.
1 July	Many states sign the nuclear non-proliferation treaty (54 in Washington, 36 in Moscow and 23 in London). The Soviet Union and the USA state they will begin strategic arms limitation talks (SALT).

14 July	Warsaw meeting of the Soviet Union, Poland, East Germany, Hungary and Bulgaria to discuss situation in Czechoslovakia and demand meeting with Czechoslovaks.
29 July–1 August	Meeting of the Politburo of the CC, CPSU and the Presidium of the CC, Communist Party of Czechoslovakia in Cierna nad Tisu to discuss the reforms in Czechoslovakia (Prague spring and socialism with a human face).
21 August	Invasion of Czechoslovakia by Warsaw Pact forces, headed by the Soviet Union, with smaller contingents from the GDR, Poland, Hungary and Bulgaria. Romania, Yugoslavia, China and Albania protest against the invasion. The reform politicians are dragged off to Moscow, but return on 27 August.
26 September	As the Warsaw Pact excludes intervention in the internal affairs of member states (article 8), the CPSU, in *Pravda*, advances the thesis of the 'limited sovereignty of socialist states in case of danger for the world socialist system'. Brezhnev advances the same concept on 6 November and it becomes known as the Brezhnev doctrine.
12 November	Leonid Brezhnev, in Warsaw, introduces the Brezhnev doctrine of limited sovereignty of communist pro-Moscow states.
1969	
2 March	Armed conflict between Chinese and Soviet forces on the islands in the Ussuri River. There is further fighting on 14–15 March.
28–29 March	The defeat of the Soviet team by the Czechoslovaks in the ice hockey world championship in Stockholm leads to celebrations in Czechoslovakia and attacks on Soviet soldiers and buildings. On 30 March Deputy Soviet Foreign Minister Semenov is sent to Prague to force through changes in the Communist Party of Czechoslovakia (CPCz) leadership.
17 April	Alexander Dubcek and other reform communists are voted off the CC, Communist Party of Czechoslovakia as a result of massive Soviet pressure. Gustav Husak becomes the new Party leader.
13 August	More Soviet–Chinese fighting along the Xinjiang border with Central Asia.

17 November–22 December	First rounds of talks on limiting atomic armaments between the Soviet Union and the USA in Helsinki (SALT). Further meetings rotate between Helsinki and Geneva.

1970

6 May	Soviet–Czechoslovak 'normalisation' treaty of friendship, cooperation and mutual assistance, in which the Brezhnev doctrine is included.
12 August	Aleksei Kosygin and Andrei Gromyko, Soviet Foreign Minister, and Chancellor Willy Brandt and Walter Scheel, West German Foreign Minister, sign the Soviet–West German Moscow Treaty which begins Bonn's *Ostpolitik*. This states that European frontiers can only be changed by negotiation. The treaty is followed by the Warsaw Treaty of 7 December 1970.
20 September	The space probe Luna 16 lands on the moon, collects some stone fragments and returns to earth.
17 November	Luna 17 places the first moon vehicle, Lunokhod 1, on the moon and it can be guided from earth.
15 December	The space probe Venus 7, weighing 1.2 tonnes, lands after 120 days on Venus and transmits information for 25 minutes.

1971

11 February	The Soviet Union, the USA and Great Britain, in Moscow, Washington and London, sign the treaty on banning nuclear weapons and other weapons of mass destruction in the sea, on the seabed and underwater.
7 June	The space capsule, Soyuz 11, docks with the space station, Salyut 1, launched on 19 April. Three cosmonauts transfer to the station and work there for 23 days and 18 hours.
3 September	Four-power Berlin treaty regulates the status of West Berlin (transit of civil goods and persons, expansion of links with West Germany, representation of West Berlin abroad). After GDR–West German agreements, a final protocol is added on 3 June 1972. The treaty then becomes law.
2 December	The space probe Mars 3 (launched 28 May) ejects a capsule which lands on Mars and sends back signals for a short time.

12 December	Hotline between the Kremlin and the White House used for the first time under Nixon amid fears of Soviet (pro-Indian) or Chinese (pro-Pakistani) intervention in the war over Bangladesh; the US fleet is ordered to the Bay of Bengal.

1972

22–30 May	Official state visit by President Richard Nixon to the Soviet Union, during which the SALT treaty is signed (26 May). Relations between the superpowers are to be based on peaceful coexistence and détente.
3 June	The USA, USSR, Britain and France sign an agreement on the future of Berlin.
5–10 June	During a visit to the Soviet Union, Tito is showered with awards and honours, even though it is unclear whether the differences between the USSR and Yugoslavia have been resolved.
18 July	Differences between Cairo and Moscow result in 17,000 Soviet military and other advisers being expelled from Egypt.
3 October	President Nixon and Andrei Gromyko sign the Anti-Ballistic Missile (ABM) Treaty.
18 October	US–Soviet trade agreement signed.
22 November–8 June 1973	Talks in Helsinki – with some breaks – on preparing a European conference on security and cooperation (CSCE). The United States and Canada join 32 European states in discussions.

1973

18–22 May	Leonid Brezhnev makes the first visit by a Soviet leader to West Germany; signs a ten-year agreement on economic cooperation.
18–25 June	During the visit of Leonid Brezhnev to the United States, agreement is reached on the basic principles of talks cutting back further on strategic offensive weapons (21 June) and avoiding military confrontation and a missile war (22 June).
3 July	The conference on security and cooperation in Europe (CSCE) opens in Helsinki.
25–31 October	A conference on the peaceful use of atomic energy is attended by over 3,000 representatives from 143 countries. Brezhnev addresses it and presents Soviet foreign policy (26 October).

1974

27 June–3 July	During the visit of President Nixon to the Soviet Union, several agreements on limiting strategic arms and cooperation between the two countries are signed.
4 July	Iraq expels 80 Soviet advisers (linked to the rapprochement with the USA and the desire for US weapons).
24 November	During a meeting between Leonid Brezhnev and President Gerald Ford in Vladivostok, it is agreed to conclude a treaty on limiting strategic arms over the period October 1977 to December 1985.
25 November	An agreement is signed by the Soviet Union, the USA and Japan on the exploitation of Siberian natural gas. It never takes effect because the USA refuses to grant the Soviet Union the necessary credits.

1975

3 January	President Ford signs the Trade Reform Act which lays down the condition that trade between the Soviet Union and the USA can only expand (the Jackson–Vanik amendment) if Moscow permits greater Jewish emigration.
18 June	The Soviet Union warns China not to interfere in Soviet–Japanese relations (rejected by Japan on 19 June and China on 21 June).
17–19 July	Joint US–Soviet space mission, agreed in 1972, takes place.
29 July–1 August	Brezhnev attends the conclusion of the third round of the CSCE negotiations and has meetings with leading politicians as well: Tito on 29 July, Pierre Trudeau (Canada) on 31 July, Demirel (Turkey) and Chancellor Helmut Schmidt on 1 August, Moro (Italy), Harold Wilson on 30 July and President Gerald Ford on 2 August.
1 August	The Helsinki Final Act is signed by heads of states and governments.
20 October	US–Soviet agreement which obliges the USSR to import 30 million tonnes of grain over five years from the USA and the Soviet Union is to deliver at least 10 million tonnes of oil annually to the USA.
1–5 December	President Ford visits China and meets Mao Ze Dong who criticises US–Soviet détente.

1976

13 May	Nine Soviet dissidents announce the setting up of a group to monitor the implementation of the Helsinki Agreement by the Soviet Union (Helsinki Group), led by Academician Yury Orlov (other members include Elena Bonner (Sakharov's wife), Aleksandr Ginzburg and Petr Grigorenko).
28 May	The USA and the Soviet Union agree to limit the size of certain underground nuclear tests.
6–26 September	Arthur Schlesinger, a former US Secretary of State, visits China and offers Beijing an alliance against the Soviet Union and analyses the weaknesses of the Chinese air defence system.
18 December	The Soviet Union and Chile exchange the Soviet dissident Bukovsky for the General Secretary of the Communist Party of Chile, Corvalan.

1977

27–30 February	US Secretary of State, Cyrus Vance, visits Moscow but Andrei Gromyko, Soviet Foreign Minister, states that there can be no major revision of the agreement on SALT at Vladivostok in 1974; he also opposes US interference in domestic Soviet politics.
4–14 October	CSCE talks begin in Belgrade as a follow-up meeting to the Helsinki agreements of 1975. They continue until 9 March 1989.
7 October	The USSR Supreme Soviet adopts the new Soviet constitution unanimously. It replaces the 1936 Stalin constitution and introduces the concept of the Soviet Union as the state of all the people (article 1). The USSR is a 'unitary multi-national federal state' (article 2) and the CPSU is the 'leading and guiding force of Soviet society' and the 'core of its political system' (article 6). The Party is also the party of the whole people.

1978

8 March	In Belgrade the final document of the CSCE follow-up meeting is signed. Talks are to continue in Madrid in November 1980.
26 April	Arkady Shevchenko, the top Soviet UN official, asks for political asylum in the USA.
13 July	Soviet dissidents Anatoly Shcharansky and Aleksandr Ginsburg are sent to prison.

1979

15–18 June	SALT II is signed at a Soviet–US summit in Vienna between President Carter and Leonid Brezhnev.
12 December	In response to the stationing of SS-20 medium-range missiles in the western regions of the Soviet Union, the NATO states agree, in Brussels, to station American Cruise and Pershing 2 missiles in western Europe from 1984. NATO adopts a double-track policy; if negotiations with the Soviet Union are successful the missiles need not be put in place.
26–27 December	Soviet troops intervene in Afghanistan and Hafissulah Amin, Afghan leader, is overthrown and murdered with the aid of Soviet troops. The new pro-Soviet leader is Babrak Karmal.

1980

4 January	In response to the Soviet invasion of Afghanistan, President Jimmy Carter imposes a trade embargo for grain and advanced technology; he also suspends the ratification of the SALT II treaty and promises greater aid to Pakistan.
19 July	The 22nd Olympic Games begin in Moscow with 81 nations participating. Over 40 states boycott the games.
11 October	The cosmonauts Leonid Popov and Valery Ryumin land in Kazakhstan after a record flight of 185 days in space. They took off from Baikonur on 9 April 1980 aboard Soyuz 35 and the following day transferred to the space station Salyut 6 which had been circling the earth for over three years.

1981

24 April	President Reagan lifts the grain embargo against the Soviet Union because it is not in the interests of American farmers.
6 August	President Reagan announces the stockpiling of neutron bombs by the USA.
23 September	Andrei Gromyko and General Alexander Haig, US Secretary of State, agree to begin talks on intermediate-range nuclear (INF) weapons.
16 October	President Reagan claims that Moscow plans to fight and win a nuclear war; Brezhnev denies this on 20 October.

18 November	President Reagan proposes a new disarmament agenda, including the complete elimination of INF weapons; this is the first time the 'zero option' is articulated.

1982

30 May	President Reagan promises the USA will adhere to SALT II as long as the Soviet Union does.
29 June	The USSR and USA begin START talks in Geneva.
10 November	Leonid Brezhnev dies.
12 November	Yury Andropov is elected General Secretary of the CC, CPSU.

1983

9 March	President Reagan describes the Soviet Union as the 'evil empire'.
23 March	President Reagan announces the strategic defence initiative (SDI), also called the Star Wars programme.
1 September	South Korean airliner, KAL007, is shot down after straying into Soviet air space.
9 September	Marshal Nikolai Ogarkov, Chief of the General Staff, appears at an international press conference to explain the shooting down of the Korean KAL007 airliner and expresses no regrets.
15 December	Mutually balanced force reduction (MBFR) talks, on conventional forces, end without agreement on further meetings.

1984

9 February	Yury Andropov dies.
13 February	Konstantin Chernenko is elected General Secretary of the CC, CPSU. Mikhail Gorbachev is regarded as his second-in-command.
28 September	President Reagan meets Andrei Gromyko for the first time, in Washington, while the latter is attending the UN.
22 November	It is announced that Andrei Gromyko and George Shultz, the US Secretary of State, will meet in January 1985 to discuss disarmament.
15–21 December	Mikhail Gorbachev visits Great Britain and Mrs Margaret Thatcher, Prime Minister, regards him as 'a man one can do business with'.

1985

7–8 January	Gromyko and Shultz agree in Geneva on three sets of talks: START, INF and defensive systems, including those based in space.
10 March	Konstantin Chernenko dies.
11 March	Mikhail Gorbachev is elected General Secretary of the CC, CPSU.
7 April	Gorbachev halts Soviet missile deployment but insists they will restart in November if NATO does not stop its deployment.
2 July	Andrei Gromyko becomes Chair of the Presidium of the USSR Supreme Soviet, Head of State, and Shevardnadze succeeds him as Foreign Minister.
25–27 September	Edvard Shevardnadze visits the US to prepare the ground for a Reagan–Gorbachev summit.
2–5 October	Gorbachev visits France, his first official visit to the west as leader. He uses the term 'reasonable sufficiency' for the first time, does not link INF negotiations to anything else and rejects ideology as the basis of foreign policy. He proposes that the superpowers reduce their strategic arsenals by half.
19–21 November	Summit meeting in Geneva between Mikhail Gorbachev and President Ronald Reagan; they agree to meet again in the future.

1986

25 February–6 March	The 27th Party Congress opens with a long keynote speech by Gorbachev in which he advocates the radical reform of the economic mechanism. He refers to the war in Afghanistan as a 'bleeding wound' and the Brezhnev era as 'years of stagnation'.
26 April	An explosion at the Chernobyl nuclear reactor, Ukraine, turns out to be the worst in Soviet history. However, the initial response of the leadership is to play down its extent.
28 July	Gorbachev arrives in Vladivostok to tour the Soviet Far East and states that six regiments will be withdrawn from Afghanistan and that talks have begun with Mongolia on the withdrawal of Soviet troops.

10 October	Gorbachev arrives in Reykjavik for a two-day summit with President Reagan. They agree on most arms reduction issues. They almost agree on substantial cuts in offensive arms and even the elimination of nuclear weapons.
19 October	Five US diplomats are expelled from the Soviet Union in retaliation for the expulsion of Soviet UN officials.
21 October	The USA expels 55 Soviet diplomats from the Soviet Embassy in Washington and the Soviet Consulate General in San Francisco.
22 October	The USSR expels five more US diplomats and withdraws Soviet employees from the US Embassy and Consulate General.
6 November	The USSR Ministry of Defence states that the withdrawal of six regiments (about 6,000 men) has been completed and they will not be replaced.
28 November	The USA deploys the new B52 bomber which violates the START II treaty.

1987

28 March–1 April	British Prime Minister, Margaret Thatcher, visits the Soviet Union and stresses human rights and calls for the withdrawal of Soviet troops from Afghanistan.
1 November	Gorbachev's book, *Perestroika and the New Political Thinking*, is published in Moscow. It is translated into many languages and is a huge best seller.
5 December	Gorbachev travels to London and meets Margaret Thatcher.
7–10 December	Gorbachev in Washington for meetings with President Ronald Reagan. In Washington, he signs the treaty banning intermediate range nuclear missiles (INF) (8 December). It is his first visit to the United States and becomes a huge personal triumph. 'Gorbymania' has arrived.

1988

14 April	Agreements on the ending of the Afghan war are signed in Geneva. The Soviet Union and the USA guarantee the agreements and promise not to interfere in the domestic affairs of Afghanistan and Pakistan.

29 May–2 June	President Reagan visits Moscow to meet Gorbachev for their fourth summit. Reagan also meets dissidents and praises freedom in an address to students at Moscow State University.
25 July	Shevardnadze, addressing a conference in the USSR Ministry of Foreign Affairs, rejects the class struggle as the basis of Soviet foreign policy.
7 December	Gorbachev, at the UN, announces that the Soviet Union will reduce its armed forces by 500,000 within two years without requiring reciprocal moves by the USA or its allies. He also stresses that the common interests of mankind and freedom of choice are universal human principles. Later, he meets Reagan and President-Elect Bush on Governors Island. Marshal Sergei Akhromeev resigns as Chief of the General Staff and Deputy Minister of Defence. Armenia is hit by a massive earthquake with over 50,000 dead. Gorbachev abandons his planned trip to Cuba and flies home.

1989

17–19 January	The CSCE Review Conference concludes in Vienna with agreement to begin negotiations on the reduction of conventional forces in Europe (CFE).
15 February	The last Soviet troops leave Afghanistan; the Najibullah regime survives until 1992. Najibullah is killed by Taliban forces in September 1996.
26 March	Elections are held to the USSR Congress of People's Deputies. Many Party candidates lose and the pro-independence parties win in the Baltic States. Boris Yeltsin wins in Moscow.
25 April	Soviet troops begin leaving Hungary.
15–19 May	Gorbachev visits China and announces the normalisation of relations between the two states.
6 July	Gorbachev addresses the Council of Europe in Strasbourg and states that the Soviet Union will not stand in the way of reform in eastern Europe.
22–23 September	James Baker, US Secretary of State, and Shevardnadze meet in Jackson Hole, Wyoming. Shevardnadze drops the Soviet demand which links reduction in strategic missiles to limits on the strategic defence initiative (SDI) or Star Wars.
25–26 September	President Bush and Edvard Shevardnadze, at the UN, propose the elimination of chemical weapons.

7 October	Gorbachev, in East Berlin, tells the crowds that 'life punishes those who fall behind' and this further undermines the authority of Erich Honecker, the GDR leader. He is replaced by Egon Krenz on 18 October.
9 November	The Berlin Wall comes down.
1 December	Gorbachev has an audience with Pope John Paul II in the Vatican and states that a law on freedom of conscience will be passed and that the Ukrainian (Greek) Catholic Church will be recognised again.
2–3 December	Gorbachev and Bush meet in Malta and Gorbachev states that force will not be used to ensure that east European communist regimes remain in power. Bush agrees to remove most controls on US–Soviet trade.
24 December	The USSR Supreme Soviet declares the secret protocol to the Nazi–Soviet pact invalid but does not comment on the incorporation of the Baltic States and other territories acquired by the Soviet Union as part of this agreement.

1990

8 February	James Baker visits Moscow and proposes 2 (East and West Germany) + 4 (the USA, USSR, Britain and France) negotiations to discuss German unification.
10 February	Chancellor Kohl, in Moscow, gets an agreement in principle on German reunification.
12 February	The foreign ministers of the 2 + 4, meeting in Ottawa, agree to begin discussions on German unification.
28 March	First free elections in Hungary since 1945.
30 May–4 June	Gorbachev travels to Washington for his second summit with Bush, then visits Minneapolis-St Paul and San Francisco.
August 2	Iraq invades Kuwait.
August 3	Baker and Shevardnadze sign a joint statement in Moscow condemning the Iraqi invasion.
22 August	Turkmenistan and Armenia declare sovereignty.
9 September	Gorbachev and Bush meet for a one-day summit in Helsinki and agree to cooperate to end Iraqi aggression in Kuwait.

12 September	The 2 + 4 treaty is signed in Moscow ending four-power control over Germany.
3 October	Germany is reunited.
19 November	The treaty on Conventional Forces in Europe (CFE) is signed in Paris.
23 November	The draft treaty of a new union is published, to be called the Union of Sovereign Soviet Republics. Most republican leaders criticise it.
20 December	Edvard Shevardnadze, Minister of Foreign Affairs, resigns and warns of the threat of dictatorship.

1991

15 January	Operation Desert Storm, to remove Iraq from Kuwait, begins in the Persian Gulf.
24 February	The US-led ground offensive begins against Iraq.
25 February	The Warsaw Pact agrees to annul all military agreements, effective as of 31 March, but to continue voluntary political links.
28 February	All military operations against Iraq are suspended.
14–16 March	Baker visits Moscow for discussions and meets Baltic leaders and other republican heads.
31 March	The Warsaw Pact is formally dissolved.
23 April	In Novo-Ogarevo, the President's dacha outside Moscow, President Gorbachev and the heads of state of nine republics sign a joint statement on speeding up a new union agreement (the 9 + 1 agreement).
12 June	Boris Yeltsin is elected President of the RSFSR in Russia's first democratic elections.
20 June	The US ambassador warns Gorbachev of a conspiracy to remove him.
30 June	The last Soviet soldier leaves Czechoslovakia (they had invaded on 21 August 1968).
17 July	Gorbachev meets G7 leaders in London but receives little support.
30–31 July	President Bush visits Moscow, meets Gorbachev and Nazarbaev, and pays a separate visit to Yeltsin.
1 August	President Bush visits Kiev and meets Leonid Kravchuk.
17 August	Several senior Party officials demand that Gorbachev hand over power to them temporarily and if he refuses, to detain him and take control.

18 August	Gorbachev rejects the demands of the delegation sent to persuade him at Foros to agree to the takeover. Shortly before midnight, Vice-President Gennady Yanaev agrees to support the takeover and signs a decree assuming the powers of the President.
21 August	The attempted coup fails; Gorbachev returns to Moscow.
8 December	In Belovezh forest, near Minsk, the presidents and prime ministers of Russia, Ukraine and Belarus declare the USSR dissolved and found a Commonwealth of Independent States (CIS). Gorbachev describes the move 'dangerous and illegal'.
12 December	Central Asian leaders, meeting in Ashkhabad (Ashghabat) request membership of the CIS as founding members.
17 December	Yeltsin and Gorbachev agree that by 1 January 1992 the Soviet Union will no longer exist.
21–22 December	Eleven former Soviet republics meet in Almaty and the CIS is extended (Estonia, Latvia, Lithuania and Georgia did not attend).
25 December	USSR President Gorbachev resigns and the Russian flag replaces the Soviet flag over the Kremlin.
31 December	The Soviet Union officially ceases to exist.

PART ONE   CONTEXT

CHAPTER ONE

INTRODUCTION: THE PROBLEM

A static power declines but a dynamic power expands. Is this statement a sophism, in other words false, or does it reveal the underlying causes of the monumental conflict which engulfed the Soviet Union and the United States for over four decades after 1945? Both America and Russia were revolutionary powers. They possessed universal visions of how to improve the lot of humankind. From a Marxist perspective to be a static power meant that one's state was in decline. The goal of communism required an expansionary policy and this would continue until the goal of a communist society worldwide had been achieved. Likewise the United States understood that its prosperity depended on what happened outside its borders. President Harry Truman put it very succinctly: 'If communism is allowed to absorb the free nations then we would be isolated from our sources of supply and detached from our friends. Then we would have to take defense measures which might really bankrupt our economy, and change our way of life so that we couldn't recognize it as American any longer' (Leffler 1992, pp. 13–14). Was this just rhetoric to gain popular support for higher taxes to fund the Marshall Plan, extend military help to states facing a communist threat and promote business opportunities abroad or was it a core belief of the Truman administration? The thrust of this book is that the Americans linked liberty, justice and freedom to a liberal market economy and the right of the individual to self-betterment. By the same token, a communist society was collectivist. The Soviet version had almost eliminated private property and private trade. The state dominated the economy. A small group of decision makers enjoyed the right to decide how the economy developed. In ideology, there was a ruling party and a ruling ideology. This party had a monopoly of political power. No dissenting voices were permitted. Where the American way was pluralistic and there were myriad economic decision makers, the Soviet way was to mobilise the population from the top down.

In 1945 no one could say for certain which revolutionary path, the Soviet or the American, would prove victorious. Europe was in ruins. Germany, its leading economy, was in total collapse. The same applied to Japan. Korea and

3

south east Asia were economic cripples. There was a widespread feeling in Europe that old-style capitalism was finished. It had led the continent into a disastrous, fratricidal war. The new order would have to attend to the people's demands for economic and social change. President Truman was warned in 1945 that if action were not taken to alleviate the suffering in Europe, the whole region could fall to communism. Desperate people were willing to adopt desperate solutions. However, it was only in 1947 that large-scale economic programmes, the Marshall Plan, got under way. Likewise in Japan, in 1947, America switched from nurturing reform of political and economic institutions to reviving the Japanese economy. This was based on securing raw materials supplies (Japan is a resource-poor country) in east and south east Asia and markets in the United States. Hence, we can say that in 1947 key economic decisions were taken which conditioned political and military policy decisions. In order for the market economy to develop, stability and security were essential. The task of the politicians and military was to provide this. The Americans perceived that political and military actions would be ineffective without rising living standards. Marx, and his latter-day apostle Lenin, had recognised this decades before. What became known later as consumerism would decide the titanic battle between the two revolutionary models. It was only in the 1970s that the Americans could feel that they had won the contest economically.

The opening of the archives in Russia, eastern Europe and China has resulted in a flood of publications. Has recent scholarship solved problems such as who was responsible for the Cold War, why it broke out, whether it was an accident or entirely predictable, whether it could have ended in the 1950s or the 1960s had the opportunities been grasped, given the massive arsenals on both sides why a nuclear war did not break out and why it ended as it did? Did the military confrontation between the superpowers destroy the Soviet Union or was its collapse due to other factors? The answer is that the more there is published the more opaque the problems become. Monocausal answers are no longer acceptable. What is clear is that the conflict was immensely complex and worldwide. Asia came into the equation in the 1950s, Africa in the 1960s and Latin America was embroiled in the same decade with Castro's revolution in Cuba.

The contest was billed as one between superpowers and only two were regarded as such. However, in reality, for much of the Cold War there was only one superpower, the United States. The gross domestic product in the Soviet Union was never more than 40 per cent of that of the American. It was not an equal race. In 1945 the Soviet economy was shattered and the American economy was experiencing a war-fuelled boom. The Soviets needed eastern Europe and China as sources of raw materials. Needless to say, it could not pay world market prices. This was bound to cause resentment sooner or later. The Americans could pay world market prices for anything they needed. The Soviet Union, by concentrating investment in certain sectors, was astonishingly innovative and successful until the 1970s. It acquired atomic and hydrogen bombs, it put the first man, woman and dog into space and it was ahead in rocket technology. This led the Americans to acknowledge nuclear parity by the early 1970s. However, just at the moment of its greatest triumph, its economy began to decline. The American economy, by way of contrast, accelerated and this forced the Soviets to switch more and more resources from the civil to the military sector of the economy. In 1985 Mikhail Gorbachev acknowledged that the Soviet Union could no longer compete militarily with the United States. Many agreements on strategic arms resulted but they could not save the country from collapse.

Another insight is that the world was not really bipolar (Russia v America): from at least the mid-1950s it was multipolar. The major power here was the People's Republic of China. Fraternal relations between Moscow and Beijing fractured in 1958 and were never repaired. Eventually China sought an understanding with the United States in its conflict with the Soviet Union. East and West Germany influenced western thinking and helped to cement the division of Europe. However, the West German policy of *Ostpolitik* (policy towards the east) began a process which culminated in the Helsinki Final Act in 1975. This was a forerunner of Gorbachev's new political thinking after 1985.

Three major factors conditioned the Cold War: ideas and beliefs; security; and culture.

IDEAS AND BELIEFS

As you approach New York, you encounter the Statue of Liberty. Liberty is the core American belief. The American idea of liberty evolved from the English revolutionary ideas of the seventeenth century, from the history of two civil wars and, first and foremost, from the philosophy of John Locke. The Americans have always been battling for liberty. In the 1770s they fought and won a war against Great Britain in order to become a free people. (Although they did have some help from the French.) Psychologically, from an American point of view, liberty has to be defended by deeds and arms whenever necessary. Liberty fosters democracy which is a continuous process. Basic to democracy are freedom of speech and economic activity or free enterprise and independence from external threats. Secure property rights are the cornerstone of liberty. The rule of law is necessary in order to regulate political, economic and social life. The United States has been the engine of global liberation since 1917 when it intervened in World War I and tipped the balance against imperial Germany. The result was that Germany and many other states could begin building democratic societies. In 1941 Washington was forced into World War II and in 1945 Japan, Germany and a host of other states could choose the democratic road of development. Soviet and American arms contributed most to the defeat of imperial Japan and national socialist Germany. Without American military intervention Japan and Germany might now dominate Asia and Europe. The American presence in western Europe after 1945 ensured that the Soviets never launched a military attack, thus permitting the democracies to develop and mature. When General Franco died in 1975, there was only one viable model for Spain: democracy.

The American founding fathers sought to guard individual liberties by restricting the powers of the state. This was in marked contrast to France, another revolutionary power, where the state seized enormous power in an attempt to implement the people's will. The American and French revolutionaries admired one another but their paths soon diverged. It was the French revolution which inspired Marx's socialist model, not the American. France's vision of making its values universal ended at Waterloo in 1815 with the defeat of Napoleon. It has continued to the present day but is now mainly confined to providing the European Union with a vision of the future. American universalism, however, goes from strength to strength.

The only time American idealism was dented was during the 1970s and this was not as a result of a defeat at the hands of the Soviets but, rather, one by the communist Vietnamese. Defeat and expulsion from Saigon in 1975 were a chastening lesson. They had reluctantly entered the Indochina conflict at the invitation of the French who were incapable of maintaining their military presence. The result was that America drew back from trying to change the world in its own image. Henry Kissinger's hardnosed *Realpolitik* suited the new mood of restraint. He treated the Soviet Union as an equal, acknowledged that it had legitimate security needs and tried to get Moscow to play by Washington rules. As a Republican he did not possess the reforming zeal of the Democrats. Détente opened up vistas of mutual benefit but was soon perceived by many Americans as all give and no take. The Soviet Union appeared to regard détente as a licence to intervene everywhere, especially in support of revolutionary regimes in Africa. Intervention in Afghanistan in 1979 was the last straw. The backlash brought to power President Reagan who insulted the Soviet Union by describing it as the 'evil empire'. The striking fact was that Reagan was a Republican and his party was changing course. Traditionally, they had rarely been interested in saving the world. That was usually a Democratic project. Republicans favoured stability and being left in peace to pursue their economic interests. The world out there was a place to do business in, not to transform through democratic revolution. The New Right, as they became known, were gradually infusing the Republican party with the zeal of the left and setting revolutionary goals. President George Bush Senior was, however, a very cautious leader but gradually warmed to Gorbachev. The missionary zeal of the Republicans to change the world came back with a bang under President George Bush Junior. The 'evil empire' of his father gave way to the 'axis of evil' (Iraq, Iran and North Korea). In April 2003 Iraq's Saddam Hussein disappeared from the political map.

Stalin's view of the world was seen through the prism of Marxism–Leninism. Recent scholarship has underlined the importance of his belief system when it came to taking decisions involving foreign policy. The Marxist vision was based on endemic hostility between socialism and capitalism which would eventually result in the victory of socialism. Conflict was inevitable and could spill over into war. It was only in 1952 that Georgy Malenkov began talking of peaceful coexistence being possible due to both superpowers possessing nuclear weapons. Stalin became more utopian after 1948. Then he launched various programmes involving the transformation of nature which involved planting million of trees in the dry steppes of southern Russia to fend off the deprivations caused by the hot winds. Another project was to irrigate over 6 million ha of land. Genetics he concluded was a pseudo-science and it was banned – until 1966. The most ambitious project was in the field of economics. From 1948 onwards teams of specialists engaged in mapping out the route to a communist society. Stalin regarded the present stage as the first fruits of communism. Full communism could arrive by about 1970. This involved the abolition of the law of value and money. The gulf between the countryside and the town and between industry and agriculture were to melt away. Another discipline in which Stalin took a passionate interest was linguistics and it continued to fascinate him until his death. It is astonishing that, in a world in which the Soviet Union was desperately trying to recover from wartime deprivations, build an empire in eastern Europe and hold the American 'beast' at bay, the master of the Kremlin spent an inordinate amount of time mulling over the origin and development of language.

The striking fact about all these concerns – the transformation of nature; irrigation; genetics; the leap into communism; and linguistics – was that he was completely wrong. They were all crass misjudgements. The Marxist nature of his thinking is clear from a reading of the *Economics of Socialism in the USSR*, finally published in 1952. His thinking was clearly utopian. Over the last years of his life nationality policy favoured the Great Russians at the expense especially of the Jews. There appears to have been a plan to move all Jews from European Russia to Kazakhstan and Siberia. Israel, to name but one state, wondered whether Stalin was gearing up to fight World War III. It would appear that he wanted everything speeded up, perhaps sensing that his days were numbered.

In domestic affairs, however, he was a hard-headed realist. The Leningrad Affair took the lives of the leading economist Nikolai Voznesensky and many Party and government officials in the second capital. The *gulag* (prison camp) filled up as many veterans who had fought bravely but had become prisoners of war were sent directly to camps on their return to the motherland. Alexander Solzhenitsyn was one of the many officers sent to the gulag for criticising

Stalin. The question remains about whether Stalin was misled by his advisers or whether he was the mastermind behind the mayhem. No one yet understands why Voznesensky, for example, was shot in 1950.

Stalin made some egregious foreign policy mistakes. His greatest blunder was the Berlin blockade which hastened the formation of a West German state and NATO. In Turkey, he overplayed his hand by demanding territory and the scrapping of the Montreux Convention which gave Turkey the major say on whether warships could pass through the Straits. The Soviet Union, according to Stalin, would be the dominant voice in the future. Molotov, in retirement, conceded that Stalin had overplayed his hand and put it down to overconfidence. Stalin's behaviour was a major reason why the United States decided to play a major role in the eastern Mediterranean and eventually to establish a naval presence there.

The question arises whether Stalin's conduct was the result of his ideological convictions or whether he was acting as a Great Russian nationalist imperialist. There is no doubt that Stalin, in 1945, believed that the tide of history was flowing in the direction of the Soviet Union. He held tenaciously to his belief that the capitalist powers would not resolve their post-war economic problems and that war between them was on the cards. Every country that chose the path of socialism reduced the source of raw materials and markets for the United States. A shrinking capitalist world would exacerbate tensions within capitalist states. Given the economic mess that Europe, Japan and other states were in, one can understand the grounds for Stalin's optimism. It would appear that his Marxist mode of analysis led him to underestimate the dynamism of capitalism which, after all, is used to cyclical crises. All we can say is that his Marxism and his Great Russian nationalism reinforced one another. Russian nationalism feared contagion from outside, primarily from the United States. The Russian view was that it did not need any help or advice from other states. All the wisdom needed to make a great nation even greater already resided in the country. A Marxist analysis fitted this fear of the outside world perfectly. Russia, indeed socialism, would only be safe when the capitalist 'beast' was no more. Stalin, most of the time, appeared to be cautious and to believe that time was on his side. On other occasions, in Turkey and Berlin, he wanted to speed history up. There are those who believe he was even contemplating a third world war at the end of his life to secure the final victory of communism throughout the world.

Khrushchev made no secret of the fact that he was wedded to Marxism–Leninism. It was his compass. The problem was that he had a very unsophisticated understanding of Marxism. His core beliefs were that socialism would prove victorious over capitalism; conflict with the Americans, indeed the whole capitalist world, was inevitable; the socialist economic model was superior to the capitalist – the fact that living standards in the USA were higher than in the Soviet Union was merely a spur to catch up with and surpass the Americans; threats were an effective weapon in foreign affairs; revolutionary movements in the Third World should be supported since every country that escaped from capitalism or capitalist influence diminished capitalist influence and markets in the world. He always believed he occupied the moral high ground and represented the future of humankind. He was as utopian as Stalin. He thought communism would arrive in 1980, ten years later than Stalin. However, he had a horror of modern warfare, especially a nuclear war. His wartime experiences had convinced him that war had to be avoided if possible. How, then, can we explain his high-risk policies, especially in Cuba in 1962? The answer seems to be that he did not think his policies through and had no back-up position if his initial sallies failed. He was overconfident. In the Berlin crises of 1958–63 he acted first and hoped the opposition would cave in. When the west refused to budge he was nonplussed but eventually accepted a peaceful solution. Was his rashness and impetuosity due to his Marxist beliefs or the result of the Soviet Union's striking successes in space and in missile technology? The answer seems to be that both fused to form a whole.

Brezhnev was not very bright and this meant he was not an innovator. However, he did sign the Helsinki Final Act in 1975 and regarded it as his greatest triumph. It cemented the division of Europe which had resulted from World War II. However, he also accepted Basket III on human and civil rights. This was his undoing. It permitted foreign states to take a legitimate interest in human and civil rights in the Soviet Union and its allies. The Soviets found themselves in the embarrassing position of having to respond to criticisms based on Marx's writings. Brezhnev had a doctrine named after him. The Brezhnev doctrine, fashioned to legitimise the Soviet-led invasion of Czechoslovakia in 1968, stated that Moscow was the final arbiter of what constituted a threat to socialism. This underlined the fact that its allies enjoyed only limited sovereignty. Recent research has revealed that the Brezhnev leadership lost its nerve afterwards and decided that intervening militarily to prop up a communist party was no longer a viable policy. Poland, for example, was left to work out its own solutions. The greatest error perpetrated by the Brezhnev regime was the invasion of Afghanistan in December 1979. Again Moscow failed completely to gauge western reaction. It was pained to discover that the whole Islamic world was also against it. By the end of the 1970s Moscow had concluded that the Americans might launch a nuclear first strike. Ideology as a legitimising instrument collapsed. The way was open for Mikhail Gorbachev who opted out of the arms race. He tried to marry Marxism–Leninism and western social democracy and, predictably, failed.

Mao Zedong fashioned Chinese perceptions of the outside world. His thought is an eclectic mixture of Marxism and traditional Chinese thinking. Stalin always kept him at arm's length and would have preferred the civil war in China to have continued until he felt he could control a future socialist

China. In the beginning Mao worshipped Stalin. Despite Stalin's deliberate attempts to downgrade him when he came to Moscow to negotiate a friendship treaty, including economic aid, Mao retained his high opinion of the Soviet dictator. After Stalin's death, Mao thought that he was the natural successor and was deeply offended by Khrushchev's crude behaviour. The Secret Speech marked a watershed and Mao began to criticise not only Khrushchev but Stalin. The way was open to break with the Soviet model and to advance a Chinese model that would eventually sweep across the world. Chinese policy was instinctively anti-imperialist and anti-hegemonist. China, which means Middle Kingdom, saw itself facing dangerous enemies whose goal was to turn China into a colony. This had occurred to many parts of China in the nineteenth century and it was like an open wound to Mao and his advisers. The Chinese believe themselves to have no equals in the world and the failure of China to protect itself against foreign domination was deeply insulting. The main enemy from 1949 was, of course, the United States. Mao worried that the Americans might try to establish bases on Chinese soil to wage war against the communist regime. There was close ideological contact between the Soviet, Chinese and North Korean communist parties immediately in and after 1949. Stalin had a low opinion of the Koreans and was suspicious of Chinese intentions but permitted Kim Il Sung, the North Korean leader, to launch the Korean war in 1950. By the late 1950s Mao had turned into a harsh critic of Moscow. The turning point was the Taiwan Straits crisis of 1958. The Chinese shelled the islands of Quemoy and Matsu (Jinmen and Mazu) without informing the Soviets first. Beijing turned down Khrushchev's offer of nuclear protection. The following year Khrushchev pressured the Chinese to desist from military action against Taiwan and indirectly to acknowledge the independence of Taiwan. China concluded that it could no longer rely on the Soviet Union unless it was willing to dilute its own sovereignty. Beijing now feared that Washington and Moscow could come together to emasculate China. The shock that China had to consider Moscow a hostile power led Mao to the belief that China had to be prepared to fight a war for survival. The need to galvanise the country for war may have been a major reason for the launching of the Cultural Revolution. China turned in on itself and engaged in ideological self-purging. Those with education were suspect and pupils humiliated their teachers. The Great Leap Forward was a vain attempt rapidly to increase steel output, among other things. Famine stalked the land and perhaps up to 30 million died. If there is an explanation, it appears to have been Mao's desire to destroy the interest groups that had formed in heavy industrial regions, such as the north east. Perhaps he reasoned they might not be willing to follow him in the event of war.

Sino-Soviet relations descended to a new low in the late 1960s when border clashes resulted in many deaths. Beijing immediately played the Washington card and Sino-American relations were normalised in 1973.

China declared itself opposed to Soviet 'hegemony' in the Asia Pacific region. However, China's room for manoeuvre was limited. From the mid-1950s to the late 1970s China devoted most of its attention to relations with the Third World. It said it was its 'international duty'. It worked hard in Africa, Asia and Latin America to promote the advance of revolutionary regimes and to prove that China was a more faithful ally than the Soviet Union. It offered Castro help, for example, but he chose the Soviet Union. The Chinese attitude to conflict resolution was to be prepared to use force. The Chinese were always extremely sensitive to criticism and wished to be accepted as major players on the world stage. The fact that, economically at least, China was a dwarf until the 1990s was ignored.

SECURITY

The Americans perceived that the Soviets had certain advantages at the beginning of the Cold War. They could tax and exploit their population and, gradually, the states under its domination in eastern Europe. China could provide useful sources of raw materials. The sheer size of the populations and economies conferred on Moscow and its allies the ability to mobilise military manpower and resources to the point where it was doubtful if the west could contain an attack, if launched. Another factor was that the Soviets were willing to sacrifice soldiers in pursuit of military goals. There was no way the Americans and their allies could match the Soviets and their allies man for man, weapon for weapon, tonne for tonne so they had to counterbalance the perceived advantages of the communist states in other ways. The route chosen was to substitute firepower for manpower, capital for labour and quality for quantity. By the early 1950s this new strategic doctrine was in place. Emotive language was used to underline the problem. Politicians and the military referred to Russian and then Chinese soldiers as 'hordes from the east'. There was no way the west could meet 'hordes with hordes'.

In the late 1940s and early 1950s America became more and more reliant on nuclear and thermonuclear weapons. However, the Soviets were capable of developing these weapons as well so it would be self-defeating to rely on a single 'wonder' weapon. The Americans and their allies had to develop and deploy a continual stream of new military systems. Washington had to gain technological superiority not only in conventional (non-nuclear) but also in nuclear technology and retain that superiority indefinitely. The Americans thought that they glimpsed a chink in the communist armour. The highly centralised political and economic system which made possible the exploitation of the population and its resources, would find it difficult to react to sudden changes in western military technology. Technological innovation would be a key element in the battle with the Soviets and the Americans perceived that a market economy would be much more inventive than a command economy. In this they turned out to be absolutely right. The goal was to spread innovation as widely as possible so as to oblige the Soviets to diffuse their resources. After all, the west was technologically more developed across the board than the Russians and their allies.

In order to gain and maintain a technological advantage the Americans would have to launch a vast research and development programme. But how was this to be organised? Washington would have to rely on the private sector. As it turned out the US government poured money into the development of defence, space and energy-related technologies. It expended very little on developing civilian industrial research. There was strong opposition to the government directing commercial research. Free enterprise and free markets should be permitted to decide what industry produced. The method adopted, which proved highly successful, was for the state to contract out research. This permitted vigorous competition for contracts and the state could choose to continue funding the most successful.

Until the mid-1960s the technologies being developed for the defence sector were either unrelated to or far in advance of those being designed for the private sector. Intercontinental ballistic missiles and thermonuclear weapons had no clear civilian use and state funding promoted such things as jet engines and nuclear power plants. President Dwight Eisenhower, a Republican and a former military commander, was wary of a particular interest group that had emerged. It consisted of the Pentagon and industrial companies which were gaining defence contracts. He coined the expression the 'military–industrial complex' to describe this lobby which had its own agenda: greater and greater defence spending. He tried to contain its influence as long as he was in the White House. Needless to say the military–industrial complex tended to favour greater tension between the superpowers and had little interest in bringing the Cold War to an end.

In the 1960s and 1970s things began to change dramatically as the computer and semiconductor industries expanded rapidly in response to civilian, commercial demand. These industries had been promoted initially by government funding. By the mid-1970s advances in electronics, telecommunications and computers were being driven by the civilian sector. The term 'spin-off' was coined to describe the process by which the private sector seized on technologies in the military sphere and developed them for commercial advantage. Hence, by the mid-1970s, high technology was being driven by the private and not the military sector. The combination of military–commercial innovation promoted technological change more rapidly than would have otherwise been the case (Westad 2000, Chapter 9 et passim).

In the 1970s and 1980s the existence of a dynamic private technological sector turned out to be a major strategic advantage for the west. A reverse spin-off occurred. Unlike the 1950s and 1960s the civilian high technology sector was now providing tangible benefits for defence. From the 1970s onwards the Soviets began to fall further and further behind in crucial high technology areas. They were brilliant in some sectors, such as lasers and rocket technology, but could simply not compete across the board with the Americans. American security now rested on high tech weapons. The key sector was electronics. No one has been able yet to explain convincingly why the Soviets were weak in electronics and electrical engineering and brilliant in other spheres. They were to pay dearly for these weaknesses.

Sputnik, launched in 1957, was a wake-up call for the Americans. There was a danger that the Soviets would win the battle for technological superiority. Paradoxically the Soviet Union's greatest success proved its undoing. Washington simply had to match Sputnik and improve on it. The outcome of the space race could be that the Russians get to the moon first. Fortunately for the west, the Sputnik shock stimulated great technological innovation in the private sector and the Soviets were left behind. A major difference between the Soviet and American (as well as the Japanese and west European) economies was that the spin-off from the military to the civilian sector in the Soviet Union was almost non-existent. Something like two-thirds of the top scientific and engineering talent in the Soviet Union worked in the defence sector. That sector had first call on national resources. If something produced in the military sector failed a quality test it was placed in the civilian economy. Transistor radios are a simple example.

As the technology gap widened some Americans began to feel that there was no limit to what they could do. When President Ronald Reagan launched his strategic defence initiative (SDI or Star Wars) most of the US scientific community was taken aback. There were very few who believed it technologically feasible. It is now clear that he, a non-scientist, promoted the programme without consulting many in the technical world. It was his baby and he clung on to it like grim death. Gorbachev did his best to get it dropped but in the end the Soviets dropped their opposition to it. They adopted a paradoxical position. They claimed that it was unworkable yet launched a major propaganda campaign against it. What appeared to unnerve them was that in developing the programme the Americans might invent other advanced weapons. This was the spin-off that Moscow feared.

The Americans were beginning, in the 1970s, to gain a technological advantage over the Soviets. Why did they then acknowledge Soviet strategic nuclear parity and suggest that the arms race be regulated? The main reason was that, once both superpowers had built up arsenals which could not only destroy one another but also the whole planet, there was no point in adding more and more weapons. Technological research would provide more and more sophisticated weapons but they could not be used since sufficient lower grade weapons existed to wipe out everyone. The fear was that one side or the other would perceive that a breakthrough afforded them an advantage and launch a first strike. The other side of the coin was that the Soviets might conclude that they were falling dangerously far behind and adopt desperate measures, including war, to redress the balance. It was possible to conceive of a situation where new technologies could actually reduce American security because they could lead the Soviets to act rashly. Arms agreements until the Gorbachev era were designed to slow down the expansion of arsenals. Under Gorbachev weapons were actually cut.

From the Soviet point of view, in 1945, Soviet security depended on the two defeated powers, Japan and Germany. Stalin's nightmare was that both would recover, rearm and begin to think about revenge. The Soviet generation that had experienced the war could never think of these countries without regarding them as a threat. Russia had suffered invasion from eastern Europe three times in just over a century: in 1812 by Napoleon, in 1914 by the German kaiser and in 1941 by Hitler. This left a permanent scar on the Russian mind. This was not really appreciated by the Americans after 1945. Stalin and his successors wanted a security or buffer zone in eastern Europe which would preclude another invasion. The American decision, in 1947, to begin rebuilding the Japanese economy sent shock waves through Moscow. Stalin's decision to permit Kim Il Sung to invade South Korea, in 1950, may have been influenced by the calculation that if the whole of Korea were under Soviet influence, this would afford greater protection against a resurgent Japan.

Neither the Soviets nor the Americans believed that the Germans would tolerate the division of their country on a permanent basis. Stalin only grudgingly conceded Walter Ulbricht's wish to build socialism in the German Democratic Republic (East Germany) after the failure of his notes of 10 March and 9 April 1952 to the western allies to elicit the desired response. Stalin had proposed that free elections should follow the withdrawal of the four occupying powers. He was willing to contemplate a neutral Germany which would not be communist. This, in his eyes, was preferable to a rearmed West Germany forming part of a western alliance. After his death, Soviet leaders again saw a united, neutral Germany as the best option. In May 1953, Vyacheslav Molotov, Foreign Minister, submitted a draft resolution to the government proposing free elections after the withdrawal of the occupying powers.

If Stalin and his successors were prepared to accept a neutral, capitalist Germany why did it not come about? Others did not want a united, neutral Germany, first and foremost the Americans. The western allies feared the attractiveness of Soviet socialism. Liberal capitalism was only in its infancy in 1952–3 and it was only in the later 1950s that one could say that, due to the rapid growth of the economy and living standards, it would survive. Germany was the key country in Europe from both a Soviet and western point of view. A united, capitalist Germany which was part of a western alliance had to be prevented at all costs. It would pose a security threat of the first magnitude to

Russia. From an American point of view a united, neutral Germany was not to be trusted as it could ally with the Soviet Union. France was very keen to prevent the unification of Germany, mindful of its inability to compete economically with a new German state. Great Britain similarly did not favour a united Germany as it would gradually become a formidable competitor in Britain's export markets. There was another determined opponent of a united, neutral Germany: Konrad Adenauer, the first West German Chancellor. As early as the summer of 1945 he had concluded that the eastern, occupied part of Germany was lost to the Soviets for the foreseeable future. He saw West Germany as an integral part of western Europe and worked indefatigably to achieve this. He also feared the attractiveness of communism. The most effective way to prevent the expansion of Soviet influence in West Germany was to integrate it firmly in western Europe. Someone else who favoured this path was Kurt Schumacher, the leader of the West German Social Democratic Party (SPD). He disagreed strongly with Adenauer on many issues but on the question of West Germany they concurred completely. Schumacher resolutely opposed the establishment of a pan-German SPD, regarding social democratic activity under Soviet occupation as well nigh impossible. By being strongly anti-communist he hoped to gain influence with the western allies. Adenauer pushed hard for West German rearmament and he used the Korean war to emphasise the need to be better prepared militarily. He begged western governments not to accept the proposals set out in Stalin's notes of March and April 1952. He argued that if the west now stood firm the Soviets would eventually concede freedom to both East Germans and east Europeans. One presumes that he said this with tongue in cheek, given his fear of Soviet power. He did not provide a timeframe for this but, of course, eventually he was proved right.

Another determined opponent of a united, neutral Germany was Walter Ulbricht. The chances of his playing a major role in a pan-German state were slim, given that he was regarded by Germans in both east and west as Moscow's man. Some even called him Stalin's lackey. Stalin held him back until April 1952. After the master's death Ulbricht faced an uncertain future. Lavrenty Beria and other Soviet leaders favoured a united, neutral Germany but the June 1953 uprising in East Berlin and East Germany saved Ulbricht. The Soviets could not stand idly by and permit the 'achievements of socialism' to be swept away. At the Geneva Summit, in July 1955, Nikolai Bulganin, the Soviet Prime Minister, and Nikita Khrushchev, the Party leader, indicated that they were prepared to negotiate. The concept of a united, neutral Germany was still not dead. Not achieving any tangible results, Khrushchev abandoned the concept and in East Berlin, en route to Moscow, he made it clear that the German question would not be resolved at the expense of the GDR. This was the first time that a Soviet leader had guaranteed the further existence of East Germany. Afterwards Khrushchev's goal was to get the western Allies out of

West Berlin. He was furious when they did not bend the knee and leave. The Berlin crises of 1958–63 are essentially about this simple policy objective. It is now known that he had no fallback position and hence the conflict could have escalated out of control. The building of the Berlin Wall, in August 1961, was a confession of weakness. The GDR could not compete successfully with West Berlin and West Germany with an open frontier in Berlin. An agreement on Berlin had to wait until Leonid Brezhnev occupied the Kremlin.

Khrushchev's negotiating technique often backfired. In the traditional Russian manner, he issued threats and believed that he could achieve his goals by frightening the opposition. He overlooked the fact that whereas at home he could send the KGB (political police) to bring a recalcitrant to heel, this could not be done abroad. He overstated the Soviet nuclear capability and this spurred the Americans on to acquire more weapons. His tantrums harmed the image of the Soviet Union and gave the impression it was being headed by someone who was unstable and erratic. He was often obscene and extremely rude. After meeting Harold Macmillan, the sad-eyed British Prime Minister, in the Kremlin, he remarked laconically to an aide: 'I have just fucked him with a telegraph pole.'

A constant of Soviet thinking about security was that small states on its borders had to acknowledge the priority of Soviet needs. It was difficult for a Soviet leader to take small states seriously. After all some of them would have fitted into a minor Soviet province. Only the United States was big enough for Moscow to think of it as an equal. Territorial acquisition was always an objective, continuing a long Russian imperialist tradition. When Mao Zedong came to negotiate a friendship treaty, in 1950, Stalin could not resist imposing some territorial conditions. The Soviets were to have a privileged position in part of north east China and Xinjiang, in the west, and foreigners were not to enter these territories. The Soviets also wanted facilities at Port Arthur (Dairen). These demands deeply offended the Chinese who were extremely sensitive about their sovereignty. Khrushchev was eventually forced to give them up. The Soviet decision not to help the Chinese acquire a nuclear potential infuriated the Chinese. After all the Russians had promised to make Beijing a member of the nuclear club. Moscow, after some deliberation, concluded that it was not in its interests to make China a nuclear power. This fuelled resentment and ensured that China would redouble its efforts to build its own nuclear bomb. Brezhnev apparently asked the Americans how they would react if Moscow took out the Chinese nuclear centre. When talking to Americans he always warned them about the Chinese who were fiendishly unreliable. Hong Kong (British) and Macao (Portuguese) were other blemishes but they would revert to China since they had only been leased to the foreigners. Taiwan was another case. Beijing, like Khrushchev, employed threats to enhance its case. It shelled islands in the Taiwan Straits to warn off the Americans. China's insecurity led to an abrasive foreign policy towards Russia and

America. Then it all changed in the 1970s and the United States soon became China's leading export market. This meant that they had to get along together.

CULTURE

America's history has provided it with a culture which is based on the freedom of the individual. Before emancipation America consisted of two societies: one free and the other enslaved. The antithesis of freedom was slavery but the free men were those who were responsible for slavery. This extraordinary paradox shaped American thinking and made the term slavery an emotive word. In 1945 the Americans talked of freedom and slavery but this was soon replaced by freedom and totalitarianism. Freedom was virtuous but totalitarianism was evil. The Judeo-Christian tradition in the United States reinforced this dichotomy. God conferred freedom on the good American but there was always an enemy, hidden or in the open: evil. It could be personified as the Devil or the Anti-Christ. In Protestant thinking the first and greatest Anti-Christ was the Pope, the head of the Roman Catholic Church. American political thinking is heavily influenced by Protestant thinking. It is striking that there has only been one Catholic President, John F. Kennedy, so far. Catholicism only became fully acceptable politically during World War II. Evil is ever present but is sent by God to test his people. If they rise to the challenge and defeat evil they acquire virtue and will be blessed by God. Subconsciously, there is always a desire to identify an evil in order to combat it. It permits the leaders of the nation to mobilise the people and thereby make them stronger and more united. Communism fitted nicely into the frame. It was the personification of evil. It denied the existence of God, it denied individual freedom, it denied the right of a person to act autonomously, it abolished the free market and it vowed to destroy the free world. It was a mortal enemy, an Anti-Christ. It was collectivist and spoke of the masses and not of individuals. Needless to say, it persecuted believers and did not permit any evangelical activity. It followed that the only sure way of overcoming the communist threat was to destroy it. It was vain to believe that the threat would simply go away or that one could negotiate a truce with it. The Devil is the Devil and he never changes. As such he is a mortal enemy and must be destroyed. Détente was only a hiatus while America recovered its strength and self-confidence. The natural order of things between America and Russia was hostility.

The first phase of the Cold War ended in 1963 when President Kennedy recognised the Soviet Union as a normal state with legitimate security needs. He dropped the rhetoric of good and evil and saw Soviet society as neither. The major reason for this change in American perception was an awareness that American power was quite limited. The Sino-Soviet split, the division of Germany which appeared to be permanent and the Cuban Missile Crisis led to a more sober analysis. Détente followed but President Nixon and his Secretary of State, Henry Kissinger, both Republicans, found that Americans increasingly refused to accept their *Realpolitik* approach to foreign affairs. This was based on pursuing policies which corresponded to American state interests. Americans thought that they had a mission in life: to extend to the rest of the world the benefits of American society. The Soviet invasion of Afghanistan was seized on to discredit President Jimmy Carter's non-confrontational foreign policy. Carter, a Democrat, gave way to Reagan, a Republican. Back came the rhetoric of good and evil and the Soviet Union became the 'evil empire'. Predictably, he increased defence spending rapidly and called on the nation to unite against the threat which emanated from the communist world. The Soviet Union could not compete and admitted defeat. Reagan responded quickly to Gorbachev's proposals and dropped the concept of the 'evil empire' but his successor, George Bush Senior, took his time. It was as if he could not really believe what Gorbachev was saying. It sounded too good to be true. A communist leader actually meaning what he said was something novel to a man brought up on a diet of anti-communism.

When the challenge of modernisation, understood as Russia becoming more like the leading powers of the day, came to Russia in the second half of the nineteenth century, the shock produced two responses. One group, the Slavophiles, rejected the western course of development and clung to a vision of Russia shaping its own future. They saw the outside world as hostile and lamented the materialism, corruption and licentiousness which they identified there. It was not a coincidence that many of the leading Slavophiles were Orthodox Christians. They preferred the Russian way which was collectivist, anti-individualist and regarded the acquisition of wealth as a by-product, not the driving force, of one's existence. Hence, Slavophiles had an instinctive dislike of capitalism. They wished to choose the Russian way not the American way.

Westernisers, by way of contrast, were keen to embrace what Europe and America had to offer. The Russian way only led to stagnation and posed a threat to Russian security. There was a great risk that if Russia did not follow the same path of development as the other leading world states it could end up as a colony of one or several of them. The westernisers paid little attention to God and sought other gods: first and foremost Karl Marx. Marxism became the dominant political ideology from the 1890s onwards. One commentator has ruefully commented that the Russian love affair with German philosophy was based on this maxim: the more abstruse and incomprehensible it is, the more attractive it becomes. All Russia's problems, the key one being backwardness, could be solved by applying western remedies. They were working in the west so why should they not work in the east? The most successful westernisers turned out to be the Bolsheviks. According to orthodox Marxism it should have been the Mensheviks who predominated. Russia was economically weak and industrially underdeveloped. According to Marx, the workers, the proletariat, would take power when capitalism had developed to the point where it could develop no further. It was quite clear in 1917 that Russia was only beginning its journey along the capitalist road. Lenin's victory in 1917 was a triumph of politics over economics. The Russian state collapsed and the Bolsheviks seized the opportunity to take power. Private capitalism would give way to state capitalism which would speed up Russia's industrial development. However, Russia could not build socialism on its own; it would have to rely on more developed states to help it. He always thought that Berlin would be the natural capital of socialism. When the desired socialist revolution in Germany was not forthcoming, Lenin was faced with an agonising choice: abandon the revolution or start on the onerous task of making Russia an industrial power. He took the fateful decision to build socialism in one country. Given the sacrifices involved, it would be impossible to achieve this by democratic means. Most of the working class were not prepared to make the sacrifices involved. The rest of the population, perhaps 80 per cent, were equally unenthusiastic. There were no successful socialist revolutions outside Russia. This meant that Russia found itself as a small island in a large capitalist sea. Internationalism had to take a back seat and the only way forward was to revert to Russian nationalism as a way of mobilising the population. Coercion had to be applied in order to drive this vision forward.

Hence the Marxist contempt for capitalism was wedded to Russian national contempt for outside powers. Contempt was based on fear and jealousy. The Stalinist system, which saved Russia from annihilation at the hands of Hitler's Wehrmacht, was an amalgam of Russian and Marxist thinking. The inferior position of the Soviet Union meant that it had to lie, cheat and spy in order to redress the balance with the more powerful capitalist states. They were mortally hostile to Soviet socialism and hell bent on destroying it. This was because socialism was superior to capitalism and the more powerful the socialist world became the weaker the capitalists felt. Their lifeblood were markets and sources of raw materials abroad. Cut them off and it would be like cutting off oxygen to a dying man.

Marxism, as a secular religion, complemented Russian Slavophile thinking neatly. The elect, the chosen people, were the working class, first and foremost the Russian working class. They were guided by a church which provided an ideology, Marxism, which represented truth in the world. It had sacred texts. In the beginning these were Lenin's writings but eventually Stalin replaced him as the fount of universal wisdom. Deviance from these texts was heresy and could, and often was, punished by death. At the head of the church and state stood the benevolent tsar: first Lenin, then Stalin and later Khrushchev and others. Lenin and Stalin were worshipped as gods. However, that is where it stopped. No one ever thought of Khrushchev or Brezhnev or even Gorbachev as a god.

Soviet ideology, in order to mobilise the population, needed external and internal enemies. In the 1920s it was Great Britain and Poland, in the late 1930s it was Germany, for ever after it was the United States. The wicked capitalists were always hell bent on turning back the wheel of history and enslaving the Soviet people. Again one finds this dichotomy: freedom is socialism, slavery is capitalism. Marxism, as a global doctrine, looked forward to a world without capitalism. Marx had not excluded that capitalism might vanquish socialism but it would only be for a season. The final victory of socialism was inevitable. This utopian vision had great power and it was only in the 1970s that the United States could rest assured that capitalism would prove the superior economic system.

Domestically, Soviet leaders always feared the appeal of capitalism. The essence of capitalism was the private ownership of the means of production, distribution and exchange. Hence, the Soviet state had to take these over and ban private enterprise. Stalin demonised his political enemies as agents of western capitalism. Even Trotsky was accused of being in league with Hitler to bring down socialism in the Soviet Union. Western thinking, western influence had to be eliminated as the new Soviet man and woman came into being. Western thought was heresy and had to be rooted out. If not, it would be the cancer that could kill socialism. Stalin's analysis of fascism misled him about the potential of capitalism to survive. He defined it as the most extreme form of monopoly capitalism. Since its class base was very narrow it was doomed to extinction. However, in its final phase it was potentially very dangerous. It could become desperate and launch a war in an attempt to survive. Hence, one of the primary goals of Stalin's foreign policy was to prevent the outbreak of fascism anywhere. He set out to ensure that capitalism died a slow, peaceful death. It is instructive that Soviet opposition to the Marshall Plan was centered on 'peace' and 'national independence'. One might have thought that socialism and revolution would have been Stalin's policies. It appears that Stalin thought that a peace movement would be a more effective way of blunting the fangs of capitalism. Promoting revolution and socialism might provoke a violent response.

The Cold War was a contest between two global doctrines which owe their origin to the European Enlightenment. The most optimistic Soviet leader was Khrushchev who was convinced of the final victory of communism. He was taken aback by American material wealth but comforted himself with the insight that all that glisters is not gold. Faced with the vastly greater productivity of American agriculture, his only comment was that the Soviet collectivist system was superior because it was more socially advanced. Collectivism to him was more advanced than individual enterprise. He did not like jazz, jeans, Hollywood chorus girls, indeed there was little about American culture which appealed to him. He was very disappointed when he could not enjoy

Disneyland, apparently because his personal security could not be guaranteed. Donald Duck might have shot him!

Khrushchev's major problem was that Soviet citizens were greatly attracted to American culture and consumer goods. The problem with demonising the enemy is that it risks making him very attractive. Moscow did its best to exclude western influence but its defences were gradually breached. It was the transistor revolution that broke down the barriers between east and west. Jazz and pop music became enormously attractive. Western fashion fascinated Soviet women and they all wanted to dress like their western counterparts. Under Brezhnev it was permitted to discuss western ideas in private but not to propagate them in public. One could tell political jokes at Brezhnev's expense provided it was done in private. They were, of course, not very flattering to the Soviet leader. Here's one example: Brezhnev arrives in the Kremlin one morning. His secretary is very embarrassed. 'But, Comrade Brezhnev, one of your shoes is red and the other blue.' Brezhnev's face lights up, 'Yes, and I have another pair just like these at home!' Such jokes herald the death of Marxism–Leninism. In 1969, this writer was in Krasnodar, in the north Caucasus. The head of Intourist was an intelligent, well-educated woman. Keen to discuss the mysteries of Marxism–Leninism he broached the subject. The reply was devastating. 'No intelligent person discusses Marxism–Leninism!' Hence, one can say that, by the 1960s, Soviet ideology had failed. Its worldview and mission were not treated seriously by those who were responsible for taking the country forward to communism. Khrushchev did enormous harm to the ideology by his boorish behaviour abroad and at home, his constant bragging about Soviet achievements and, worst of all, his promise that the foothills of communism would be reached in 1980. Once, while in the Soviet Union, *Pravda* published flattering figures about Soviet economic growth. The writer asked a Party member if he was impressed. His reply was: 'I look in the shops.' He took it for granted that the party newspaper would exaggerate economic growth and welfare.

Russian nationalism replaced ideological conviction. The same applied to non-Russian republics. Traditional values surfaced. Despite the fact that few thought that communism was achievable, anti-Americanism and anti-western attitudes were widespread. This was traditionally a Russian attitude but one reinforced by communist ideology. What was Russian was best was still the dominant attitude. This began to change in the 1970s and 1980s as Soviet citizens realised how wide the gap was between living standards in east and west. Even more embarrassing for Moscow, the standard of living in many east European countries was higher than that in the Soviet Union. Western materialism became an irresistible magnet. Especially among youth, the belief began to gain ground that the west was a paradise. The revolution of rising expectations swept aside Marxist–Leninist ideology. However, certain core ideas of socialism remained: education and social security should be provided by the state. Everyone had the right to a job and housing and the state should look after these. The traditional friend–foe dichotomy broke down under Gorbachev. Most of the younger generation no longer conceived of the United States as the mortal enemy, waiting to launch a nuclear strike against them. Arguably Coca-Cola, jeans, Walkmans, CDs and the paraphernalia of western consumer culture did more to undermine the appeal of socialism and normalise relations than any number of books and propaganda broadcasts.

CHAPTER TWO

THE COLD WAR IN PERSPECTIVE

The term 'Cold War' was popularised by the US columnist Walter Lippmann and entered general usage in 1947. The Truman doctrine, proclaimed in March 1947, underlined US willingness to help counter the communist threat in Greece and Turkey, but in reality, it was a general commitment to come to the aid of states facing a communist takeover. Its economic arm, the Marshall Plan, announced in June 1947, was to provide aid and thereby to revive the flagging market economies of Europe. Economic prosperity was perceived as the most effective antidote to the attractiveness of communism.

The expression 'cold war' had been coined by the fourteenth-century Spanish writer Don Juan Manuel. He was describing the conflict between Christendom and Islam and observed that hot and cold wars were mainly distinguishable by the ways in which they ended: 'War that is very fierce and very hot ends either with death or peace, whereas a cold war neither brings peace nor confers honour on those who wage it.' Before 1990 neither east nor west had proved victorious, but communists could point to the reunification of Vietnam in 1975 as evidence that the tide was flowing in their direction. The other partitions which symbolised the conflict – Germany and Korea – remained. But in 1990 the tide seemed to be turning, as the communist regime in East Germany fell and Germany was reunited. Then in 1991 came the unexpected collapse of the Soviet Union. One of the reasons for this collapse was that the economic burden of being a superpower became unbearable. The Soviet Union imploded. The irony was that the last President of the Soviet Union, Mikhail Gorbachev, had brought the Cold War to an end, realising that his country could sustain it no longer. In doing so he destroyed his own state. By the late 1990s only the division of Korea remains as testament to past tensions.

The Cold War can be divided into four main periods. The first, Cold War I, spans the last years of Stalin and concludes with his death in 1953. Russian foreign policy during these years was low risk or risk averse. Then follows the second period, one of danger and confrontation, from the death of Stalin until détente breaks out in 1969. Central to this is the high-risk diplomacy of

Khrushchev who was much too confident of the Soviet Union's growing power. Then follows the third period, one of détente and the desire of both superpowers to normalise their relations and reduce the risk of confrontation. This era ends with the misjudged Soviet invasion of Afghanistan in 1979, arguably the most disastrous mistake Moscow made in foreign policy during the whole Soviet era. Russian advisers even informed their leaders that the continued Soviet presence in Afghanistan could lead to a third world war [*Doc. 11*]. The ensuing fourth period, Cold War II, saw an acceleration in the arms race and a rising political temperature. This was only halted by the fresh vision of Gorbachev, who wanted to reassess fundamentally the goals of foreign policy and to negotiate a new relationship with America, one which would remove ideology from Russian foreign policy formation. Moscow would no longer support communism and national liberation movements around the globe and interdependence became a guiding light of Moscow's policy as it set out to build a new world order in partnership with Washington. However, all the gains accrued to America and the demise of the Soviet Union followed swiftly on the end of the Cold War.

COLD WAR I

Some scholars regard the Cold War as beginning in 1917 when the Bolsheviks established the first communist state. As early as 1918 Lenin had sought an accommodation (co-habitation) with the capitalist world, believing that the preservation of Soviet power was a key element in promoting world revolution. Soviet foreign policy until the outbreak of World War II was therefore defensive. However, Stalin subscribed to the Marxist belief that war between capitalism and communism was inevitable eventually, so the Soviet Union had to become militarily strong enough to win such a conflict. Given this and the expectation that wars would be fought on foreign territory, Soviet military doctrine was offensive.

World War II transformed Russia into the leading European military power and a great power, an actor on the world stage for the first time. Its only real rival was America and managing the relationship with Washington assumed vital significance for Moscow. In 1945 a partnership for peace appeared possible. Moscow played a full role in the negotiations which led to the formation of the International Monetary Fund (IMF) and the World Bank and positive analyses of the benefits of membership were being forwarded to Stalin as late as December 1945. However, the IMF stipulation that its employees should have access to sensitive economic data, including gold reserves, before any loan could be extended proved too much for Moscow. Stalin did not want the west to realise how economically weak the Soviet Union was in 1945.

In the aftermath of the war, Stalin did not wish to provoke a conflict with America and ordered communist parties in Europe to participate in government wherever possible, for example in France and Italy, but not to attempt to seize power. The strongly anti-communist British Foreign Secretary, Ernest Bevin, was alarmed at the waxing of communist influence. As early as 1946 he was prepared to accept the division of Europe, but it had to appear that the Russians were to blame. The consolidation of communist power in eastern and south eastern Europe in 1946, and the possibility that the communists would win the civil war in Greece, eventually led to the Truman doctrine and the Marshall Plan.

Moscow saw the world divided into two antagonistic camps, the socialist and the capitalist, with countries such as India and Indonesia outside both. The communist takeover in Czechoslovakia in February 1948, more due to miscalculations by local politicians than to Moscow's machinations, convinced many in the west that the communist steamroller was moving westwards. The Berlin blockade, which began in June 1948, a bad miscalculation by Stalin, added fuel to the flames. A direct result of the blockade was the establishment of West Germany and, almost immediately afterwards, of the German Democratic Republic in the east. The founding of the People's Republic of China in October 1949 brought into being a second potential communist giant. In response to this situation NATO was formed at the request of the west Europeans. In June 1950 there were further communist advances in Asia, as North Korea invaded South Korea, and in Vietnam the communists went on the offensive against the French and defeated them finally at Dien Bien Phu in 1954.

BRINKMANSHIP

The death of Stalin in March 1953 and the election of President Eisenhower, committed to ending the Korean war, signalled a phase of negotiation between east and west and the ending of Cold War I. Moscow had already launched the doctrine of peaceful coexistence in 1952, following the successful explosion of its atomic bomb. War ceased to be inevitable because it was so destructive. The Russians toyed with the concept of a united, neutral Germany, but this was opposed by West Germany and France, among others. An armistice was signed in Korea in July 1953 and a ceasefire in Indochina in 1954. A new mood of optimism was abroad and negotiations between east and west were held in 1954 and 1955, the first since 1947, covering Germany, Austria, Korea and Indochina. The Soviets agreed to leave Austria, with the peace treaty describing Austria as a neutral state. There was no agreement on Germany but Moscow held to its goal of a united, neutral Germany until 1955, when Khrushchev declared that the socialist achievements of the GDR could not be negotiated away. Korea and Vietnam also remained divided, as there was no victor in the contest between capitalism and communism.

This optimism soon lapsed, however, and the period 1953–69 became one of dangerous conflicts and brinkmanship, with relations between east and west quite volatile. The Hungarian uprising and the Anglo-French invasion of Egypt occurred in 1956, the latter leading to the Russians threatening to intervene on the Egyptian side. Another period of negotiations was initiated by Khrushchev's visit to America in 1959 and the emergence of the Camp David spirit (an early version of détente) between him and Eisenhower, but this ended abruptly in 1960 at the Paris Summit, which was wrecked by the fallout from the Russian shooting down of an American U2 reconnaissance aircraft. Relations continued frosty in 1961 in the wake of the Laos and Berlin crises (which saw the erection of the Berlin Wall).

The most dangerous incident turned out to be the Cuban Missile Crisis of October 1962, which brought the world close to nuclear war. It resulted from the over-optimism of Khrushchev, who believed that the final victory of communism over capitalism was in sight and that he had the measure of President John F. Kennedy. Whereas Stalin had been a low-risk negotiator, Khrushchev was a high-risk negotiator, although he did eventually back down in the face of a critical situation. The crisis had a sobering effect, with a nuclear test ban treaty signed in 1963 and a hotline between Moscow and Washington established. When Khrushchev was removed in 1964, Kosygin took over as chief negotiator and summits continued until 1967.

Tensions were high elsewhere in the world. In 1965 the USA took the fateful decision to intervene in Vietnam and also went into the Dominican Republic. The third Arab–Israeli war erupted in 1967, with the Soviet Union and the USA committed to opposing sides. The 1968 Warsaw Pact invasion of Czechoslovakia – after President Johnson had assured Moscow that the country was within the latter's sphere of influence – spread fear in West Germany and raised tension elsewhere. It also split western communist parties and fatally weakened the attractiveness of Soviet socialism. This era of brink-manship eventually came to a close with the advent of President Nixon in 1969, beginning a sustained period of negotiations, called détente.

DÉTENTE

This phase lasted a decade, from 1969 to 1979, and produced many accords. The recognition by the USA that the Soviet Union and the USA enjoyed nuclear parity led to the SALT I agreement in 1972. The Conference on Security and Co-operation in Europe (CSCE) in 1975 finished with the signing of the Helsinki Final Act. The Soviets attained one goal – the recognition of the inviolability of the post-1945 frontiers in Europe – but acknowledged that human rights were a matter for legitimate international concern. The Paris Accords permitted the USA to withdraw its troops from Indochina and close an unhappy chapter in its history. Détente ended in 1979 with the Soviet invasion of Afghanistan, although it had already been the butt of conservative critics in the USA for conceding too much to Moscow. The move into Afghanistan was the result of two Soviet miscalculations: that the operation would only take a few weeks and that the Americans would not raise any major objections. President Carter confessed that the invasion had opened his eyes about the real nature of the Soviet Union.

COLD WAR II AND THE END OF THE COLD WAR

Cold War II covered the period from the invasion of Afghanistan to the advent of Mikhail Gorbachev in March 1985. It was marked by rapidly rising military expenditures as both sides spoke of the need to be prepared for war should the other side strike. War became more likely. Hence the use of force in international relations became legitimate. In the USA President Reagan promised to restore military superiority, making it clear that he was willing to intervene in Third World states, such as Libya, Cuba and Nicaragua, to promote pro-western values. The Soviets responded in kind and, among other things, installed SS-20s in eastern Europe. The influence of the Soviet military on security policy in the late Brezhnev period was unprecedented.

The temperature of the polemics between east and west during this period was reminiscent of Cold War I. The Soviet Union was pilloried and described as the 'evil empire' by President Reagan and was also accused of supporting international terrorism and even attempting to assassinate the Pope. Washington began to see Moscow's hand behind all the unrest throughout the world. Superpower relations became a zero-sum game: if the Soviet Union gained an advantage anywhere then the USA was the loser and vice versa. One of the reasons for this was the wave of communist states that had come into existence in and after 1974 in the Middle East, Africa and Central America. The United States and its allies determined to redress the balance. The USA used trade boycotts (for example, ending grain shipments to the USSR) as a weapon and pulled out of the 1980 Olympics in Moscow. (The Soviets failed to turn up in Los Angeles in 1984.)

The arrival of Andropov as Soviet leader in 1982 elicited little change in Soviet attitudes. His belief that the peace movement was influential enough to force the West German government to rethink its policy of installing Pershing and Cruise missiles was misplaced. East–west talks continued, however, (unlike in Cold War I) in Geneva on intermediate-range nuclear weapons and strategic arms reductions, in Madrid on CSCE, and in Vienna on mutual and balance force reductions in Europe.

The election of Mikhail Gorbachev as Soviet leader in March 1985 introduced a sea change to international relations. Convinced that the arms race was crippling his country, he afforded primacy to foreign policy and spoke of the new political thinking. This acknowledged that security could not be achieved by military means alone, that all states were interdependent, that nuclear weapons should be abolished by the year 2000 and that ideology should be banished from foreign and security policy making. Together with Edvard Shevardnadze, his Foreign Minister, he launched a charm offensive and bowled the west over. His first meeting with President Reagan, in Geneva in November 1985, led to a joint statement that proposed that the superpowers' nuclear arsenal be cut by 50 per cent. The next summit took place in Reykjavik in October 1986, but on this occasion disagreement over the strategic defence initiative (SDI or Star Wars) could not be overcome. The third summit, in Washington DC in December 1987, was historic. It produced an agreement to eliminate a whole category of nuclear weapons: land based, intermediate and shorter range missiles. This was the Intermediate Range Nuclear Forces (INF) Treaty, signed by Reagan and Gorbachev at their final summit in Moscow in May–June 1988. Serious difficulties continued to exist, however, especially over verification of the implementation of the treaty. The two presidents did not discuss SDI: the Soviets had conceded defeat.

One of the agreements reached at Geneva had been on the withdrawal of Soviet troops from Afghanistan, completed in February 1989. Soviet relations with President Bush were good and produced two historic agreements: the CFE Treaty, signed in November 1990, and the START Treaty, signed in July 1991. However, opposition from the Soviet General Staff undermined the CFE Treaty and the dissolution of the USSR halted progress on the START Treaty. The Cold War was over because the USSR had become a supplicant, with Gorbachev seeking in vain to raise vast credits in the west to shore up the old system.

Did the Cold War end in 1990 or 1991? Those who regard the Cold War as merely another term for superpower competition between Russia and America would say 1990, when Gorbachev declared it to be over. However, those who see it as a systemic struggle, between capitalism and communism, between democracy and authoritarianism, would plump for 1991, when the Soviet Union ceased to exist.

CHARACTERISTICS OF THE COLD WAR

During Cold War I there was a military build-up, the division of Europe, and eventually the world, into two camps, and no meaningful negotiations between east and west (the Soviet Union even boycotted the United Nations for a time). The conflict was restricted to Europe in the first phase and then moved to east Asia in the latter stage. Stalin wanted an accommodation with the west but was too pessimistic about the Soviet Union's ability to resist the allures of western capitalism. In eastern Europe he would probably have settled for the Finnish solution – benevolent neutrality. He always kept his options open on Germany and again would have preferred a united, neutral, demilitarised Germany. The west misjudged the Soviet Union's strength and intentions, with the USA initially perceiving Moscow as posing no threat to its security, then regarding it as a horrendous threat. This hysteria produced McCarthyism and deeply coloured the debate until the demise of the Soviet Union. Western Europe was weak after 1945 and fearful of the attractiveness of Marxist solutions and Soviet intentions. The Berlin blockade (Stalin could have had an advantageous agreement but overplayed his hand) reinforced western concern about Soviet expansionism. Hence, although Stalin always sought dialogue and put forward various proposals on Germany, he met constantly with a lukewarm response.

In the early postwar period the USA was the dominant economic power and enjoyed a nuclear monopoly for a short time, but by the mid-1950s the USSR believed that it was catching up and was capable of putting America in the shade. The utopianism of Khrushchev surfaced in 1961, when he proclaimed that the foundations of a communist society (very high living standards for all) would be built by 1980. Partly because of this optimism, Soviet policy under Khrushchev became much more unpredictable and he was keen to make use of the Soviet nuclear arsenal as a bargaining chip. He sought a solution to the Berlin situation (West Berlin would gradually fall under communist control) and then acceded to the GDR wish to build the Berlin Wall. He also expanded the range of Soviet foreign policy by visiting Asia, especially India, and the Middle East and offering an alternative to western capitalism.

However, it was under Khrushchev, for the first time, that the communist monolith began to crack (the Sino-Soviet conflict) and it was no longer accurate to see the world in bipolar terms. The Cuban revolution of 1959 was not communist in origin but Castro was forced to seek aid and protection from Moscow because of American threats. Later, in 1962, the Cuban Missile Crisis resulted from Khrushchev wishing to counter American dominance in intercontinental ballistic missiles by placing Soviet missiles on Cuba. Soviet commanders later claimed that they had authority to launch a nuclear strike on the USA if they perceived they were under nuclear attack. One consequence of the Soviet climb-down was to exacerbate relations with Beijing.

Détente marked the apogee of Soviet power. It is ironic that at the moment the USA conceded nuclear parity Russia began to decline economically. The late 1970s saw the influence of the Soviet military on the rise as Moscow began to get involved in the communist Third World. Post-colonial Africa appeared to welcome communism (Angola, Mozambique, for instance) and Ethiopia also joined the band. Those in the west who had been warning of Soviet expansionism seized upon the invasion of Afghanistan in 1979 to demand greater defence preparedness.

Cold War II differed from Cold War I in that by 1979 the west had lost its fear of communism as an ideology. Instead, it had become a military and security threat. The violent suppression of the Prague spring had been the death knell of Marxism and the ensuing period saw virulent propaganda campaigns, even more so than after 1946. One of the most vigorous debates was about the health of the Russian economy. It is now clear that the Russian economy was in a state of terminal decline, but at the time those who supported the vast rise in US defence spending could not concede that the Soviet Union might collapse. There were those who believed that the most appropriate way to overcome Russia was to increase defence spending to the point where the Russians would be ruined by being forced to keep up, since the Russian GDP was about 40 per cent of the American. One of the unexpected side-effects of this eventually successful policy was a huge US budget deficit.

There are many theories about the reasons for the Cold War [Halliday 1983, pp. 24–8]:

- *The Russian threat.* All the conflicts and crises originated with the Soviet Union and were caused by Russian expansionism. This in turn was part and parcel of Marxist–Leninist ideology which envisaged the world victory of socialism over capitalism. Hence, one state is blamed for all the problems that arise in international relations.
- *American imperialism.* This is the mirror image of the previous view, with Washington the root of all evil, emanating from predatory, expansionist capitalism. Again responsibility is ascribed to the actions of one state with the other trying to avoid armed conflict. Capitalism is viewed as requiring confrontation and military production to survive.
- *The superpowers theory.* Developed by the Chinese in the 1960s to demonstrate that Moscow had departed from the true Marxist–Leninist path, this view regards the superpowers as colluding and competing in an attempt to rule the world. This underlines the break between Beijing and Moscow and reveals Chinese insecurity. In the 1970s there is rapprochement with America, which in turn alarms Russia.
- *The theory of the arms race.* The build-up of nuclear weapons had reached proportions where it appeared to be out of control. Both east and west were responsible. Hence, the stopping and reversing of the arms race was of paramount importance. This theory was especially popular among those in the peace movement.
- *North–south theory.* Proponents of this view perceive the main conflict in the world as that between north and south, between rich and poor nations and between dominant and dominated states. The contest for the leading position in the Third World is the motive behind all conflict.
- *West–west theory.* World politics is dominated by conflicts among rich capitalist states. The Russian–American conflict is a smoke screen for the real conflict: that between the USA, Japan and the European Union. The origins of Cold War II are to be found in the increasingly sharp conflicts

among rich capitalist states. These, in turn, promote and exacerbate conflicts within the Third World.

- *Intrastate theory.* The domestic policies of states determine their foreign policy. Changes in foreign policy are related to movements in internal power relations, new economic weaknesses and alterations in social composition. Politicians use international events to resolve internal tensions and overcome domestic competitors.
- *Class conflict.* This is based on the Marxist analysis of class conflict as the motor of change. Tension is the product of the ebb and flow of social revolution. The conflict between capitalism and communism is expressed in tensions between the superpowers. The revolutionary movement in the Third World inevitably sucks in the superpowers.

These various explanations can be accompanied by other ways of analysing the reasons for the Cold War [Leffler 1992, pp. 9–30]:

- *The orthodox or traditional view.* This corresponds to the Russian threat thesis (just examined). Russia was always hostile to the west and only cooperated when it was tactically necessary. It was, by definition, an expansionary power.
- *The revisionist view.* This adopts the same analysis as the thesis about American imperialism (just examined).
- *Post-revisionist interpretations.* These seek to avoid monocausal reasons for conflict and overcome the weaknesses of the preceding two views. The orthodox interpretation pays little attention to the legitimate security needs of Russia and the revisionist fails to lay stress on changes in Russian approaches which led to changes in American policy. Access to official documents led to a flood of post-revisionist studies which attempt to achieve some detachment from the conflict and assess the responsibility of both sides for the tension. These studies can be called post-revisionist (mark 1).

The post-revisionist (mark 2) approach is by John Lewis Gaddis who, while taking into consideration these studies, develops a sophisticated analysis based on containment before and after Kennan (see following) [Gaddis 1998]. America and Britain needed Russia as an ally to defeat Germany, but in so doing created another threat to their security. Containment, the term used to describe American policy towards Russia after 1945, may be viewed as an attempt to cope with the consequences of the bargain entered into during World War II. The goal of containment was to ensure that Russia did not reshape the international order in such a manner as to make it hostile to the west. The term 'containment' was coined by George Kennan in July 1947, when he advocated a 'long-term, patient but firm and vigilant containment of Russian expansive tendencies'. This led to the Truman doctrine and the

Marshall Plan. The US administration had no desire to oppose communism on a world scale, only expansionary Soviet communism, and began to use the term 'totalitarian' rather than 'communist'.

Halliday's view [Halliday 1983] can be classified as a post-revisionist (mark 3) analysis. He reveals the weaknesses of both the Russian threat and American imperialist interpretations. Whereas analyses of the Cold War during the 1940s have concentrated on Russian–American rivalry for influence, the conflict gradually spread until it embraced the whole world. Hence this study of the Cold War, beginning in 1949, will consider superpower rivalry throughout the world. The bipolar world of the 1940s became a multipolar world from the 1950s onwards.

PART TWO   ANALYSIS

CHAPTER THREE

COLD WAR I: 1949–1953

THE BERLIN BLOCKADE

The first time that war between Russia and America became a possibility was during the Berlin blockade. Stalin's response to the fusing of the western zones of Germany, the end of de-Nazification, the resurrection of German industrial power and the introduction of the German mark (Deutsche Mark or DM) in June 1948 was defensive. His advisers had not envisaged that West Berlin could be supplied by air so he felt confident that the western allies would eventually be forced to leave West Berlin. Stalin's goal was to ensure communist control over all Berlin and end access by the western powers, as had been agreed by Russia, America, Britain and France in 1945. The Russians began interfering with traffic to West Berlin but on 24 June imposed a ban on all traffic flows. In response, the American military in West Germany advocated the use of military force to clear the routes to Berlin. There were those in the US air force who did not believe that West Berlin could be supplied by air.

President Truman decided not to risk war in an election year, but he had to appear tough and not be seen to be caving in to Stalin, particularly since the fall of Czechoslovakia in February 1948 fuelled the arguments of the American right that communism was on the march. The resultant Berlin airlift was a spectacular success, with the allied air forces keeping the western part of the city alive. At its peak, they flew in 13,000 tons of supplies daily and kept going for 324 days. Stalin's emissaries in Berlin reported that they expected the airlift to fail and this may have misled Stalin into continuing the blockade. He eventually conceded defeat in May 1949, but the conflict changed Russian–American relations. There was a general feeling in America that had war come, the atomic bomb would have been used. Neither Moscow nor Washington wanted war but both now prepared for it. The two leading world powers had clearly become adversaries and the term 'cold war' is an apt description of their relations from this point.

The airlift transformed Harry Truman's political fortunes. Trailing badly in the race for the presidency with the Republican, Thomas E. Dewey, he gradually caught up and surprised most analysts by winning. The conflict over Berlin allowed him to demonstrate that he was a strong, resolute leader, a man who could stand up to Stalin and communism. The right had failed to drive home their charge that he had 'lost' eastern and south eastern Europe to the communists. Berlin had demonstrated that Stalin would be circumspect in future about challenging American power. West Europeans, happy with Marshall Aid, wanted more than economic aid. They desired security and wanted to shelter under the American umbrella. Uncle Sam was the only one who could frighten away the big, bad Moscow wolf from their door. They began pressing for a military alliance in early 1948 and it came to fruition in April 1949 as the North Atlantic Treaty Organisation (NATO).

Stalin's response to these events was to stoke up the fires of Russian nationalism at home. A mood of xenophobia was generated by the authorities as they sought to wean Russians away from western influence. All cultural influences from the west were deemed nefarious and designed to weaken Russia's resolve to defend its culture and traditions. This also applied to scientific contacts, which were now off-limits. Successful spying (especially the acquisition of atomic bomb secrets) replaced open contacts. It also made it possible to explain why living standards were not rising as rapidly as expected and why ideological vigilance was necessary and desirable. Jews were caught in this vice as anti-Semitism waxed. After the death of Andrei Zhdanov in 1948 there were purges targeted at his Leningrad political base. In eastern Europe show trials saw many people executed, particularly Jews. The Stalinist leadership was making Russia and eastern Europe safe for its brand of communism. The only one who got away, Yugoslavia's Tito, remained a thorn in Moscow's flesh. The peoples of the new Russian empire were paying a heavy price for the tension between Moscow and Washington.

CHINA

The United States found Chiang Kai-shek a frustrating ally. Considerable aid had been extended to the Chinese nationalist leader to do battle with the occupying Japanese, but he preferred to keep his powder dry for his long-running battle with the Chinese communists, led by Mao Zedong, and simply avoided pitched battles with the Japanese. The Americans attempted to negotiate a modus vivendi between the two Chinese leaders but Chiang believed he could rout and destroy Mao's troops, later to be known as the People's Liberation Army. This was a fatal misjudgement and despite Chiang's great military advantage on paper, he was soon facing disaster. When Chiang pleaded for much more war matériel, US advisers judged that he could not be saved. President Truman did not perceive China to be of any strategic significance for the United States and consequently left Chiang to his fate. The People's Republic of China was proclaimed on 1 October 1949. Mao put out feelers to the United States but Washington looked the other way. The Truman administration declared it would not recognise communist China and so Mao had no other way to turn than to Russia. Was a historic opportunity lost? Only in 1972 did Washington change its mind and rapprochement between China and America get under way.

US Republicans seized on Chiang's expulsion from mainland China – he repaired to Taiwan to re-establish himself and plot his return to the mainland – to pillory the Truman administration for the 'loss' of China. Alger Hiss was tried and found guilty, finally and not until January 1950, of passing classified information to the Russians in the late 1930s. A major role in turning up evidence from a previous decade was played by the up and coming congressman, Richard M. Nixon. Anxiety was compounded by the TASS announcement in September 1949 of the explosion of a Russian atomic bomb. This took the American military by surprise as it had expected the Russians to take a few more years to produce a nuclear device. For some, the explanation for the rapid Soviet advance in nuclear technology was simple: there were traitors in America who were passing on nuclear secrets. President Truman ordered that the development of the hydrogen bomb be speeded up.

In February 1950 the British announced that an espionage ring, headed by one Klaus Fuchs, had been caught passing on atomic secrets to the Russians. In the same month, a junior senator from Wisconsin, Joseph McCarthy, declared dramatically that he had evidence that the Department of State was seething with communists. He had a list of no fewer than 205 Communist Party members in the institution which shaped American foreign policy. He had no such evidence, in actual fact, but since his claim came at a propitious time, the American public was willing to believe the accusation. His claims were dismissed by the Truman administration, but they were nevertheless embarrassing. The senator's brilliant but short career had begun.

Since he could not hope for any help from America, Mao was obliged to repair to Moscow to entreat Stalin to fund the transformation of China. Stalin was not amused by Mao's victory as he would have welcomed a divided China, with the communists dependent on him. The self-confident Mao would be difficult to influence and would bridle at being expected to kowtow to Stalin's brand of communism. When Mao came to Moscow, in December 1949, to negotiate a friendship and mutual assistance treaty, Stalin kept him waiting, to underline who was the supplicant and who was the master.

Mao wanted the earth, but in the treaty of February 1950 Stalin fobbed him off with US$300 million trade credits over five years and charged him interest. Mao did get Stalin to promise to surrender Russia's special rights in Manchurian ports and the east Chinese railway, also in Manchuria, despite the fact that Stalin had been eyeing Manchuria and inner Mongolia. But there were concessions: the Soviets were granted economic rights in Xinjiang and Mao had to agree to mixed companies as a way of tapping Russian technical expertise. Foreigners were not permitted in Manchuria and Xinjiang and Soviet troops could cross Manchuria to Port Arthur at will and without informing the Chinese beforehand. Mao also asked for an atomic bomb but was turned down. As a parting gift, Stalin handed Mao his man in the Politburo of the Communist Party of China, Kao Kang, on a plate, or rather to the firing squad. Kao had been Stalin's main Chinese spy and was immediately executed. Although Mao had enormous respect for Stalin, he was very sensitive about Chinese sovereignty and wished to be master in his own house. The seeds of the future conflict between the communist giants had been sown. One explanation for Stalin's cool reception was that he was fearful that Mao might turn out to be another Tito. Until his death Stalin dealt with all relations, large and small, with the Chinese communists. China was too important to be left to others. A doubt that gnawed away at Stalin's mind was that the Chinese comrades were not really Marxists at all.

NSC-68

In early 1950 President Truman instructed the National Security Council to undertake a fundamental reappraisal of US Cold War policy. This document, which was only declassified in the 1970s and became known as NSC-68, had a formative influence on the way America waged the Cold War, until it was superseded by the changed environment of détente. It viewed the world as bipolar: Russian and American. The scenario it sketched was apocalyptic: Russia was 'animated by a new fanatic faith, antithetical to our own, and seeks to impose its absolute authority . . . In the minds of the Soviet leaders, however, achievement of this design requires the dynamic extension of their authority and the ultimate elimination of any effective opposition to their authority . . . Soviet efforts are now directed toward the domination of the Eurasian land mass' [quoted in LaFeber 1993, p. 96]. Kennan, proponent of 'containment', did his best to undermine this analysis. He simply did not believe that Stalin had a blueprint for the conquest of the world.

Dean Acheson, Secretary of State, disregarded this view. As a politician, he needed to seize the initiative and an open invitation was extended him in the document. Having outlined the threat, NSC-68 spelled out the solution: America was to take the lead in fashioning a viable political and economic system throughout the non-communist world or, in the terms of the document, throughout the free world. Limited wars were justified if they achieved America's objectives. The document was based on a worst case scenario for the United States. What should America now do? [LaFeber 1993, p. 97]. There was no point in negotiating with Moscow as the balance of forces was such that the Russians could not be coerced into concessions. Instead America had to prepare for possible military confrontation: the hydrogen bomb had to be available for deployment by 1954, since the Russians were also capable of making one; conventional forces were to be expanded rapidly to defend US power without resorting to nuclear weapons; taxes were to be increased rapidly to pay for the expensive military establishment; American society was to be mobilised to make the necessary sacrifices to implement these goals; and strong, American-led alliances should be formed around the globe. The ultimate aim was that communism should be undermined within Russia and Russians won over to the American side.

The official mood in the USA had changed dramatically. Containment – accepting that the Russians were not a long-term threat to America – now gave way to the view that communist power had to be confronted and rolled back. The average American's aversion to paying taxes, let alone increased taxes, threatened to make NSC-68 just another policy document, so the administration needed a dramatic event to make its implementation irresistible. On 25 June 1950 North Korea invaded the South. The situation was transformed: 'Korea came along and saved us' [LaFeber 1993, p. 98], Acheson later admitted. On reflection, it is clear that NSC-68 presented a view of the Soviet threat which would permit increased defence expenditure. It was not an objective analysis of the Soviet Union. For instance, no attempt was made to consult Soviet experts in the US administration or in the academic world.

THE WAR IN KOREA

With its tradition of anti-imperialism, America favoured the emergence of independent states in east and south east Asia. The locals would not welcome the return of their colonial masters and would fight for their independence. Would independence movements be friendly to the United States or would they fall under the influence of communists? America played its part in ensuring the Dutch did not re-establish their empire in the East Indies and an independent, non-communist Indonesia emerged. In Indochina the French attempted to resurrect their empire but had to contend with resistance groups which had emerged under Japanese occupation. In Japan the Americans, having smashed the Japanese military, began to promote a vibrant market economy. Security remained firmly in the hands of Washington. The Philippines were granted independence but the Americans retained strategic military bases and helped in the suppression of a communist uprising.

The USA knew little about Korea as it had been under Japanese rule from 1905 until they were driven out in 1945 by Russian and American forces. Koreans wanted to be independent and resented the new occupation. Since Korea bordered on Russia, Stalin wanted to ensure that no military threat emanated from there again. The Russians and Americans began to train Koreans in the martial arts. Separate governments were formed in 1948 and in 1949 it was decided to withdraw US troops from Korea. Although Syngman Rhee, the dictator in South Korea, was unpopular, and it was possible that a united communist Korea might follow American withdrawal, Washington judged that the Asian mainland was outside the American defence perimeter.

Everything pointed to American lack of interest in the inevitable Korean civil war. Stalin provided the North Koreans with offensive weapons and, in so doing, promoted the invasion of the South, but he had completely misjudged the reaction of the Americans. Korea had to be saved from communism and this provided the bandwagon that the Truman administration, the US military and the right had been waiting for. It soured relations between the super-powers and held back détente for 20 years. It also set in train an arms race which would ruin Russia and contribute to the collapse of communism in 1991. The superpower confrontation spread to all corners of the globe. Vast stockpiles of nuclear weapons, which could never be used except to destroy the planet, were built up. The Korean war stimulated a cancer which gnawed away at the vitals of the world for 40 years.

The onset of the Korean civil war was inevitable. It just happened that Kim Il Sung invaded the South before Rhee had girded his loins to invade the North. The fact that Kim Il Sung had beaten Rhee to the draw transformed the situation. A Rhee invasion of the North would almost certainly have resulted in a united, communist Korea. The Americans had abandoned Chiang Kai-shek to his fate, so presumably they would have done the same to Rhee. Some viewed Kim's invasion as aggression and it was up to the United Nations to punish aggressors; otherwise the world could sink into anarchy.

The Truman administration grasped its opportunity with both hands. Kim's invasion – it was taken for granted that he had been sent south by Stalin – was the first real test for American resolve when confronted by Russian aggression. The domino theory was favoured: if Stalin were not stopped in Korea he would advance and states would fall in succession to communism until it dominated Europe and Asia or started a third world war. If Stalin went unchecked, US promises to resist communist aggression in Europe and Asia would turn out to be hollow. The credibility of American foreign policy was at stake; Truman would become a lame duck president. The UN Security Council voted to intervene in Korea, led by the American military. Russia absented itself during the crucial vote in the Security Council, but could have cast its veto had it been present. Was Moscow absent in order to avoid a confrontation with Washington?

It is now clear that the driving force behind the war was Kim Il Sung. He travelled to Moscow in late March and stayed until April 1950 arguing his case that the South Korean chicken was ripe for plucking. Stalin had his reservations but eventually gave in. On paper it looked a walkover as North Korean forces were greatly superior. For example, they had twice as many troops and artillery pieces. Whereas he had turned down Kim Il Sung's request to attack the South in 1949 he now gave the go-ahead. Soviet generals planned operations using their own equipment.

Brilliantly led by General MacArthur, UN forces routed the communists in three months. Having reached the 38th parallel, the border between North and South, should UN forces cross it, overrun the North and unite Korea under a more acceptable leader than Rhee? The Truman administration decided it should invade the North, assuming that Stalin would abandon it for fear of precipitating a third world war. The Chinese were written off as weak and their threats of intervention discounted. There were dissenting voices in Washington, one of whom was Paul Nitze, the driving force behind NSC-68, who thought the time was not ripe to risk a war with Russia. It would be better to wait until the NSC-68 recommendations had been implemented. But Truman could not resist using the mailed fist to refute the claim that he was soft on communism.

Mao and the Chinese leadership were in a quandary. They had no direct diplomatic links with the US and relied on the *New York Times* for information on American intentions. They gained the impression that the Americans, after defeating the communists in Korea, would then turn on China. Mao wanted to avoid war with the USA, but was convinced the Americans would force him into a conflict and so decided to fight on Korean rather than Chinese soil. About 200,000 Chinese troops invaded in October and, in November, UN forces had been routed and the Chinese poured across the 38th parallel. The North Koreans and Chinese took tremendous losses, partly due to American air supremacy, but the war became more and more unpopular in the United States.

All the while US military power was growing, especially in nuclear weapons, guided by NSC-68, and in late 1952 the American military perceived they could confront and defeat Russia. The generals concluded that the balance of power had moved in their direction. The fact that Russia did nothing to prevent its Chinese and Korean clients from being defeated in South Korea was taken as conclusive evidence. America came to believe that it could act aggressively in pursuit of its perceived interests.

Stalin provided military equipment to the Chinese, at prices the Chinese viewed as extortionate, but did not provide the air cover he had promised them. Moscow did not intervene itself in the conflict (which eventually claimed the lives of about 3 million people) or threaten to extend the war into other theatres. Through excellent sources of intelligence (spies) in Washington and London, Stalin was aware that the Americans had decided against invading China and using nuclear weapons and he was convinced that the Americans could not win a conventional war in North Korea given the vast manpower resources of China. Stalin conducted a low-risk strategy, evidenced by his reneging on the deal to supply the Chinese with air cover. He was determined to deny the Americans the opportunity to attack him.

The Korean war fuelled anti-communism in America and made it impossible to propose a balanced policy towards communist states. Policy towards

China was completely reversed. The Chinese had killed tens of thousands of American boys and were now regarded as full members of Stalin's evil communist empire. There could be no question of diplomatic recognition of the Beijing regime. Some nervous Europeans worried that if the communists had attempted to unite Korea by force, might they not try the same in Germany? Measures were needed to forestall this. NATO needed more European troops and West Germany could provide them. General Dwight D. Eisenhower was appointed Supreme Commander of allied forces in Europe and more US divisions were to be moved to Europe. The Korean war thus led to the decision to remilitarise West Germany.

The war also transformed the fortunes of Japan, which had supplied the lion's share of the provisions required by the UN forces in Korea. A tangible reward was soon forthcoming. In September 1951, in San Francisco, a peace treaty was signed which envisaged American withdrawal in May 1952. All belligerent countries signed, except, of course, the Soviet Union, China, North Korea and other communist states. The USA kept some military bases but Japanese security was guaranteed by Washington. Japan had joined the anti-communist club. The Philippines, Japan, Australia and New Zealand signed security pacts with Washington. In Europe, Greece and Turkey joined NATO. The Americans prepared to expand their influence in the Middle East. Russia was gradually being surrounded by states relying on the United States for their security and the outlook seemed bleak for Stalin. Instead of devoting resources to vitally needed reconstruction and development at home, he was being forced to invest more and more in security [Cohen 1993, pp. 58–80; LaFeber 1993, pp. 99–145].

CHAPTER FOUR

TO THE BRINK AND BACK: 1953–1969

THE SEARCH FOR A NEW RELATIONSHIP

Stalin was reported dead on 5 March 1953. The people mourned, but some in the leadership, especially Lavrenty Beria, celebrated. Stalin's last years had been replete with suspicion and fear. At the 19th Party Congress, in October 1952, there was a call for vigilance in the face of the 'threat of a new war'. The Politburo was replaced by a Presidium, with twice as many members as the old Politburo. Was Stalin preparing a purge of the old guard so as to clear the way for a new, young, Stalin-dedicated cohort?

Tension was heightened in January 1953 when *Pravda* announced the discovery of a Doctors' Plot. Over the years since 1945 several prominent politicians had already been murdered by a group of doctors, most of whom were supposedly linked to a Jewish organisation run by the Americans. One of the accused confessed that he had received orders to 'eliminate the leading cadres of the Soviet Union'. This included Comrade Stalin. The newspaper assured its readers that documentary evidence, conclusively proving the case, was available. Ministries were accused of slackness and the party and Komsomol of lacking vigilance. Then suddenly, on 23 February, the whole campaign was dropped. Shortly after Stalin's death, the so-called plot was acknowledged as a fabrication and the deputy minister of state security was blamed and shot.

A collective leadership of Malenkov, Molotov and Beria would 'prevent any kind of disorder or panic'. They hastened to relax tension at home and abroad, which was of imperative importance during the domestic power struggle. Georgy Malenkov had already called for peaceful coexistence in 1952. He now promised the Russian population a better life. Internationally, he reiterated his offer of peaceful coexistence and held out the olive branch to Tito and sent soothing words to countries bordering on the Soviet Union. Beria also launched a few initiatives. He proposed the promotion of non-Russians (he himself was Georgian) in non-Russian republics and the unification of Germany as a neutral state. The uprising in East Berlin and Beria's arrest, both in June 1953, removed him from the scene. An intriguing question remains: had he become dominant in Moscow, would Germany have been reunited and the situation in eastern Europe transformed? In retrospect, this would have served Russia better than a divided Germany and an accelerated arms race.

KHRUSHCHEV TAKES OVER

Stalin had been cautious and keen to reduce risk to a minimum in his foreign policy. He was extremely well informed about the policies and intentions of his capitalist adversaries through his highly successful spy network, although it is not yet clear how much of this excellent reporting he believed. As a Marxist, he expected the capitalist world to sink into crisis and the socialist world to remain outside these conflicts and then benefit from them. Khrushchev was a man of quite a different mould. He was a risk taker in foreign affairs as he believed that Soviet socialism would eventually prevail everywhere. He also had the atomic bomb and, by August 1953, the hydrogen bomb. Russian rocketry was developing rapidly and there was a huge Russian scientific community servicing military ends. Khrushchev was made Party leader in September 1953 and forced Malenkov to resign as Prime Minister in February 1955.

Khrushchev's knowledge of the outside world had been garnered as a rising star under Stalin. He was a frequent guest at Stalin's home and his memoirs reveal a reasonable understanding of world politics. Of course, he suffered from the besetting sin of Russian leaders: arrogance towards other socialist states. He, like Stalin, expected their leaders to defer to him. He quickly found out that the Chinese and Yugoslavs had no intention of acknowledging his precedence. His confrontation with the Chinese was eventually to split the world communist movement and then provoke border skirmishes with Beijing.

The demise of Stalin and the change of president in America made it possible to negotiate an armistice agreement in Korea, along the 38th parallel, the status quo ante, on 27 July 1953. During the struggle for primacy with Malenkov, Khrushchev could not visit any leading capitalist state as head of a delegation. That was the prerogative of the Prime Minister, Malenkov, and the Foreign Minister, Molotov. Instead, he could lead a delegation to any socialist state as relations with these countries came under the Communist Party. Relations with them were fraternal, not foreign. His first stab at diplomacy was therefore in Beijing, in September 1954, when Molotov, much to his chagrin, was left at home. Mao enjoyed playing cat and mouse with Khrushchev, who found some of Mao's statements to be opaque, others so mundane as to be blindingly obvious. There was little respect on either side. Mao thought that he was the natural successor to Stalin as the leader of the communist world, but such an idea was deeply offensive to Khrushchev. Mao got the better of the exchanges: the Russians gave up their Chinese ports and dissolved their joint stock companies. Mao even asked for Outer Mongolia (the Mongolian People's Republic, Chinese until 1911) but was put in his place.

In May 1955 Khrushchev and company made for Belgrade to bring Yugoslavia back into the Russian fold. Again, Molotov was left at home. Khrushchev blamed all the misunderstandings during the years since 1948, when Yugoslavia had been expelled from the Cominform, on Beria, but Tito was not taken in. Only in 1956 could Comrade Stalin be blamed for his policy mistakes. Khrushchev wanted to restore inter-Party relations: in other words the Yugoslavs were to recognise the leadership of the Communist Party of the Soviet Union, but Tito would not bite and offered instead to restore interstate relations.

Russia was seeking to mend all its fences with the outside world. It was mindful of the need to restrict its military budget so as to strengthen its economy and raise living standards. It wanted peace with everyone. Nuclear weapons promised to make it possible to cut the defence budget, but would the Americans play ball? There was precious little trust between the two superpowers [*Doc. 1*]. No successful agreement had been negotiated during the Cold War so far and a major problem for both sides was lack of knowledge of the other. It would take until the Gorbachev era before both sides could feel completely comfortable with one another.

When Stalin died there was a new president in the White House, General Dwight Eisenhower, and a new secretary of state, John Foster Dulles: Eisenhower was a war hero and had served as NATO Commander-in-Chief; Dulles was steeped in foreign affairs and had served under Truman. The presidential campaign had been dirty. Eisenhower's vice-president was Richard Nixon, skilled at muck raking. Joseph McCarthy campaigned for Eisenhower and dragged George Marshall's name in the mud. He and all his kind, McCarthy claimed, had betrayed America, refusing to stand up to the communists. Dulles called the containment policy 'immoral' and spoke of the 'liberation of captive nations' and the rollback of communism in eastern Europe and east Asia. The American right was on a roll.

Fortunately for America, Eisenhower and Dulles were level headed, cautious and reasonable. The vast increase in defence spending in the early 1950s increased self-confidence and Eisenhower was able to quieten those in the military who advocated a pre-emptive strike against the Russians. Apprehensive about the growth of what he termed the 'military–industrial complex', in the United States, he wanted to reduce military spending and eventually balance the budget. Eisenhower chose to concentrate on air and nuclear power. The Americans might use nuclear weapons to counter a Russian conventional attack and Dulles spoke of 'massive retaliation' at the slightest provocation. Despite this rhetoric, Eisenhower was keen to reduce the risk of nuclear war.

Russian policy in Europe centred on Germany and the aim was to ensure that Germany did not rearm and become a threat. Until 1955, Austrian and German policy went hand in hand. The goal was to create unified, neutral states, but all Moscow's blandishments in Germany came to nothing as the west feared that a united, neutral Germany might slide into the Russian orbit. In May 1955 Moscow decided to separate the two states and accept a united, neutral Austria. The Austrian Peace Treaty was signed by the four occupying powers or Big Four (America, Russia, Britain and France) and resulted in the withdrawal of all foreign troops. This was the first instance on which Russian soldiers had voluntarily left a country they had occupied in 1945. There was a bonus for Moscow: NATO could no longer use Austria as a link between West Germany and Italy. The occupation of West Germany came to an end and it joined NATO, also in May 1955. The GDR was admitted to the Warsaw Pact, the Russian response to NATO.

THE GENEVA SUMMIT

Despite this, the Big Four agreed to meet in Geneva in July 1955 to discuss nuclear weapons and the German question. Eisenhower put forward what later became known as the 'open skies' proposal. He suggested each side provide the other with a list of its military installations and that aerial reconnaissance be permitted to check that no attack was imminent. Khrushchev backed off, but when he offered partial reconnaissance two years later it was the Americans who backed off. At Geneva, the two leaders agreed on a moratorium on nuclear testing, without, of course, permitting any verification.

Nevertheless it was a landmark: the two sides were talking to one another constructively, for the first time since 1945. After the flat beer of the previous years, the Geneva spirit was quite inebriating. On Germany, Khrushchev talked about all-German elections. On his way home, however, he dropped in on Walter Ulbricht, the GDR leader, in East Berlin and assured him that the 'socialist achievements' of the GDR would be preserved. In other words, Moscow, for the first time, formally gave up its dream of a united Germany. Khrushchev had decided that increasing trade with West Germany came before everything else. Konrad Adenauer was invited to Moscow in September 1955 and diplomatic relations were established. He tried to 'buy' the GDR by offering generous credits and reparations but Khrushchev resisted the temptation. The Russians had to accept a divided Germany and a divided Europe – for the time being.

In February 1956 Khrushchev shocked communists and non-communists alike by denouncing Stalin. The self-confident Party leader declared that peaceful coexistence was the basis of relations with the capitalist world. This, however, did not mean that Moscow accepted a static world order. The class struggle, between the oppressed and the oppressors worldwide, would continue. There would be no peaceful coexistence as far as ideology was concerned. In April 1956 the Cominform was dissolved. This was one of the preconditions which Tito demanded for the normalisation of relations. Its activities were transferred to the Central Committee Secretariat and a department for liaison with communist and workers' parties was eventually set up.

THE HUNGARIAN REVOLUTION

Khrushchev's rapprochement with Tito and his declaration that there were national roads to communism fuelled hopes in eastern Europe that Russian control might be loosened. This was particularly so in Poland and Hungary. Eventually, the Poles forced the Russians to accept their choice of leader, Gomulka, in October. No resolution to the tension in Hungary could be brokered, however. On 23 October police fired on a peaceful demonstration which was demanding the return to power of Imre Nagy, the former prime minister. The revolution was under way. Nagy was appointed Prime Minister and on 1 November declared that Hungary had left the Warsaw Pact and called on the UN to recognise Hungary as a neutral state.

Khrushchev and the Russian leadership were in a quandary about whether to intervene or not. On 28 October, and again on 30 October, the Presidium (Politburo) resolved to seek a peaceful solution by withdrawing the Russian army. But on 31 October this decision was reversed and Moscow chose the military option. The reason for the change of mind appears to have been strong Chinese support for the military option. Tito also favoured using force. Another reason for the intervention was Khrushchev's fear that if he abandoned the Hungarian comrades (and Nasser during the Suez conflict which was being fought out at the same time), the decision could split the Presidium and, possibly, lead to his removal. Despite strong oral American support for the Hungarians, the United States was not willing to risk a third world war by intervening militarily.

ASIA

There were also serious tensions in Asia. The French were determined to stay in Indochina but the Viet Minh communists, led by Ho Chi Minh, were equally determined to defeat and expel them from the region. The guerrilla tactics of the Viet Minh were proving successful and, far from home, the French found it ever more difficult to provision the existing troops and provide fresh ones for the conflict. In France there was political instability and governments changed often, rendering a coherent colonial policy in south east Asia more difficult. There was also the burgeoning financial burden which

France was ill equipped to bear. The war went badly until, facing disaster at Dien Bien Phu in March 1954, the French were obliged to call for American intervention. In 1954 the Americans were paying about 70 per cent of the French military budget and had advisors in Indochina. Eisenhower and Dulles feared that if the French were defeated, the whole of Indochina would fall to the communists. The same might happen in Malaya, Indonesia, Taiwan and South Korea. A US general recommended the use of a few small, atomic bombs. Sir Winston Churchill refused to come to France's aid, seeing it as a lost cause.

The American military did not want another Korea with their men dying on foreign fields. If the USA intervened, would China also come in? In the event, the French surrendered and a new government in Paris negotiated peace in Indochina: Ho Chi Minh controlled about two-thirds of Vietnam but agreed to withdraw north of the 17th parallel; and there were to be national elections within two years to unify the country. The pro-communist Pathet Lao forces were given free rein in Laos and there were to be national elections in Cambodia. Ho concentrated on reconstructing North Vietnam, with Russian assistance. He was certain to win the national elections. The USA was not a party to the peace agreement and refused to acknowledge it. Given the anti-communist mood in America, Eisenhower and Dulles deemed it wise not to concede communist control over North Vietnam. The Americans decided to channel their aid directly to the South Vietnamese, cutting out the French. They began training a South Vietnamese army. In July 1955, with most of the French gone, Diem, the American-picked head of government, announced that national elections would not take place.

Dulles believed that an alliance, similar to NATO in Europe, was needed to prevent the spread of communism in Asia and so, on 8 September 1954, the United States, France, Great Britain, Australia, New Zealand, Thailand, Pakistan and the Philippines agreed to establish the South East Asia Treaty Organisation (SEATO). South Vietnam, Laos and Cambodia were of special concern. Indonesia, India and Burma declined to join. They did not view the communist threat in the same apocalyptic terms as the Americans. American forces, Dulles assured the Senate, would only be committed when communists were clearly in the ascendancy and the Senate would approve intervention. Initial involvement would be by the air force, not the army. Significantly, the treaty provided for the deployment of American military might to prevent a communist party successfully challenging for power in a state. The other members of the alliance made clear they would not intervene in such a case. Fateful decisions had been taken.

The Taiwan problem caused Eisenhower and Dulles endless problems. The latter profoundly mistrusted Chiang Kai-shek, suspecting that he was angling to embroil the USA in a conflict with China, in which Chiang could take over as ruler of China after American troops had cleared the mainland of communists. Mao was alarmed by the formation of SEATO and he thought the USA was planning to separate Taiwan from the mainland. Consequently China began bombing some of the offshore islands and thought this would make the Americans wary of committing themselves to Chiang. It had the opposite effect: Washington could not be seen to be abandoning Taiwan as it would send the wrong messages throughout east and south east Asia. A defence pact was signed with Chiang but the latter had to promise not to attack the mainland without Washington's consent. The USA would also not defend the offshore islands held by Chiang.

Washington pressed Beijing to renounce the use of force to regain Taiwan but the Chinese demurred, seeing the matter as the uncompleted part of the civil war. In 1957 the Americans broke off the talks. Mao began to press Khrushchev for support for an offensive against the offshore islands Jinmen (Quemoy) and Mazu (Matsu). The Americans threatened nuclear retaliation and the Chinese desisted. One of the reasons for the Chinese backdown was Russia's refusal to provide offensive military aid to China. They would only help if America invaded China. This caused great anger in Beijing as it became clear that the Russians would not risk a conflict with the Americans to help the Chinese.

It would not take long for the communist giants to fall out [*Doc. 2*]. According to the Chinese, the Russians, on 20 June 1959, unilaterally 'tore up the agreement on new technology' and 'refused to provide China with a sample atomic bomb and technical data concerning its manufacture'. The first Chinese–Indian border skirmish, on 9 September 1959, resulted in Moscow adopting a neutral stance, to the chagrin of the Chinese. When Khrushchev visited Beijing, on his way home from a summit with President Eisenhower, he asked for a Russian radio base to keep in touch with its submarines in the Pacific. Mao countered with a request for atomic data. Neither got anything. The festering Sino-Soviet conflict burst into public view at a Congress of the Romanian Party, in Bucharest, in June 1960. Ostensibly it was about socialism and de-Stalinisation (Mao had expected Khrushchev to consult him before debunking Stalin), but in reality it was about leadership of the communist movement and international status. Khrushchev informed the Russian public about the divorce at the 22nd Party Congress, in February 1961.

THE MIDDLE EAST

Oil made the Middle East strategically important, since about two-thirds of the oil available to the west was there. The region was overwhelmingly Arab and Muslim. When Israel was established in 1948, logically America should have supported the Arabs, but there was a powerful Jewish political lobby in America. The British and French had dominated the region in the interwar years; after 1945 France faded away but Britain remained. It controlled

Iranian oil and the Iranian government sought every opportunity to acquire control over its most important asset. When Prime Minister Mossadeq nationalised the Anglo-Iranian oil company, oil exports stopped and the Iranian economy declined and there were rumours of a Russian loan for Mossadeq. Dulles, after a visit to the region, was alarmed by the neutral stance of states in the conflict between 'slavery' and 'freedom'. The USA and Britain helped the Shah to reassert himself in August 1953 and the British were forced to give up their oil monopoly. In a new consortium America and Britain obtained 40 per cent each: for the Americans it was good politics and good business.

The Americans were seeking ways to fashion an alliance system in the Middle East to prevent Russian expansion but always ran up against the problem of Israel. Washington was perceived by Arab states as siding with the Israelis against the Palestinians, indeed as taking the Jewish side in the Arab–Israeli conflict. The Jewish lobby in Washington was strong and US Jews also channelled financial aid to Israel. Israel was, however, America's main ally in the Middle East. Eventually, in February 1956, Turkey and Iraq signed what later became known as the Baghdad Pact, and Great Britain, Pakistan and Iran joined later the same year. The United States never joined. The pact antagonised those Arabs, first and foremost Egypt's Nasser, who believed the region should not become involved in the Cold War.

The Americans wanted to step into the vacuum left by the exit of the British from Egypt but Nasser was calling for Arab socialism and war against Israel. Russia was also keen to step into the vacuum and Czechoslovak arms were soon on their way to Cairo. Nasser had proved he could play off east against west. But he came unstuck when arranging finance to construct the Aswan dam, to provide irrigation water and power. The Americans backed out and Nasser nationalised the Suez canal, run by an Anglo-French company, to raise funds. Anthony Eden (later Lord Avon), the British Prime Minister, overreacted, seeing Nasser as another Hitler who could only be stopped by force. France, Israel and Britain secretly coordinated war plans and on 29 October 1956, while Khrushchev was agonising in Moscow over the Russian response to the Hungarian revolution, they struck against Egypt.

What was the USA to do? Traditionally an anti-imperialist power, could Washington side with its allies and alienate the Arabs? Eisenhower and Dulles decided that their long-term goals in the Middle East came first and sided with Russia in the United Nations. The war was to end and the belligerents to go home. Khrushchev, secure in the knowledge that the Americans would not come to the aid of the British and French, threatened them with nuclear missiles if they did not go home. It was the end of British and French power in the Middle East and also Eden's political career. He had made the fatal mistake of assuming the Americans would remain neutral.

Afterwards, Congress declared the Middle East a region of vital national interest and the President could come to the aid of any state under threat. It became known as the Eisenhower doctrine. In 1957, when King Hussein of Jordan felt threatened by pro-Nasser forces in his country, the Americans stepped in and he received US$10 million in aid. It paid to be America's friend. In 1958 American marines landed in Lebanon to help the President against pro-Nasser opponents. In Iraq, the pro-western king and government were overthrown and a nationalist, anti-western regime took over. Khrushchev threatened to intervene militarily if the Americans did not leave, but Washington left when it decided Arab nationalism would not sell out to Moscow.

OTHER THIRD WORLD STATES

Khrushchev was looking for ways of establishing contact with Asian Third World states in order to counter American influence. The Bandung Conference of Afro-Asian states, in Bandung, Indonesia, condemned racism and colonialism. This was a breakthrough for the Russian leader and he was attracted by its anti-western credentials. In November–December 1955 he and Prime Minister Bulganin visited India, where the crowds were so great they were almost crushed to death, as well as Burma and Afghanistan. President Sukarno of Indonesia was invited to Moscow and promised arms and technical assistance. Communists in Indonesia supported him and made Dulles nervous. Washington provided assistance and aid but Sukarno was very ambitious and played east off against west. In 1958 Eisenhower used the CIA to promote Sumatran secession as the Americans believed many island states were preferable to one Indonesia. The attempt failed but America was caught red handed. Khrushchev beamed and increased military aid.

Khrushchev's first foray into black Africa was in the Republic of the Congo, the former Belgian Congo, where Patrice Lumumba became the Prime Minister on independence in June 1960. Mineral resources, especially copper, in Katanga province proved too valuable to abandon and the Belgians promoted its secession. Lumumba appealed to the USA, the UN and Russia to help reunify the country and the UN passed a resolution appealing to the Belgians to leave and granting military assistance for Lumumba. Nothing happened, confirming the rule that the UN only deploys troops when the USA is in favour. The Congo was a long way away and of little interest.

Lumumba appealed again to Moscow. This time, Khrushchev jumped in and sent military equipment and technicians. This sent alarm bells ringing in Washington and UN troops flew in. There was a risk that the Congo could go communist and begin a chain reaction in the region. The CIA considered assassinating Lumumba but he was dismissed from office in September 1960. He then attempted a coup but UN forces closed Kinshasa airport and prevented the Russians airlifting in pro-Lumumba forces. He was replaced by Joseph Mobotu, acceptable to the Americans (until eventually forced into exile in 1997). Lumumba was killed in 1961 and became a hero in the Soviet bloc. A university for Third World students in Moscow was named after him. When the cards were down, far from home, the Americans could always beat the Russians. Khrushchev could rant and rave, in the UN and elsewhere, against American imperialism and threaten them with his missiles. All he achieved was the acceleration of the arms race [Cohen 1993, pp. 85–120; Cohen and Iriye 1990, pp. 121–42; Khrushchev 1971; LaFeber 1993, pp. 146–94].

BRINKMANSHIP: BERLIN

The space age was launched on 4 October 1957 when Sputnik circumnavigated the globe every 96 minutes. It was a staggering achievement for Russian science to propel an 83.6 kg satellite into space for three months. Then it returned to the earth's atmosphere and burned out. However, it was not a bolt from the blue. It was followed by another eight Sputniks which scored a dazzling list of firsts: the first dog in space and so on. Russian rocket technology was the best in the world and threatened to alter the balance of world power. Khrushchev exulted and Russians felt proud. They had put one over on the Americans. As events were to show, Khrushchev became dangerously overconfident. Everything was not as it seemed. Eisenhower had actually prevented America from being the first in space. The capacity had been there but the US President was concerned about sending a space vehicle over enemy territory. He wanted the Russians to go first and then the Americans would follow. Had the USA gone first, it might have lowered the tension of the ensuing five years.

Convinced he had secured the upper hand in missiles, Khrushchev resolved to push America to the limit. He was riding high after successfully seeing off the Anti-Party group which had attempted to remove him in June 1957. He then became a strong, national leader. The Prime Minister, Marshal Bulganin, had sided with the losers and was left in power for appearance's sake. As the Yugoslav ambassador, Micunovic, remarked to Khrushchev, it would not be advisable to give the impression that he had become Stalin, mark II. In early 1958 Khrushchev pushed Bulganin aside and became Prime Minister himself. He was the supreme decision maker until the Cuban Missile Crisis of 1962 weakened him, when his opponents began to plot his downfall.

Berlin was the west's Achilles's heel. Khrushchev, in his down-to-earth language, called it the west's 'balls'. Every 'time I squeeze them, the west squeals'. Rustic but right. West Germany was now a member of NATO and the Russians were concerned that Bonn might acquire access to nuclear weapons, since it was provided with nuclear-capable artillery and fighter bombers. The USA was building up tactical (short-range) nuclear weapons and ballistic missiles which could reach the Soviet Union. They were intended to counter Russia's superiority in conventional (non-nuclear) forces. In 1958

NATO thought of providing West Germany with 'defensive' nuclear weapons [Kaplan 1994, p. 94].

As a strong, national leader, Khrushchev had three goals: to ensure the economy expanded as rapidly as possible; to increase Russia's security; and to expand communism throughout the world. Russia's security held the key. The greater defence spending, the less investment there would be for the civilian economy and for raising living standards. Rocket superiority promised a solution. Perhaps the USA could be forced into disarmament negotiations and rockets could replace some ground forces in Russia.

The Berlin crises of 1958–63 were provoked by Khrushchev. It is clear, from the archives, that Khrushchev launched the Berlin crisis because he felt that Berlin was within the Soviet sphere of influence and the west should acknowledge this. What would happen if the west stood firm? Khrushchev did not have a back-up plan. He made up policy as the need arose. When one avenue closed, he chose another. Khrushchev accepted Ulbricht's point that if the open boundary with West Berlin were not closed, the GDR would not achieve its economic potential. Workers, scientists and other professionals could simply vote with their feet if they thought the sacrifices being demanded of them were too great. The Soviet side did understand that one of the options the United States might choose was to go to war. Khrushchev read Adenauer's statement, in March 1958, that an 'Austrian solution' (unified, neutral state) to the German question was acceptable to him, as a sign of the increasing weakness of the west. During the Berlin crisis, the GDR consistently argued for a vigorous, confrontational pose.

On 27 November 1958 the Soviet Union issued its first Berlin ultimatum. All Russian rights in Berlin were to be transferred to the GDR within six months, West Berlin was to become an 'independent, political entity, a free city'. If no such agreement were reached, the allies' access to West Berlin would be regulated by the GDR. The allies replied, on 31 December, that they regarded the previous arrangements as still in force and refused to negotiate with the GDR authorities (the west did not recognise the GDR in international law). Khrushchev warned the USA that if it used force in Berlin, a third world war would result. Recognition of the GDR and the prevention of West German access to nuclear weapons were some of the goals being pursued by the Russian leadership. Talks were held in Geneva in the summer of 1959, but no progress was made. The Russians reiterated, on numerous occasions, their demand that West Berlin become a 'demilitarised, free city'.

Khrushchev had always been fascinated by America and sought an invitation to visit his main adversary. The Americans thought that by inviting him he would become more amenable to a Berlin settlement which would end confrontation. In September 1959 he became the first Soviet leader to visit the USA. Talks at Camp David with President Eisenhower papered over some of the cracks and Khrushchev withdrew his Berlin ultimatum. The greatest disappointment for Khrushchev was that his ardent desire to visit Disneyland was frustrated – the Americans said they could not guarantee his safety.

The west did not budge on Berlin but Khrushchev was sanguine that the problem could be resolved at the Paris Summit in May 1960. Bonn was strongly against any concessions on Berlin. By early 1960 US spy planes had confirmed that Khrushchev's talk of intercontinental ballistic missile (ICBM) superiority was nothing but Russian *vrane* (boastful lies). On 1 May 1960 the Russians announced the downing of a U2 spy plane, with pilot Gary Powers taken alive, near Sverdlovsk (now Ekaterinburg). This confirmed that Russian missiles had become more effective but it also demonstrated to Khrushchev that the Americans knew he was engaging in missile bluff. He torpedoed the Paris Summit of the Big Four (Russia, America, Britain and France), on European security, by demanding that Eisenhower personally apologise for the U2 incident. Khrushchev had gained the upper hand diplomatically by contradicting Eisenhower's statement that no spy plane had been flying over the Urals. He showed photographs and revealed that the pilot had been captured alive. The British Prime Minister, Harold Macmillan, pointed out to Khrushchev that it was unrealistic to expect the President of the USA to apologise in such a humiliating situation. One major reason for Khrushchev's action appears to have been the rapidly deteriorating relationship with China. Mao opposed a rapprochement with the west and advocated aggressive nuclear diplomacy, so Khrushchev's belligerence may have been partly designed to reassure him.

In the Berlin crisis, Khrushchev informed Ulbricht on 30 November 1960 that, in order to protect the prestige of the Soviet Union, his threat of concluding a separate peace treaty with the GDR would have to be made good. Ulbricht objected that this might lead to a trade boycott by the West Germans which would cripple the GDR. Khrushchev countered, without making any calculations, that the Soviet Union would make up the deficit (later it proved incapable of doing this). Ulbricht was now in a no-lose situation and could always counsel confrontation. In a letter to Khrushchev, on 18 January 1961, Ulbricht requested a Warsaw Pact conference to strengthen the position of the GDR and to force the west to make concessions on Berlin. The increasing flow of refugees to West Berlin was making these more urgent. Khrushchev replied that he wanted first to discuss the matter with Kennedy. If the President did not make any concessions, Khrushchev would discuss the implementation of their agreed measures with Ulbricht. The Warsaw Pact conference took place on 28–29 March 1961 but no one was willing to agree to the full GDR demands. Khrushchev concluded that Yury Gagarin's first flight in space, in April 1961, and the Bay of Pigs disaster, in May 1961, had weakened Kennedy.

Khrushchev met the new American President, John F. Kennedy, in Vienna in June 1961 and thought he had taken his measure. Kennedy made it clear that he did not want war but would not concede on Berlin. Khrushchev responded that if war were to come, it should come sooner rather than later, when the weapons would be even more terrifying. Kennedy did not take Khrushchev's outburst about war all that seriously. The Russian leader judged that the young American president might buckle under pressure and was soon to put him under immense pressure over Cuba.

Khrushchev then informed Ulbricht he wanted a Warsaw Pact conference as soon as possible to advance matters. At the end of June, Khrushchev permitted Ulbricht to begin making preparations to divide Berlin. Kennedy addressed the American nation on television on 25 July 1961 and underlined that the real question was not West Berlin but American credibility throughout the world. Access to West Berlin, the garrisons there and the viability of the city would be defended. The President, however, did not state that access from West to East Berlin would be defended. Here was a way out for Moscow. Khrushchev's first reaction to the speech was to declare that it was a declaration of war, but he soon calmed down.

The Warsaw Pact summit on 3–5 August decided to divide the city, initially with barbed wire, and then, if the west did not react, with a wall. This was all the GDR would be permitted to undertake, it was not to move a 'millimeter beyond this'. The GDR was not to prevent western military personnel entering East Berlin since this would have led to Soviet personnel being barred from West Berlin. On 13 August 1961 sealing West Berlin off from East Berlin and the GDR began. The west did not intervene. Kennedy and Khrushchev were both relieved.

On 15 September Ulbricht wrote to Khrushchev informing him that he was drafting a peace treaty. Khrushchev, in his reply of 28 September, failed to mention the peace treaty. Khrushchev and Ulbricht did not give up. In February and March 1962 Soviet military aircraft interfered with traffic in the air corridors to West Berlin and the west began to fear that the land routes would be blocked. Just why these moves occurred is not clear, neither are the reasons why Moscow suddenly backed off. In September 1962 the Russians stopped a US military convoy en route to West Berlin. The Americans warned Moscow they would not take this lying down. Again the Russians backed down. The GDR, in January 1963, dropped all mention of West Berlin and a separate treaty and began to propose a confederation with West Germany. This was not the end of the matter. Again, in October–November 1963 the Russians halted US military convoys but after protests allowed them to proceed.

It appeared that if the west were resolute, it could outstare Khrushchev. His diplomacy consisted of an eclectic mix of threats and calls for negotiations. This made him unpredictable and, consequently, not a leader one could trust. The Americans, predictably, concluded that the best policy was to negotiate from strength. Afterwards when tension increased over Berlin, talks always defused the tension. In 1969 Andrei Gromyko signalled that the Soviet

Union desired to negotiate a Berlin agreement with America, Britain and France, and this led to the quadripartite agreement of 3 September 1971. The recognition of the GDR by the west and West Germany followed and the Berlin issue ceased to be peace threatening [Beschloss 1991; Harrison 1993; Zubok and Pleshakov 1996].

BRINKMANSHIP: CUBA

Superpower brinkmanship on Berlin consisted in the west repeatedly making clear that its position in Berlin was non-negotiable and the Soviet Union trying initiative after initiative to force concessions. America was asking for nothing but to be left alone. It was Moscow that was trying to change the balance. But the Berlin crisis rarely threatened to escalate into a third world war. Cuba, however, was quite different and brought the world very close to nuclear war [*Doc. 4*]. Brinkmanship almost tipped over the edge. There, America was attempting to get Moscow to remove its medium-range nuclear missiles by escalating its threats. In Cuba, the United States was, once more, the status quo power wishing to revert to a pre-crisis situation. The Soviet Union, again, was attempting to change the strategic balance.

At the Bay of Pigs in April 1961, Cuban exiles supported by the CIA failed ignominiously to overthrow Fidel Castro. However, it was a self-inflicted disaster as the President was mainly to blame. The Joint Chiefs of Staff informed him that the mission by 1,500 Cubans to overthrow Castro had 'little chance of success'. This assessment was repeated on several occasions. The President chose to back the CIA, which was very optimistic that the Cubans, trained by them, would succeed. He personally took the decision to move the invasion from the east coast to the swampy Bay of Pigs on the southern coast and also to reduce cover from the air force and navy. The whole episode was a disaster, as 300 Cubans were killed and 1,179 captured. A humiliated Kennedy was forced to negotiate with Castro and it took 20 months and a ransom of US$53 million, paid in baby food, medicine and medical equipment, to get them released. There was now the danger that Kennedy would again try to topple Castro. At the 22nd Party Congress, Marshal Malinovsky, the Minister of Defence, reiterated Soviet claims to military superiority.

On 30 November 1961 President Kennedy authorised Operation Mongoose, to 'help Cuba overthrow the communist regime'. Fidel's Cubans infiltrated the CIA and obtained a document which stated that if Castro had not gone by October 1962, tougher measures would have to be taken. Robert McNamara, Defence Secretary, ordered that preparations be made so as to make the invasion of Cuba by 20 October possible. The USA had conclusive proof that the Russians were building missile sites on Cuba and on 22 October warned Khrushchev that an attack from Cuba would be construed by America as an attack by the Soviet Union. A quarantine was imposed to prevent any more missiles being shipped to Cuba – in reality they were already all in place. The word quarantine was chosen instead of blockade which was regarded as a word of war.

There were 42,000 Russian troops on Cuba, armed with tactical nuclear weapons, at the disposal of local Russian commanders. The Russians speeded up the construction of missile sites. A showdown was approaching. On 25 October Russian ships making for Cuba were turned back. The USA made it clear it would attack before the missile sites became operational. Plans for an air strike on 29 or 30 October were in full swing. On 26 October Khrushchev cabled Kennedy expressing his readiness to negotiate. The same evening, Robert Kennedy met Anatoly Dobrynin, who informed him that the removal of American missiles in Turkey might contribute to the resolution of the conflict. The President stated that he expected the missiles to go after the crisis. (This meeting was kept secret for over 25 years.)

The most dangerous day was 27 October. Robert Kennedy, US Attorney General, told Anatoly Dobrynin that day: 'The situation may get out of control, with irreversible consequences. A real war will begin, in which millions of Americans and Russians will die.' Robert Kennedy was very prescient. Things almost slipped out of control. Unknown to American intelligence, a Soviet B-59 submarine and three others patrolling the waters around the island carried nuclear weapons. The same day the Soviets shot down a US U2 spy plane over eastern Cuba. In the B-59, with communication to superiors impossible and US destroyers regularly dropping depth charges, one of the submarine officers ordered a nuclear torpedo assembled. The submarine's oxygen supply was running out and temperatures were over 30°. At this point, another officer, Second Captain Vasily Aleksandrovich Arkhipov, intervened and insisted that requirements for the firing of the torpedo, including damage to the hull, had not been met. He prevented the firing of the torpedo and in so doing saved the world from nuclear war.

On 28 October Khrushchev announced that he had ordered the dismantling of the offensive weapons and their shipment back to Russia. The Americans declined formally to promise that they would never invade Cuba but informally kept to this understanding. American Jupiter missiles were to be removed from Turkey (only revealed to the American public in 1968). The Russian leader felt humiliated but he had chosen peace, not war. Castro was furious. He called the Soviet leader a 'son of a bitch... bastard... asshole... *no cojones* [balls]... *maricón* [homosexual]' (Taubman 2003, p. 579).

Castro had wanted the Soviets to oust the Americans from Guantanimo Bay, among other things. Khrushchev dispatched Anastas Mikoyan to Havana to mollify Castro even though Mikoyan's wife was dying. Che Guevara told Mikoyan that the Soviets had 'offended our feelings by not consulting us' about the withdrawal of the missiles. When Mikoyan's wife died he stayed on. This touched Castro and relations became slightly easier. Khrushchev worried about the reactions of the 'irrational' Castro. He could stoke up tension with the United States and drag the Soviet Union into war with the Americans. Khrushchev wrote to his diplomats in Cuba, on 16 November 1962, that Castro 'wants to drag us along on a leash and wants to pull us into a war with America by his actions'. [Beschloss 1991; Cohen 1993, pp. 131–44; Garthoff 1989; Zubok and Pleshakov 1996.]

The shock of the crisis transformed Russian–American relations. A hotline was put in place as a result of the difficulty of direct contact between the two leaders. There was also now a desire to avoid confrontation and for détente. From now on, conflict was transferred to the Third World, to Vietnam, Ethiopia, Somalia, Angola, Mozambique, Afghanistan and elsewhere. It led to defeat for America in Vietnam and Russia in Afghanistan. No one gained from these conflicts, everyone was the poorer for them. The need to intervene was fuelled by the zero-sum mentality: if the opposition gains ascendancy in a state, then the other is the loser. Only Gorbachev was brave enough to break this vicious circle.

THE WAR IN VIETNAM

The Americans came to regard Indochina as indispensable for their security [*Doc. 3*]. The region must not be allowed to go communist, otherwise communism might become unstoppable in south east and south Asia. Vietnam north of the 17th parallel was conceded to the communists but everything else had to be held. Eisenhower did not want to become the President who had 'lost' Indochina. Kennedy shared these views. However, he took a relaxed view of Laos and eventually America recognised it as neutral, even though pro-communist forces were in the ascendancy.

Vietnam was quite a different matter. No Democrat could win the presidential election in 1964 if Vietnam went red. Kennedy increased the number of US military advisers and permitted them to engage in combat; they could use napalm and defoliate the forests. Then combat troops began trickling in. There were over 16,000 by the time Kennedy was assassinated in November 1963. The Americans deluded themselves into believing they could defeat the communists by military force, but the real battle in South Vietnam was political, economic and social. Unless the Diem regime offered something superior to communism, it would lose.

Generals vied with one another for ascendancy and Washington was happy to choose the leader. However, in 1964 the leader had no political base among the people. When the North Vietnamese attacked a US destroyer in the Gulf of Tonkin in August 1964, President Johnson was presented with a pretext to bomb the North. Congress empowered the President to use whatever force he deemed necessary to resist communism in south east Asia.

Bombing of North Vietnam began in February 1965. This gave birth to the protest movement as more and more Americans became alarmed at the extension of the war. The USA had become embroiled in a war without a debate in America or any declaration of war. America was being perceived worldwide as an aggressor, imposing its will on poor, underdeveloped Vietnam. In 1968 most Americans thought the war a mistake. In May 1968 Washington and Hanoi began peace talks and in October Johnson called off the bombing of the North. The Russians had applied pressure on the North Vietnamese (they provided the lion's share of their war equipment) and the USA forced the South Vietnamese into line. Now the struggle was to concentrate on who should rule South Vietnam.

Nixon was elected President at this point, and promised to end the war, but he did not want to become the first American President to admit military defeat. In May 1970 the USA invaded neutral Cambodia, determined to eliminate North Vietnamese supply routes to the South. The unfortunate result was that a murderous civil war ensued, with Pol Pot and the Khmer Rouge the eventual victors. In February 1971 South Vietnamese forces, supported by US air power, extended the war to Laos, again with disastrous results. As the Soviet Union and China were keen on improving relations with the USA, Hanoi had to accept a peace settlement in late 1972. The South refused to accept it and the war continued with the USA engaging in massive bombing of the North.

President Nixon and the USA got out in February 1973, providing the South with enormous amounts of war matériel. The final offensive occurred in March 1975 when Saigon fell to the communists and became Ho Chi Minh City. By then Nixon had left the White House, a victim of Watergate. Promises he had made to the South Vietnamese government went with him. Vietnam was a disaster of epic proportions for the Americans. It undermined the economy, the legitimacy of government, belief in the rightness of the nation's cause and divided the country. However, it made American policy makers more cautious about the use of force worldwide. The huge budget deficits run up during the war undermined the dollar and it eventually came off the gold standard. Other countries, such as Japan, seized their chance. Not until the 1990s would America recover its economic health and re-establish itself as the world's most powerful economy [Cohen 1993, pp. 156–81].

The Americans did have some luck in south east Asia. In 1965 the Indonesian Communist Party (PKI), with 3 million members in a population of around 100 million, appeared to be challenging for power, aided by the Chinese. An anti-Chinese, anti-communist coup by the right destroyed the party and with it the threat that Indonesia, of key strategic significance in the region, would change sides or even become a communist state. Had Indonesia gone communist, at a time when US intervention was increasing in Vietnam, it might have altered the strategic balance significantly in Indochina. The defeat of the PKI protected America's flank from attack.

CHAPTER FIVE

DÉTENTE: 1969–1979

FORGING A NEW RELATIONSHIP

When Khrushchev was removed in October 1964, he was criticised not for the direction of his foreign policy, only the means he had used. Aleksei Kosygin, the Prime Minister, took the lead in diplomacy. A cautious man, a technocrat, he was more concerned about increasing the efficiency of the domestic economy than taking risks abroad. Relations with the Chinese became more polite after Khrushchev's passing but the two leading communist powers did not come closer together.

In Hanoi, in February 1965, Kosygin counselled caution, a negotiated settlement and a long-term approach to winning control of the South. While he was there, the Americans bombed the North for the first time. The Soviet Union had to step up military deliveries. This pleased China, which would have welcomed a Russian–American nuclear confrontation. By then, however, China had succumbed to the Cultural Revolution, beginning in 1966. Mao had launched it in the belief that the existing elites were becoming too conservative and resistant to his leadership. The mayhem weakened China over the next decade and an era came to an end with Mao's death in 1976. The Arab–Israeli war in June 1967 found the two superpowers on opposite sides.

Aleksei Kosygin was invited to meet President Johnson, at Glassboro', New Jersey, just after the end of the war. When the Russians received the invitation, they looked for but could not find Glassboro' on any of their maps and began to think that the invitation was a hoax! To overcome their embarrassing ignorance of America, they decided to establish what became known as the US and Canada Institute, Academy of Sciences. Glassboro' was the only summit between America and Russia between 1961 and 1972. The two leaders discussed the Middle East and Vietnam but no progress was made. Nevertheless, President Johnson accepted a return invitation to visit Moscow.

Then came Czechoslovakia where the Prague 'spring' had given a new meaning to democratic socialism. The Czechoslovaks were edging towards social democracy but their new leader, Alexander Dubcek, did not appreciate that his espousal of greater democracy in Czechoslovakia was perceived as a threat to socialist orthodoxy in Moscow. Tension increased and Moscow enquired about the American view on the situation. President Johnson informed the Soviets that the USA would not intervene in what he considered an intra-communist polemic. The Warsaw Pact invasion of Czechoslovakia was there-fore free to go ahead in August 1968, fatally weakening the communist movement. West European parties, led by the Italians, sided with the Czecho-slovak reform communists and condemned Russian intervention.

For a brief time, Eurocommunism, the democratic face of communism, flourished in western Europe. The invasion ended hopes for greater autonomy for enterprises in the Soviet Union and the slow decline of the Soviet economy set in. The Chinese vented their anger on what they perceived to be social imperialism. This masked the apprehension that Russia might decide to inter-vene in China. The Brezhnev doctrine was born, which obliged socialist states to intervene in one another's affairs if socialism were perceived to be in danger. Who decided when socialism was in danger? Russia, of course. This in turn led to the fateful decision to intervene in Afghanistan in December 1979. It would be left to Gorbachev to extricate the Soviet Union from its expensive blunders. In June 1969 a conference of communist and workers' parties convened but the Chinese, North Vietnamese and North Koreans declined to attend. There was no world communist movement any more.

A NEW PRESIDENT AND A NEW APPROACH

The arrival of Richard Nixon in the White House in 1969, and his choice of Henry Kissinger as head of the National Security Council until 1975, and Secretary of State 1973–77, transformed the international situation. Nixon had a brilliant feel for foreign affairs. He knew that Americans wanted out of the Vietnam war as quickly as possible and had become weary of playing God throughout the world. The economy was in decline, hence it would be advis-able to cut the defence budget. But he needed the cooperation of Moscow to get a peace settlement with Hanoi. The Soviet Union had just achieved nuclear parity with the United States: perhaps the time was propitious to negotiate an arms control agreement. Nixon was the ideal man to initiate such a policy. He had made his name as a communist baiter and a ruthless critic of all those who had advocated a softer approach to Moscow. Kissinger, born a German Jew, was a leading specialist on nuclear weapons and foreign policy. Both men ardently desired to make their mark but neither was a team player.

They began with a weak hand. American society was tearing itself apart and not prepared to renew its leading role in the world. The deal they fash-ioned for Moscow came to be known as linkage: Washington would recognise the Soviet Union's strategic parity, would not attempt to interfere in the Soviet empire and would open up access to western investment and technology. In other words, the rollback of communism had been consigned to the dustbin. The Americans wanted the Russians to help them out of Vietnam and to recognise that the superpowers had mutual interests in the Third World. The key goal was stability. The superpowers had a joint responsibility to ensure that the world did not go up in flames. For the first time since 1945, the Americans were saying to the Russians: let's do a deal. Would the Russian leadership share power with the Americans or would they decide to attempt to become number one in the world? Moscow was building up a position of strength: conventional and nuclear forces were expanding, the submarine fleet was growing, an aircraft carrier was even being built to project Soviet power throughout the world. In some areas of rocketry they were world leaders. From the point of view of the Russians, the correlation of forces was moving inexorably in their favour. Vietnam had proved to be a 'bleeding wound' for America.

The American offer of arms negotiations and what became known as détente inevitably aroused suspicion in Moscow. Washington was offering arms control negotiations just when the Russians were on the point of achieving superiority. A truce in the Third World could only signify that America wanted to hold on to what it had. However, Kosygin was aware that Russian industry needed high technology inputs and that economic growth was slowing down. Gross national product during the years 1966–70 had grown 5 per cent annually but this was to fall to 3.1 per cent annually in 1971–75 (1988 calculations). Consumption per head of population was 5.3 per cent in 1966–70 but fell to 3.6 per cent in 1971–75. The Russian economist Khanin has argued that these data overstate performance.

The second half of the 1970s saw the decline continue. GNP in 1976–80 only grew by 2.2 per cent annually and consumption growth declined to 2.6 per cent annually. These are later calculations, so the question arises about whether the leadership was aware at the time of the serious decline in economic growth. Soviet defence spending increased during the 1970s and aid to the Third World also grew, for instance to Cuba and Vietnam. There were several reports which pointed out the alarming consequences for the Soviet Union if economic reform were not considered, but Brezhnev ignored them. He was living in a fool's paradise.

CHINA CHANGES SIDES: RAPPROCHEMENT WITH AMERICA

Faced with rising tension with the Soviet Union, in November 1968 the Chinese leader Zhou Enlai proposed talks with the incoming Nixon administration. However, other, more conservative leaders ensured that the discussions did not take place. In 1969 Chinese border guards along the Ussuri River fired on their Russian counterparts, killing some on several occasions.

The dispute was about which country owned islands in the river – a controversial matter since the riverbed had changed course over time. Moscow considered a nuclear strike to take out China's nuclear capacity. Beijing backed off and Zhou began again to lobby for a rapprochement with Washington.

Nixon and Kissinger were greatly taken by the idea as it promised to be very fruitful. A wedge could be driven between the two communist giants and the communist movement weakened in the rest of the world. An understanding with China removed the danger of war and American troops could gradually be extricated from south east Asia. America could concentrate its efforts on the Soviet Union and China would help to contain Moscow and Hanoi. As the Chinese were only weakly represented in the Third World, there was little danger of tension developing. Since the US public had become allergic to seeing its boys fighting and dying in other people's wars, Washington would now have to concentrate on training and arming their clients in the Third World. All these factors suggested that rapprochement with China would pay huge dividends.

President Nixon astonished the world in February 1972 when he flew to Beijing and met Mao. The main obstacle to better relations was Taiwan. The USA had practised a 'two Chinas' policy: the People's Republic on the mainland and the Republic of China on Taiwan. Beijing insisted that there could only be one China and asked for US forces to leave Taiwan. Washington accepted the logic of the argument and agreed to remove its troops and installations from Taiwan, as tension subsided. If China helped the USA to withdraw from Vietnam and refrained from belligerent acts in the straits between the mainland and Taiwan, it would promote the unification of China.

Moscow had not anticipated a Sino-American rapprochement and was very relieved to discover that no military alliance was contemplated. However, it was a bitter blow to discover that China, the most populous socialist state, had changed sides and was consorting with the class enemy. The rapprochement completely changed Moscow's view of the world. It would now have to think in multipolar terms. There were three main players: Russia, America and China. A new zero-sum game was emerging. If Russia pushed America too hard, it might drive it into a closer relationship with China. Thus Nixon's visit to China made Russia more amenable. There was the awful prospect of other socialist states following China and opposing the Soviet Union. This was a condemnation of Russian foreign policy making, but, as time would tell, Moscow did not draw the correct conclusions from the Chinese débacle.

SALT

The Nixon administration's efforts to develop an anti-ballistic missile (ABM) system worried Moscow. It was an area of technology in which the Americans were ahead and the Russians did not want to be forced to switch resources to compete. Strategic arms limitation talks (SALT) could bring benefit. There had been desultory discussions under way since 1969 but they always got bogged down in the technical detail. Nixon and Kissinger had little interest in the finer details of arms negotiations but were more concerned about the political impact of an arms deal. It would signal that the superpowers had moved from confrontation to negotiation.

The first SALT agreement was signed by Brezhnev and Nixon in Moscow in May 1972. It limited the deployment of ABM systems but little headway was made on offensive weapons systems. Agreements were signed on health and a joint space programme (the 1975 Apollo–Soyuz mission), and the two sides also agreed on certain basic principles regulating their relations, including restraint during crises and the avoidance of confrontation [Garthoff 1994, pp. 146–223]. Nevertheless Nixon had pulled off a diplomatic coup: rapprochement with the nation's two main adversaries, China and Russia. The Russians were also pleased. The Americans had made concessions and formally acknowledged nuclear parity.

Brezhnev's first trip to America resulted in another summit with Nixon, in Washington, Camp David, and San Clemente, California, in June 1973. Hearings on Watergate were suspended for the meetings, during which there were agreements on agriculture, transport and cultural exchanges, and the framework for SALT II talks. Both countries promised to contact one another if nuclear war threatened to involve one or both of them. Superpower summits were becoming part of the international agenda.

THE GERMAN PROBLEM DEFUSED

In Europe, the Berlin problem was defused by the quadripartite agreement in 1971 and the East–West German agreement of 1972. For a time it appeared that West Germany might incline more to neutrality in pursuing its *Ostpolitik* (policy towards the east) under Willy Brandt. But when he was obliged to resign in May 1974 because an East German spy was discovered in his chancellery, his successor, social democrat Helmut Schmidt, reverted to a much closer relationship with Washington and accepted NATO modernisation. This was one instance when the brilliantly successful East German spy system in Bonn scored an own goal.

THE MIDDLE EAST

In 1967 Russian agents in Syria spread false rumours of an imminent Israeli attack and the Syrians appealed to Nasser for support. The latter demanded the removal of UN forces which were separating his troops from the Israelis and advanced towards the Gulf of Aqaba. Israel attacked and the Six Day War was under way. Egyptian, Jordanian and Syrian troops were routed. Moscow threatened to intervene, replaced the lost equipment and sent thousands of advisers, in return for which the grateful Egyptians granted them naval rights in Egyptian ports and air bases. They were now in a position to counter the activities of the American Sixth Fleet in the Mediterranean. In 1969 Nasser began small-scale attacks against Israel and the latter responded in 1970 with devastating air attacks far behind Egyptian lines. The Egyptian air force was no match for the Israelis and so Nasser requested, and obtained, Russian air defence systems, missiles, aircraft and pilots. The Russian pilots flew combat missions and reversed the course of the war. Moscow acceded to American calls for a ceasefire and it was announced in August 1970.

Moscow's standing as the friend of the Arabs was never higher. Nasser died a month later and the new Egyptian leader, Anwar Sadat, called on the Soviet Union to help the Arabs recapture the land lost to the Israelis. However, Moscow was more concerned with reaching an agreement with Washington. Shortly after the Brezhnev–Nixon summit in Moscow in May 1972, Sadat suddenly expelled all Russian personnel from Egypt. A high-ranking Egyptian officer commented later that one of the reasons for the decision had been the Russian claim that bases were their territory and that Egyptians could not enter them without permission. The key reason appears to have been the Egyptian realisation that America held the key to the Middle East. Russia would always place its relations with America ahead of those with the Arabs.

Egypt and Syria had been armed for war and were determined to go ahead without direct Soviet help. The attack in October 1973 took the Israelis completely by surprise, launched on Yom Kippur, when all Israelis were observing their most important religious festival. It exploded the myth of Israeli military invincibility and Moscow immediately jumped in to resupply its clients and called on other Arab states to join in. The Americans kept their distance for a week until Golda Meir, the Israeli Prime Minister, threatened to use nuclear weapons. The Americans then flew in vast amounts of supplies and the Israelis penetrated deeply into Egypt. A ceasefire, proposed by the Russians and negotiated by Kissinger, ended the fighting. But then the Israelis broke the ceasefire and Moscow threatened to send in combat troops. Nixon placed American troops on strategic alert and the superpowers were back at one another's throats.

Washington was annoyed that Moscow had known of the imminent Arab attack on Israel and had failed to warn the USA. The Russian attempt to involve other Arab states in the war rankled. Brezhnev, on his part, was frustrated by the American alert which had stopped him in his tracks. The superpowers were as far apart as ever, at least in the Middle East. An increasing number of Americans were arguing that Moscow had not honoured its obligations under détente. Afterwards, Kissinger, in never ending diplomacy, tried to patch up a Middle East settlement and conspicuously excluded the Russians [Kissinger 1979, pp. 569–99; Garthoff 1994, pp. 404–33].

In May 1972, on their way back to America from signing the SALT I agreement, Nixon and Kissinger dropped in on the Shah of Iran. They concluded a secret agreement whereby Iran was to act to encourage Iraq to break its close ties with Moscow. In Vietnam, ferocious bombing of the North secured a peace agreement in January 1973 and American troops began leaving the South. In the Middle East, after Egypt had expelled Soviet military advisers in 1973, Moscow was deprived of its land and air bases, the most significant bases it had in the Third World.

The high hopes of détente faded as it became clear to the Americans that the Soviet Union was not willing to accept strategic inferiority. Kissinger was quite open about ensuring America's continued world hegemony. The SALT I agreement was to halt the race in ICBMs and submarine-launched ballistic missiles (SLBMs) when the USA was way ahead in nuclear warheads. This would allow the Americans rapidly to develop systems not covered by SALT: the Trident submarine, the MX missile, the B-1 bomber and the Cruise missile [Garthoff 1994, pp. 256–74]. Funding for these new weapons was a problem during the upheavals of the Vietnam war but they all went ahead, especially the Trident submarine and Cruise missile. The Nixon doctrine, declared in July 1969, aimed at arming Third World states to intervene and resist the rise of communism. This was born of the realisation that it was a bad idea to have American troops bogged down in a regional conflict far from the main Cold War areas. There was also the fact that Congress, after 1973, would not permit Nixon to dispatch troops to defend Cambodia against North Vietnam.

THE AGENDA CHANGES AS FORD TAKES OVER

Nixon's struggle for political survival in 1973–74, the death of Mao and the succession struggle which followed, slowed down the intricate Nixon–Kissinger policy of rapprochement with Russia and China. Congress reasserted itself in the light of the Watergate affair and proceeded to claw back some of the power which had passed to the President. Nixon and Kissinger had conducted their foreign policy largely out of view of Congress and the people, partly because they believed that they could achieve more on their own and partly owing to their disdain for the hurly burly of democratic politics. In 1973 Congress passed an act which aimed at restraining the president's ability to deploy American military force without a declaration of war. The legislators also ordered an end to the bombing of Cambodia and passed a law which prevented US troops from being sent to Vietnam again. Relations with the Soviet Union would be tied to human rights issues, such as the freedom of Jews to emigrate from Russia. These moves restricted the ability of Nixon and

Kissinger to keep the promises they had made in fashioning their intricate détente policies [*Doc. 5*].

Gerald Ford, when he took over in 1974, found himself in the same position. Brezhnev was disappointed that little American high technology flowed to the Soviet Union. Nixon needed the support of the right in his battle to survive and had to delay recognising China. The defence treaty with Taiwan remained, much to the satisfaction of the assertive enemies of 'Red' China. Gerald Ford could not improve relations with China either.

The Bretton Woods agreement of 1944 had seen the dollar become the world's leading currency. It was tied to gold and dollars would be converted into gold by the US government. The unwillingness or inability of American presidents to increase federal taxes to pay for social programmes, foreign defence and foreign aid meant that the federal budget was normally in deficit. The money markets could be tapped to cover the deficit. This system functioned extremely well for the quarter century after 1944. The US economy was the richest and most competitive in the world and American policy makers had an unprecedented freedom of action to fashion the world in America's image. But the profligate spending by Johnson on Vietnam, the climbing budget deficits, the rise in Japanese and West German competitiveness, all contributed to the slowdown in the American economy. Johnson's overspend in Vietnam fuelled inflation and this led, in 1971, to America recording its first balance of trade deficit in the twentieth century. Foreigners now held more dollars than could be converted into gold.

Nixon bit the bullet and abandoned convertibility, devalued the dollar against the Japanese yen and the German mark (DM) and turned the economy round – at least for a short time. The Arab–Israeli war of 1973 was another demonstration of the USA's declining power. A massive increase in the oil price by Iran and the Arab producers revealed how dependent America and Europe were on oil supplies from the Middle East. Saudi Arabia, the largest supplier, became the arbiter of oil prices and the Organisation of Petroleum Exporting Countries (OPEC) took over the market. There was even talk of the Arabs establishing their own banking system with the mountains of petrodollars now piling up.

AFRICA

In Africa, the Brezhnev era got off to an unfortunate start. Its friends fell from power: first Nkrumah in Ghana in 1966, and then Keita in Mali in 1968. However, by 1979 the situation had been transformed. There was an impressive list of states which had declared Soviet socialism as their goal: Angola, Benin (Dahomey), Congo (Brazzaville), Ethiopia, Guinea, Guinea-Bissau and Mozambique. In the post-colonial aftermath, America, China and Russia competed for influence. China was in a good position in east Africa and

Zambia. In the Nigerian civil war, in the mid-1960s, the Soviets supported the federal government and China supported, diplomatically, rebel Biafra.

The revolution in Portugal in 1974 transformed the situation. Guinea-Bissau, Mozambique and Angola were to be granted their independence after years of guerrilla warfare against the colonial power. Angola brought all the competing powers together. There was also the attraction that the country was rich in minerals and oil. The MPLA, dominated by leaders of mixed race, was partly Marxist and received support from Cuba, the Soviet Union, Algeria and some western governments. The FNLA, drawing much of its strength from the Bakongo tribe, was backed by America, China, Libya and some western governments. UNITA, centred on the Ovimbundu, received aid from China and was the favourite of South Africa. In January 1975 an agreement was reached on the transfer of power from Portugal, to take place in November 1975.

Determined to prevent the emergence of a pro-Russian government, the Chinese increased arms supplies to the FNLA, followed by the Americans. The Soviets and Cubans responded in kind and helped their client, the MPLA. Fighting followed and South Africa intervened. In November Cuba sent combat troops to prevent the capital, Luanda, falling. China withdrew and Russian and Cuban involvement deepened after Congress refused Kissinger's request for more funds. This also led to the South Africans backing out. The MPLA took over as the government in early 1996, backed by Russian, Cuban (about 17,000) and some east European troops. But the Russians and Cubans supported different factions within the MPLA leadership and civil war continued for another two decades. Cuban intervention in Angola was not the first time that Castro had sent troops to black Africa. Some had arrived in Congo (Brazzaville), Guinea and Guinea-Bissau. In the Middle East, in 1973, there were about 3,000 Cuban troops. In October 1976 Angola concluded a treaty of friendship and cooperation with the Soviet Union and Mozambique followed in March 1977. Russia supplied the separatist movements in Eritrea and the Ogaden, while it had good relations with Somalia, where bases and port facilities were made available. When Ethiopia requested help, Russia changed sides and provided the military equipment to defeat a Somali offensive in the Ogaden. Russian and Cuban commanders turned the tide. In November 1977 Somalia expelled its Soviet advisers and told them to quit their bases. Ethiopia became a pro-Soviet socialist republic.

The communist Third World was taking shape and it appeared that Moscow had scored a decisive victory over Washington. Kissinger felt very frustrated that Congress would not provide the means to counter the communist advance on the continent. All the Americans could do was to watch from the sidelines. In Angola, the Russians could not tolerate the Americans and Chinese coming out on top and felt obliged to demonstrate to the Third World that Russia, not China, was their natural ally. The Russian military, especially the navy, were also keen to expand their presence and capabilities worldwide. They wanted bases and surveillance stations everywhere in Africa, especially on the coast. If another Middle East oil crisis erupted, they wanted to have the capability to influence the flow of oil to Europe and America.

The Russians had examined the American experience in the Third World and felt certain they could avoid the pitfalls of overexposure. They were also buoyed up by the feeling that the correlation of forces was moving inexorably in their direction. America, engrossed with its own problems, appeared to have lost the will to challenge Russia. All these assumptions and decisions turned out to be false, with the Russians doomed to repeat the mistakes of the Americans. However, this was not the American view at the time. Détente was turning sour as all the benefits appeared to be accruing to the Russians. Brezhnev could see nothing wrong in his policy as he was merely doing what the Americans would have liked to have done.

THE HELSINKI ACCORD

The Brezhnev leadership pursued several objectives in western Europe: it wished gradually to detach the region from the United States and thereby weaken NATO; it needed the technology and know-how which increased trade would bring; it also wanted the borders of 1945 to be recognised as inviolable, thus confirming the Soviet victory in Europe in 1945. The non-aggression pact with West Germany in 1970 paved the way for the intra-German agreements of 1972 and the recognition of the GDR by the western world. These were European initiatives in which the Americans played a minor role. The first approach for a grand European conference was made in 1954, but Russia was never quite clear whether it would be better off with the Americans out of Europe or with them in Europe as a brake on the Germans.

In December 1971 the Atlantic Council accepted a proposal by the Warsaw Pact for a security conference on Europe. Preparatory talks got underway and a conference convened in Helsinki in July 1973, attended by 33 states, including NATO, the Warsaw Pact, the non-aligned movement and neutral states. Only Albania boycotted the proceedings. NATO participation meant that the USA and Canada were present. The Helsinki Final Act was signed on 1 August 1975 by President Gerald Ford, Leonid Brezhnev (technically, as Party leader, he should not have signed; he only became Soviet President in 1977), and other leaders.

The Russians had achieved their goal: the status quo in Europe. In order to gain their objective, the Russians had to concede, for the first time, that human rights were of a universal character and that there was to be a free exchange of ideas and people across Europe. This was Basket III and Moscow had to accept it in order to get Basket I: the inviolability of post-1945 frontiers.

Brezhnev lived to regret this concession as it led to the founding of Helsinki monitoring groups and human rights groups in the Soviet Union. He had conceded that human rights were the legitimate concern of other states. They could now use it to criticise the Russian record on human rights. A Conference on Security and Co-operation in Europe (CSCE) was to convene to monitor progress and promote further developments. The next meeting, in Belgrade in 1978, occurred at a time of rising east–west tension and there was precious little goodwill on show. The CSCE process was revived under Gorbachev.

A NEW PRESIDENT SOWS CONFUSION

Gerald Ford lost the presidential election in 1976 to Democrat Jimmy Carter, whose views on Russia and foreign policy were inchoate and uncertain. He rode to power on the backs of disillusioned voters who wanted a new start and a solution to all the political, economic and social problems facing America. But the President lacked experience in foreign affairs and had little knowledge of the complexities of nuclear strategy. As an able man, he would learn as he went along. He had, after all, served in the US navy and had had contact with nuclear submarines. He told Americans what they wanted to hear: he would do away with the old, tawdry Washington politics and base his policies on respect for human rights; he would ease the tension with the Soviet Union. But he failed to grasp that his emphasis on human rights would exacerbate tension, rather than alleviate it. On arms control, he eschewed the results of the slow, painstaking negotiations and made very radical proposals which only alarmed the Soviets.

The advice he received on foreign affairs was often contradictory as Cyrus Vance, his Secretary of State, and Zbigniew Brzezinski, National Security Adviser, were like horses pulling in different directions. They both agreed on one thing – that the Soviet Union was the key country – but they differed fundamentally on how to modify Russian behaviour. Vance advocated the renaissance of détente as this would facilitate joint efforts by the superpowers to lessen tension and solve problems throughout the world. He believed that behind the ageing Brezhnev leadership stood a younger cohort, as keen as the Americans to end the confrontation between the superpowers and to concentrate on modernising their country to compete in the modern world. SALT II should be an important objective as the USA needed to cut defence spending, reduce its budget deficit and, thereby, bring down inflation. The Russians could be afforded a larger role in the Middle East with something approaching an American–Russian condominium. This would ensure that Moscow would not succumb to the temptation of promoting extremist Arab regimes. In Africa, the Russians would soon learn what the Americans had learned in Vietnam: expending energy and resources there would lead to disillusionment. Africa was, after all, of marginal significance to the superpowers. China was not as significant as Nixon and Kissinger had believed. The danger for America was that China could cause tension which would harm the development of détente with Russia. Vance's goal, therefore, was to get the Russians to see the world through his spectacles.

Brzezinski was quite a different person. As a native Pole, he had great respect for Russians but did not trust them. Moscow would not modify its behaviour out of the goodness of its heart. It would have to be obliged to do so. To this end, America should go for strategic superiority, strengthen NATO, attract the Chinese to its side against Russia, undermine Russia's hold on eastern Europe and outface the Soviets worldwide. If SALT II were signed it would be a bonus. Brzezinski adopted the typical Polish view that the best way to deal with the Russians was to beat them. Hence, Carter got conflicting advice and, as an amateur, tried to evolve policy which reflected both viewpoints. This made him a laughing stock to many.

Vance's approach was not viable in the late 1970s. Brezhnev, now partly dependent on drugs, was becoming incoherent at top meetings and had ignored all the warnings about the need for economic reform. Those around him preferred that he stay in office as it allowed them to build up their own empires. Those who had aspirations to succeed him wanted him to stay until the propitious moment for their succession bid arrived. The gerontocrats put personal interest ahead of national interest. Nevertheless, the tide of world affairs appeared to be flowing in Moscow's direction. Communists took power in Afghanistan in April 1978, on their own initiative. The Shah of Iran had to flee his country in January 1979 and this undermined the American position in the Middle East. Ayatollah Khomeni turned out to be virulently anti-American and anti-western. In the Caribbean, Grenada became pro-communist and in Central America Guatemala sided with Moscow. It all appeared as if the Soviet Union's position in the world were strengthening and that the future would be even brighter.

Carter did register many foreign policy successes but they were almost all achieved at the expense of the Soviet Union. Anwar Sadat, of Egypt, concluding that the Soviets could not broker a Middle East peace, accepted American mediation in the conflict with Israel. This produced the Camp David Accords and Sadat astonished the world in 1977 by going to Israel to demonstrate that peace was possible between the two countries. Pushed by Carter, the Israelis agreed to return the Sinai peninsula to Egypt, which in return would recognise – the first Arab state to do so – the state of Israel. The latter had now the right to exist. This démarche annoyed the Russians as they had been expressly excluded from the peace process. Predictably, Moscow did not recognise the agreement and sided with Arab states which continued to deny Israel the right to exist. Superpower tension in the Middle East was as great as before.

The United States finally normalised its relations with the People's Republic of China in December 1978. Carter was always torn between soothing the

Soviets, Vance's preference, and demonstrating American muscle to them, Brzezinski's advice. The former had little interest in China and did not think that improving relations with Beijing at the expense of relations with Moscow was sensible. Deng Xiaoping, who emerged as China's main leader in 1978, was keen to use the Vance–Brzezinski dissonance to benefit China. Beijing was apprehensive about Soviet–American détente and wanted to give Vietnam a bloody nose, without the threat of Russian intervention.

Deng became the first Chinese leader to visit the United States, in January 1979, and the visit was a great success. He asked to visit the space centre at Houston, where he climbed into a simulator and was fascinated by the technology which brought a spacecraft down to earth. Washington turned a blind eye when Chinese forces penetrated North Vietnam. Despite criticising the course of Sino-American relations, the Russians were keen to slow down the arms race.

CARTER AND BREZHNEV REACH AGREEMENT ON SALT II BUT ON LITTLE ELSE

After seven years of endeavour, SALT II was signed by Presidents Jimmy Carter and Leonid Brezhnev in Vienna in June 1979. A draft SALT II agreement had been floated at the Vladivostok Summit between Gerald Ford and Leonid Brezhnev in November 1974, but progress had been slow thereafter due to claims that too much was being conceded to the Soviet Union under détente. The Russian invasion of Afghanistan, in December 1979, led to President Carter withdrawing the treaty for ratification in the Senate, in January 1980. However, both sides pledged to observe the treaty limits voluntarily. The next stage in arms talks, which opened in Geneva in June 1982, assumed the name of strategic arms reduction talks, or START. This was a psychological leap forward, with the superpowers now talking about *reducing* their arsenals.

Carter and Brezhnev fell out over a Soviet combat brigade in Cuba. It and other troops had been there since the Cuban Missile Crisis and this was permitted, according to the deal done to end the crisis. Pressed by the right, Carter demanded the brigade be withdrawn and Brezhnev refused. This unnecessary conflict rumbled on during the summer and autumn of 1979. However, it was soon overshadowed by a much more serious event.

In November 1979 Ayatollah Khomeni's followers seized the US embassy, holding those inside hostage (the siege lasted 14 months). This humiliated the United States and, inevitably, President Carter became another man under siege. Why could he not use American power to free the hostages in Iran? In December 1979 Carter's Soviet policy collapsed.

CHAPTER SIX

COLD WAR II: 1979–1985

DÉTENTE FAILS TO SATISFY AMERICAN ASPIRATIONS

By the mid-1970s it was clear that Kissinger's policy of détente had failed [*Doc. 5*]. It had rested on the assumption that a linkage could be established. Washington's improved relations with Moscow would depend on Moscow's willingness not to challenge Washington in the Third World. SALT I and increasing Russian–American trade should satisfy Moscow. It did not. Brezhnev could not resist helping America's enemies to press home their advantage. In Vietnam, the communist victory in 1975 owed much to the arms supplied by the Soviet Union. In Africa, Cuba and the Soviet Union embarrassed the United States. The volatility of Third World politics began to reveal that the two superpowers were no longer masters there. The USA and the Soviet Union simply did not possess the economic power to ensure that their will was done. Furthermore, western Europe and Japan were developing rapidly and demanding a greater say in international economic policy.

In Europe, the collapse of the right-wing dictatorship in Portugal in 1974, the fall of the military dictatorship in Greece, also in 1974, and the death of Franco, the Spanish dictator, in 1975, alarmed Kissinger. Communist parties were influential in all three states and it also appeared possible that the communists in France and Italy, the Eurocommunists, would enter into coalition governments. This had alarming implications for NATO as all these states, except Spain, were members. As it turned out, Kissinger's gloom was unfounded. All three states took the democratic path and Spain joined NATO. In 1976 Kissinger declared that he would no longer use the term détente. What was to succeed it – something between it and Cold War II, or Cold War II? During the 1976 election campaign, Jimmy Carter reflected the anti-military mood of the voters by criticising the one-sided emphasis on military power to achieve security. However, he also took umbrage at the weakness of Gerald Ford at Helsinki and the ground he had given to the Soviets in the SALT II memorandum, agreed at the Vladivostok Summit. Either he was confused or he was pitching for votes from the right and left.

CARTER'S MIXED RECORD

In office, Carter pursued even deeper cuts in a SALT II agreement, although he did not succeed in getting these into the agreement signed in 1979. He did not engage in the anti-Russian rhetoric which was the common currency of many previous presidents. The weakness of the US economy demanded he pay greater attention to reflation, in collaboration with the developed market economies. Human rights became important, as did north–south issues. The USA would no longer support repressive regimes simply because they were anti-communist. Government was to be more open, to heal the wounds of the Nixon–Kissinger years.

Contrariwise, Carter cancelled the B-1 bomber in 1977 and the development of Cruise missiles. The main reason was expense but the switch allowed the development of a new Stealth bomber. Defence expenditure climbed under Carter. During negotiations on a SALT II treaty, Helmut Schmidt, the West German Chancellor, and the Russians, wanted European theatre weapons (medium-range nuclear weapons) to be included. Carter, following Brzezinski's advice, declined. Cyrus Vance informed Moscow in March 1977 that these weapons would not be included in discussions.

When Schmidt finally gave way to Carter, the Soviet response was to deploy SS-20s in eastern Europe in late 1977. This was a tactical mistake by Moscow and handed the initiative to NATO, always having to find ways of balancing Soviet conventional superiority. In January 1979 the west decided to deploy Cruise and Pershing 2 missiles. Carter went on the offensive against the Soviet Union in 1977 by declaring that it could be undermined in six states: China, Vietnam, Somalia, Iraq, Algeria and Cuba. This was in sharp contrast to Kissinger's policy, which now appeared defensive.

Besides rising defence expenditure, there was the added bonus that weapons were becoming more accurate. In July 1980 Carter signed a presidential decree that placed emphasis on targeting military objectives, rather than economic targets and the population, as before. This made possible a limited war, one aimed only at certain military targets. Here the Americans had an advantage. Only about one-quarter of their ICBMs were on land, whereas the Soviets had about three-quarters on their terrain. Conventional forces were not forgotten. The President signed decrees establishing a rapid reaction force which could intervene in the Third World when the occasion arose. Carter had promised to withdraw US forces from South Korea but, in office, quickly reversed this decision. He also turned a blind eye to human rights' violations there. Another campaign promise – quickly to scale down arms deliveries to the Third World – was forgotten and El Salvador, to name just one instance, was armed to counter the Sandinistas in Nicaragua [Hamilton 1988].

Carter had downgraded the significance of China to the US, but in August 1979 Vice-President Mondane went to Beijing to sign a secret agreement permitting the Americans to install an electronic listening station in Xinjiang, in western China, near the Soviet border. China, in another agreement, reached in Beijing in January 1980, was to receive US military equipment for the first time. This alarmed the Russians and may have convinced them to sign a SALT II agreement, even though it did not include European theatre nuclear weapons.

DISASTROUS DECISION MAKING IN MOSCOW: INTERVENTION IN AFGHANISTAN

Moscow intervened in Afghanistan [*Doc. 9*] believing the mild-mannered American President would hardly raise an eyebrow. A KGB report informed Brezhnev that the country could be taken over in a few weeks, then a few months, then six months and so on. The Vietnam syndrome was this time returning to haunt the Soviet Union. Carter took Brzezinski's advice. He went over the top, described the invasion as the most serious danger to peace since 1945, halted a grain export contract with Moscow and told US athletes not to participate in the 1980 Olympic games in Moscow. Other nations should follow suit. This mortified Moscow and it responded by not sending athletes to the 1984 Los Angeles games. Only Romania broke the eastern boycott. The Carter doctrine was proclaimed, also in 1980, according to which the Persian Gulf was of vital strategic importance to America. America would deal directly with any outside force seeking to gain control of the Persian Gulf region. The Russians were not to go anywhere near it.

Russia's intervention in Afghanistan was decided by a handful of top leaders but they ignored Soviet military reservations about the wisdom of getting involved in domestic Afghan politics. Brezhnev's main worry appears to have been that a new leader might be under the influence of China or America. This might threaten the Soviet position in Central Asia. If Moscow failed to come to the aid of its friends in Afghanistan this might lead other communist leaders around the world to conclude that Moscow no longer had the will-power to counter the American threat. But the Brezhnev leadership failed completely to appreciate the negative impact the invasion would have on the Islamic world, first and foremost in the Middle East [*Doc. 11*]. At a time when America's authority was very low, Moscow was throwing Washington a lifeline by uniting the Middle East against Russia.

By 1979 only China could express any satisfaction at the evolution of events during the 1970s. The Americans and Russians were profoundly dis-illusioned: strategic parity had brought few dividends for the Soviet Union and détente had become a term of abuse in many American mouths. Moscow's drive for supremacy had crumbled and had provoked accelerated defence spending. The war in Afghanistan contributed to the election of Ronald Reagan as President. The champion of the right was unequivocal about the

Soviet Union – it was the 'evil empire'. Russians felt deeply insulted by this term [Cohen 1993, pp. 188–218; Garthoff 1994, pp. 623–85].

CARTER, BRZEZINSKI AND COLD WAR II

It was Brzezinski who articulated the thinking behind Cold War II, which can be dated from Soviet intervention in Afghanistan. He was keen to involve the Soviet Union in a military and economic race that would increase political and social strains within that country. He was not against nuclear war per se, believing that the Soviet Union would come off worse. The abandonment of détente was blamed, of course, on Moscow. Its lack of restraint in Afghanistan proved the pretext to announce the beginning of the new cold war. It marked the end of the policy of deterrence which America had pursued since the 1960s.

It is ironic that Carter continued to be perceived as a weak president. He had suffered the humiliation of the Iranian hostage crisis, the continued presence of the Soviet combat brigade in Cuba and the Russian slap in the face in invading Afghanistan. But there was another side to his presidency. He increased the military budget, created a rapid reaction force, deployed the MX missile and concluded secret military deals with the Chinese. Domestically, his greatest failure was his inability to turn the economy round. Hence, he was seen by voters as a failure, domestically and internationally. He prepared the way for Ronald Reagan who only had to promise to re-establish America's hegemony in the world and to stimulate economic growth for many voters to choose him. There was no evidence that he, uninterested in foreign and security affairs and economics, would be any more successful than Carter, but, as an actor, he was brilliant at creating an aura of optimism. Surely such an imposing, articulate man had to succeed.

A NEW PRESIDENT AND A NEW DEPARTURE

President Ronald Reagan adopted a simple black and white view of the Russians. Drugged by a utopian ideology into believing they were destined to take over the world, they were addicted to lying and cheating at every opportunity. Morality to them was relative. If a policy advanced the interests of the Soviet Union and communism worldwide, it was moral. Failure, of course, was immoral. There was no point in negotiating agreements with the Russians since they were bound to break them. The way to deal with Moscow was to build up American nuclear superiority and combat Soviet interventions in the Third World.

Reagan presided over an extraordinary expansion of the military–industrial complex in the United States. Although 1981 was a poor year economically, defence expenditure in 1982 was to increase 13 per cent, and over 8 per cent in succeeding years. The CIA budget went up even more rapidly. The American military began to think it could initiate and win a nuclear war. One option was to prepare for a six-month nuclear war with Russia. The new weapons were more accurate and could take out Soviet military and political targets with surgical strikes. Communications were being developed to function in America after a Soviet nuclear strike. The Reagan administration claimed to have discovered a window of vulnerability through which a Soviet first strike would devastate America and this highly dubious claim was used to justify the extraordinary expansion of the US arsenal in the early 1980s. In Europe, the use of the neutron bomb and chemical weapons might even be considered. The administration returned to the concept of linkage. In 1981 the United States informed the Soviet Union that the latter's response to US proposals on Afghanistan and Cambodia would be the litmus test for their relations. Washington wanted a Russian retreat there.

Despite his military's thoughts of starting and winning a nuclear war against the Soviet Union, President Reagan had a horror of such weapons. His major objective was to ensure that no Russian first strike was ever launched against America. Later he was to concur with Gorbachev's goal of eliminating nuclear weapons, all nuclear weapons.

The Russians were alarmed about the deployment of Pershing 2 and Cruise missiles, whose accuracy and speed made them extremely difficult to counter. They believed they had found a secret weapon in their battle to ensure these missiles were never deployed – the western peace movement. Anti-nuclear feeling was running very high in western Europe in the early 1980s, and consequently the west European states that were to receive the missiles only wanted them as a last resort. They would have preferred the United States to reach an agreement with the Soviet Union which would make their deployment unnecessary. If the Soviets would remove their SS-4s, SS-5s and SS-20s, there would be no need for Pershing 2 and Cruise missiles in Europe. This was a good tactic since it takes two to reach an agreement.

In Geneva the Americans began discussing an intermediate-range nuclear force (INF) agreement. Congress instructed the President to resume the SALT talks, renamed the strategic arms reduction talks (START). For the first time, the arsenals of the superpowers might be reduced. Given the attitude of the Reagan administration to the Soviet Union, these negotiations promised to be long drawn out.

There was another issue on which America's European allies did not see eye to eye with the USA. When martial law was proclaimed in Poland in 1981 [*Doc. 10*], the USA announced economic sanctions against both Poland and the Soviet Union and asked the Europeans to follow suit. One sensitive item was the natural gas pipeline to carry Soviet gas to western Europe. Washington requested that western Europe cease supplying pipes and equipment, but such was the negative European reaction that the Americans backed off and the pipeline went ahead [Halliday 1983, pp. 203–33].

Against all the odds, the chief American and Soviet negotiators, while walking in the woods near Geneva, arrived at a compromise on intermediate-range weapons. But the White House was not pleased as it wanted talks but no agreement. In the end, Washington was spared acute embarrassment by Moscow turning down the deal as well. The Brezhnev leadership had deluded itself into believing that Reagan was a president with whom they could do business. They greatly disliked Carter because of his zigzag policies, his inability to meet commitments and his violent rhetoric after their intervention in Afghanistan. As the US economy was in bad shape, it was logical that Reagan would welcome a deal to trim his defence budget. But he was a bitter disappointment to the ailing Brezhnev. The latter was unaware that it was the Soviet Union which urgently needed to cut its defence spending, rather than the USA.

ANDROPOV AND REAGAN: MISSED OPPORTUNITIES

Brezhnev died in November 1982 and was succeeded by Yury Andropov. His first priority was to increase the effectiveness of the Soviet economy by improving labour discipline. He knew that growth had slowed down (in reality, it had stopped) but was unaware that the Soviet Union was facing a systemic crisis. It was soon discovered that he was terminally ill, dying of kidney failure, however, and so he was unable to make much impact on the Soviet Union. He was a well-informed Russian leader as the country had built up a competent group of specialists on foreign policy. The military dominated security policy. The specialists were aware that the expansion of the Soviet nuclear arsenal and the penetration of the Third World had contributed to America's more belligerent stance [*Doc. 11*]. Moscow, like Washington, was attempting to gain superiority. As long as this continued, a slowing down of the arms race was unlikely. The Soviet Union would have to offer the United States something tangible to entice the latter to change its attitude to Russia.

In the early 1980s Moscow perceived, for the first time, that the burden of empire was becoming too heavy. Subsidies were required for more and more countries: Cuba, Vietnam, Afghanistan, Ethiopia, to name only the most onerous. The billions of dollars needed to support these regimes were needed to reinvigorate the domestic economy. The war in Afghanistan was unpopular at home and eroding the status of the Soviet military. It was also promoting drug addiction and trafficking and corruption in the military. Andropov placed too much reliance on the western peace movements to halt the deployment of Pershing 2 and Cruise missiles. Arms negotiations in Geneva became formal as the USA tabled proposals which it knew Moscow would not accept. Andropov's illness also contributed to a lack of flexibility in Soviet policy. On one occasion, when the American negotiators requested Moscow's latest position on arms, a Soviet delegate opened his briefcase and pulled out a copy of that day's *Pravda*. He then pushed it across the table. Needless to say, the US delegation had already been briefed on that day's *Pravda*. In November the Soviet delegation simply walked out of the INF negotiations, blaming the Americans for their breakdown.

In March 1983 President Reagan suddenly announced a startling initiative, the strategic defence initiative or Star Wars programme. He had been fascinated for a long time about the concept of protecting the United States from missile attack by erecting a shield in space. It was consistent with his horror of nuclear war. Had this been feasible, it would have been the dream weapon. Despite being called defensive, it could provide the shield behind which the US military could launch a nuclear first strike. Few US scientists took it seriously, and even fewer Russian scientists, but the Soviet military could not ignore it. The Soviet military did not wish to devote resources to it, but if the Americans went ahead they would have to. The major objection, however, remained unarticulated in public. The Russians were alarmed about the research and development implications of the SDI project: it might lead to a technological breakthrough in a related defence field. US negotiators now had a bargaining chip in dealing with the Soviets. Moscow launched violent propagandistic attacks on SDI, thereby convincing many observers that the Americans had something the Russians feared. It was illogical to claim simultaneously that SDI was science fiction and then claim it was a threat to world peace. SDI was thus at the centre of arms talks during the whole Reagan administration.

The low point during the Andropov–Reagan era was the shooting down in September 1983, by Soviet fighters, of the Korean airliner, KA007, en route from Alaska to Seoul, killing all 269 passengers and crew, including some American citizens. It had strayed into Soviet airspace and was taken for a spy plane. The Russians first of all denied shooting it down and then insisted that it was a spy plane. Reagan mirrored American and international outrage and Russia was belaboured in the United Nations. Andrei Gromyko, lost for words, simply turned his back on some film evidence shown by the Americans. The situation was compounded by the choice of Marshal Nikolai Ogarkov, the highly capable Chief of the General Staff, as the Russian spokesman. A poor diplomat, he made no attempt to express regret or apologise for the incident, merely stating that it would be repeated if another spy plane penetrated Soviet airspace. His performance was technically brilliant but sent shivers down western spines. The Soviet decision-making process was clearly in need of reform. Part of the problem had been that the Commander-in-Chief of the armed forces, Yury Andropov, was terminally ill. In Geneva in December 1983, talks on reducing conventional forces ended without agreement on further meetings.

FAILURE AND SUCCESS FOR AMERICA

A disastrous episode for American policy in the Middle East was their involvement in the Lebanese civil war. After Israel had invaded the Lebanon and ignited a civil war, the USA intervened in an attempt to restore order. In October 1983 a terrorist drove a lorry packed with explosives up to the marine compound and killed 241 Americans. Reagan then ordered those marines who had survived to ships off the coast. Moscow avoided direct involvement, unsure about US and Israeli reaction, and restricted itself to arming the Syrians who gained the upper hand in the Lebanese civil war. A mortal enemy of America and Israel, Iran, was also involved.

Things went better for the USA in Grenada, a small island in the Caribbean, the same month. A powerful American force overwhelmed the Cubans and North Koreans advising and protecting the communists who had seized power. Cuba's Castro fumed about US imperialism but Moscow did nothing – it was too risky to intervene in America's backyard. It continued to provide some arms to the Sandinistas but eschewed direct intervention [*Doc. 6*]. The USA had re-established hegemony in the Americas.

THE GROUND IS PREPARED FOR BETTER RELATIONS WITH RUSSIA

The appointment of George Shultz, in June 1982, as Secretary of State heralded a more pragmatic approach to Russia. The United States was becoming more self-confident and things were not going economically very well in the Soviet Union. Reagan, despite his reference to the Soviet Union as the 'evil empire' and calls for a crusade of freedom, was keen to visit the country, and also China. Shultz explained that an improvement in relations was necessary before a visit could take place.

Reagan had a secret meeting with Anatoly Dobrynin, the Soviet ambassador, in February 1983. He talked about constructive dialogue and reducing tension between the superpowers, but nothing happened because the Moscow establishment was, understandably, very suspicious of Reagan and, furthermore, Andropov was terminally ill. In January 1984 Reagan made an uncharacteristically hopeful speech about improving relations and George Shultz impressed on Andrei Gromyko, the Russian Foreign Minister, that Reagan meant what he said. Andropov sent a secret letter to the President informing him of his interest in promoting contact between them. Again nothing came of this as Andropov died and was succeeded by the ill Chernenko. The best way to improve superpower relations was for the leaders to meet face to face. The likelihood of this, however, was slim, given the fact that Chernenko was more concerned about breathing (he suffered from emphysema) than meeting the President.

In September 1984 Reagan met Andrei Gromyko for the first time, while the latter was attending the UN. When Reagan was re-elected President in November 1984, he and Shultz set out to improve relations with Moscow. In November it was announced that Gromyko and Shultz would meet in January 1985 to discuss arms control. In Geneva, Gromyko and Shultz agreed on three sets of talks: START, INF and defensive systems, including those based in space. Konstantin Chernenko died in March 1985 and his successor was Mikhail Sergeevich Gorbachev, the youngest member of the Russian leadership. He was destined to improve relations with the United States to an extent undreamed of by Reagan or Shultz. Cold War II was over [Cohen 1993, pp. 219–30; Garthoff 1994, pp. 1125–46; Kissinger 1982, pp. 286–320; Oberdorfer 1992, pp. 18–75].

REAGAN IMPROVES RELATIONS WITH CHINA

In April 1984 Reagan was granted his wish to visit China. Shultz managed to wean him away from seeing Taiwan as China and towards appreciating the importance of the People's Republic for the United States. Reagan's intelligence was not that of an academic but that of an actor and this placed a premium on those who wrote the script.

The President found economics, strategic theory, and all disciplines which required a long concentration span, boring. He had a sense of what the ordinary person wanted to hear and he was extremely skilled in delivering a message. Only he could present a change in policy towards Russia as something absolutely natural. Those advisers who proved most adept at gaining his ear, promised to be very influential. Shultz turned out to be one of them. As the champion of the right, Reagan had always been surrounded by those who were close to Chiang Kai-shek and Taiwan and who dreamed of one day returning to power in Beijing. As a pragmatist, Shultz knew this was nonsense, perhaps dangerous nonsense. There were advantages to Washington in good relations with Beijing, but the closeness of the later Carter years was gone and the 'China card', playing Beijing off against Moscow, existed more in theory than reality.

CHAPTER SEVEN

NEW POLITICAL THINKING AND THE END OF THE COLD WAR: 1985–1991

Gorbachev's first priority was to accelerate Soviet economic growth. He was aware that the existing order was inefficient. There were over 100 situation papers on the economy on his desk when he took over, the product of an endeavour initiated by Andropov. The major goals of reform were to strengthen the Communist Party and the country. He was aware that the military burden was too onerous (it proved impossible to quantify it accurately) and warned that if reform did not succeed the Soviet Union might lose its superpower status by 2000. The Russians thought the Americans were unlikely to sustain their rises in defence spending due to the huge rise in the budget deficits. Gorbachev thought that reforming the existing Soviet system would suffice and only realised in 1989 that the country was in systemic crisis. In order to save money on defence, he needed a meeting with Reagan to wean him away from SDI and to initiate arms negotiations which would halt and, eventually, reverse the arms race. Since the superpowers could destroy one another many times over, there was no point in making more nuclear weapons.

THE NEW POLITICAL THINKING

An early move was to remove Andrei Gromyko, known as 'grim Grom', as Foreign Minister, and replace him with Edvard Shevardnadze, a charming, volatile Georgian. The Gorbachev–Shevardnadze duo revolutionised foreign policy and won hearts and minds worldwide. They operated according to what became known as the new political thinking [*Doc. 12*]. The main components of this were:

- confrontation between the superpowers is counterproductive since any tangible gain by one side stimulates the other to match and improve on it
- military power does not guarantee security; it can only be achieved by political means and the search for common solutions
- the security of one state is not enhanced if it is achieved at the expense of another state

- the conflict between the superpowers in the Third World had brought Moscow little tangible gain, indeed it had exacerbated tension between them; Russia and America should combine their efforts to solve Third World problems together
- all states were interdependent, hence their security depended on interaction with others
- common universal values, such as human rights, the non-use of force in order to solve political problems, democracy and freedom of conscience, should inform foreign policy making
- the class approach to foreign policy formation should therefore be dropped in favour of the common interests of humankind
- the Soviet Union was a normal state which was not seeking world hegemony; it wished to work closely with all other states.

Afghanistan was a major stumbling block in this new policy as it antagonised the west and the Islamic world. The communist Third World was becoming a greater burden as not a single state appeared capable of sustainable economic growth. One estimate put the annual cost of subventioning Cuba, Vietnam, Ethiopia, Afghanistan and the others, at US\$40 billion. Furthermore, all east European states were heavily in debt to the Soviet Union.

The Reagan administration continued to combat the friends of the Soviet Union worldwide. In Nicaragua more aid was extended to the Contras, trained by the CIA. The Mujahidin were backed in Afghanistan and those opposed to the Soviet-friendly regimes in Angola, Cambodia, Mozambique and elsewhere were encouraged.

THE GORBACHEV–REAGAN SUMMITS

When Vice-President George Bush attended Chernenko's funeral he handed Gorbachev a letter from the President proposing a meeting in America. Two weeks later, Gorbachev agreed in principle, but suggested they meet in Moscow. In June, they agreed their first meeting would take place in Geneva in November 1985. During the spring and summer of 1985 Gorbachev and Reagan exchanged letters quite frequently and this permitted both sides to float proposals to discover if there were any common ground.

In October Gorbachev introduced the concept of 'reasonable sufficiency' in assessing the size of armed forces. The Soviet side devoted considerable energy to developing a position on arms control, with the Politburo drawing up a negotiating position, in consultation with the foreign and defence ministries, the international department of the Party Central Committee and the KGB. On substantive points there were guidelines on how far Gorbachev was to go. A fallback position was also worked out. On the most contentious issues – on conventional and nuclear arms cuts – the foreign ministry acted as the coordinator. It was later superseded by a special Politburo commission, chaired by Lev Zaikov, which received submissions from ministries, the KGB, academic institutes and leading specialists. Zaikov or Shevardnadze would then brief Gorbachev, who would introduce his own ideas and a final version would be submitted to the Politburo. Hence, the day-to-day evolution of Soviet foreign policy rested with Shevardnadze. It is difficult to say if proposals originated with him or Gorbachev. The Soviet leader was mainly concerned with domestic affairs but foreign affairs assumed great significance towards the end of his period in office.

The Geneva Summit was a watershed in relations. Gorbachev's attitude to Reagan was that he was more than a conservative, he was a political dinosaur. The American President reciprocated by viewing the Soviet Union as Upper Volta with missiles, but potentially a threat to the free world. He despised everything about communism. Reagan's dislike of Russia and Russians was abstract – he had never visited the country. However, the few Russians he had met, such as Dobrynin and Gromyko, he liked. Geneva was regarded as a success by both sides. The personal chemistry worked. One of the reasons for this was that Gorbachev noticed that Reagan did not like detail. So the two leaders talked in general terms and got on well. Reagan was keen to get across the message that a nuclear war could not be won, so should not be fought. The Russians proposed that the two superpowers should issue a statement that neither would be the first to launch a nuclear war. The USA objected to this as it precluded an American nuclear response to a Soviet conventional invasion of western Europe. The compromise reached was to agree to prevent any war between them, whether nuclear or conventional. They also pledged not to seek military superiority. On Afghanistan, Gorbachev made it clear that the Soviets did not intend to stay there and were seeking a political settlement.

In January 1986 the goal of a nuclear-free world was spelled out at a conference in Moscow at the Ministry of Foreign Affairs. In May 1986 the new political thinking in foreign policy was formally launched. Gennady Gerasimov, renowned for his suave performances and one-liners, such as the Sinatra doctrine 'we'll do it our way', became the foreign ministry press spokesman. The ministry had been found wanting during the Chernobyl nuclear disaster in April 1986, when it had claimed that there had been no disaster and subsequently new-style diplomats, long on persuasion and short on ideological cant, began to take over.

Reagan's commitment to SDI, reiterated at Geneva, did not deter the Russians. In the months following the summit they launched proposal after proposal to end the arms race. Everything now appeared to be negotiable and Moscow's flexibility caught Washington off guard. In January 1986 Gorbachev dramatically proposed the phasing out of nuclear weapons by 2000. On intermediate-range missiles, the Soviet position was now almost that of the

Americans. Moscow was willing to accept limits on ICBMs and the balance of conventional forces in Europe. Soviet troops, perceived as threatening by NATO, could be redeployed. The Russian military were quite happy to go along with cuts in strategic arms, if they did not make the Soviet Union vulnerable. However, they drew the line at conventional reductions and here Gorbachev had a fight on his hands. In February 1986 Gorbachev referred to Afghanistan as a 'running sore' and signalled that Russia wanted out in order to improve relations with Washington.

The American response, in April 1986, was to strike at Libya, with the intent of killing Qaddafi, the Libyan leader judged an accomplice in a bomb attack which had killed US servicemen. The CIA began to supply the Mujahidin with Stinger missiles which were promptly used to bring down Soviet helicopters. In May Reagan declared that the USA would no longer observe the unratified SALT II agreement.

The first direct conflict between the two leaders occurred in August 1986, when the Americans arrested Gennady Zakharov, a Soviet UN employee, when he was on the point of purchasing classified documents. The KGB responded by arresting Nicholas Daniloff, the Moscow correspondent of *US News and World Report*. Reagan wrote a personal letter to Gorbachev confirming that Daniloff was not a spy, but George Shultz and the editor of *US News and World Report* were aware that Daniloff had acquired secret Soviet documents and photographs and had passed them on to the State Department. Shultz was furious when he discovered that the CIA had used Daniloff as a contact with a Soviet source and had discussed him on an open telephone line; he regarded the whole episode as a CIA ploy to oppose his efforts to improve relations with the Soviet Union.

During the three weeks Gorbachev took to respond to Reagan's letter, the USA ordered 25 Soviet UN employees, whom they deemed to be engaged in intelligence gathering, out of the country. Moscow was warned that if it retaliated more would go. The Americans also demanded that Yury Orlov, a prominent human rights campaigner, be released and permitted to move to the USA, along with his wife. (They eventually left.) Shultz's excellent personal relations with Shevardnadze, which included taking the Foreign Minister on a boating trip down the Potomac and serenading him with 'Georgia on my mind', made it possible to find a solution. Daniloff was released, Zakharov was expelled and Reagan then announced the Reykjavik Summit, in October 1986. However, this was not the end of the affair. After the summit Moscow ordered out five US diplomats and Washington retaliated by sending 55 Soviet diplomats packing. Why did Gorbachev take KGB advice and order out the American diplomats? It may have been in pique after failing to get what he wanted from Reagan at the summit.

The US Congress restricted financial support for anti-communist movements throughout the world. The Reagan administration countered by seeking donations from rich supporters and foreign rulers, such as the Saudis. To secure the release of American hostages held by pro-Iranian terrorists in the Lebanon, it was decided to sell arms secretly to the Iranians and to use the proceeds to arm the Nicaraguan Contras. This began to embarrass Reagan when the story broke in late 1986.

In the run-up to the Reykjavik Summit, Gorbachev offered more and more concessions. ICBMs could be eliminated over ten years. US and Soviet tactical nuclear weapons could be removed from Europe. The sticking point, as before, was SDI. Initially, Gorbachev gained the upper hand. Noting that Reagan's answers were vague, the Russian leader then posed specific questions. The President then shuffled his cards to find the right answer but some of them fell on the floor. When he had gathered them up they were out of order. Reagan accepted Gorbachev's goal of the elimination of nuclear weapons but refused to agree that testing of SDI should be restricted to the laboratory. The President could have agreed to laboratory testing without slowing down the project, but he was unaware of this.

The two leaders came tantalisingly close to an official agreement but unofficially they had agreed on more issues than ever before. The Soviets now accepted on-site inspection and human rights as a subject for negotiation. When he returned to Moscow, Gorbachev gave vent to his frustration at a Politburo meeting, using insulting, demeaning language to describe Reagan. However, when he had calmed down, he confessed that the two leaders were 'doomed to co-operate'. Formal failure at Reykjavik resulted in a better INF agreement in 1987, when all missiles were eliminated. Britain and France would have resisted giving up their nuclear deterrents if Reagan's acceptance of the elimination of all nuclear weapons had remained [*Docs 13 and 14*].

Reagan pursued four objectives in his relations with Gorbachev: arms reduction, withdrawing from military confrontation in third countries, building respect for human rights and raising the Iron Curtain. Gradually the Soviet side came to realise that progress on these issues could be of mutual benefit. If progress were made on one issue it would not be that the Soviets had lost out to the Americans. Zero-sum diplomacy was coming to an end. The breakthrough came in November 1987, when Shultz and Shevardnadze reached agreement on verification.

In December Gorbachev travelled to Washington and he and Reagan signed the epoch-making INF agreement. It eliminated a whole class of nuclear weapons: those carried by intermediate-range ballistic missiles, over 2,500 in all. It was the first arms agreement signed by the superpowers since 1979. The verification procedures were so intrusive that American officials began to worry that the Soviets might learn too much about US defence. On the last day of his visit, on 10 December, on his way to the White House, Gorbachev suddenly instructed his driver to stop. He got out and started working the crowd. He was enthusiastically received and was exhilarated by the warmth and emotion he encountered. Over lunch, he informed everyone that his reception had made a deep impression on him.

Psychologically, this came at a vital moment for him. At home, he was finding it harder and harder to counter the populist appeal of Boris Yeltsin and opposition to perestroika in the Party and the country. As things became more complex domestically, they flowered internationally. 'Gorbymania' can be said to have been born in Washington in December 1987. He was adored and he loved it. In future, when he felt battered at home, all he had to do to recover his aplomb was to go abroad and be feted. Doubters abroad were being silenced while domestically they were becoming more strident and numerous. The Washington Summit cemented a partnership with the USA and the end of the Cold War was in sight. Things began to change also in Russia. A softer line on human rights was taken and Jews who wished to emigrate were released from detention and permitted to leave. The Russian Orthodox Church, with the support of the regime, marked the millennium of Christianity in Russia, churches were refurbished and reconsecrated.

In February 1988 Gorbachev announced that Soviet forces would be withdrawn from Afghanistan and an agreement on this was signed in April. In May Russian troops began to leave Mongolia and it was hinted that they could soon begin quitting eastern Europe. Reagan travelled to Moscow for his last summit with Gorbachev and on 1 June they exchanged the instruments of ratification which implemented the INF treaty. Reagan strolled in Red Square with Gorbachev and when asked by journalists if he still regarded the Soviet Union as an evil empire, answered in the negative. He had changed his mind, as had many Americans. Only 30 per cent now saw Russia as evil and threatening.

In December 1988 at the UN, Gorbachev announced that the Soviet Union would reduce unilaterally its forces by half a million within two years. Soviet troops stationed in the GDR, Czechoslovakia and Hungary would be gradually withdrawn. Astonishingly, he did not expect the United States to reciprocate. The remarkable thing about this speech was that neither Gorbachev nor Shevardnadze had consulted the defence ministry before announcing the cuts. In protest, Marshal Akhromeev, Chief of the General Staff, announced his resignation the same day. He had gone along with strategic arms reductions but drew the line at conventional reductions, with America reciprocating. Gorbachev was engaged in a high-wire act with his own military.

Gorbachev used the UN forum to elucidate his view of universal human values. He stressed that freedom of choice was a universal principle. Many wondered if this also extended to eastern Europe. Afterwards, he met President Reagan and President-Elect George Bush on Governors Island. The Armenian earthquake disaster intervened and Gorbachev had to cut short his visit and return to Moscow.

THE BUSH–GORBACHEV RELATIONSHIP IS SLOW TO DEVELOP

The impetus in Russian–American relations was now lost as President Bush, after assuming office in January 1989, took his time to elaborate his foreign policy priorities. Bush felt that Reagan had been too quick to deal with Moscow and had been too accommodating. This revealed the difficulty the new President was having in comprehending the sea change in Soviet foreign policy. The conservative Bush administration did not want to believe that many of its cherished beliefs about the Soviet Union were dissolving before its eyes. In May 1989 Marlon Fitzwater, the White House spokesman, dismissed Gorbachev as a 'drugstore cowboy'. But George Bush changed his mind during his extensive tour of eastern and western Europe in July 1989. Everyone pressed him to meet Mikhail Gorbachev as momentous events were taking place. The relationship eventually became very close and Gorbachev remarked, on one occasion, that it was not in the interests of the Soviet Union to diminish the role of America in the world. On some occasions he excluded his own Russian interpreter from meetings with Bush, relying entirely on the American interpreter. This behaviour was puzzling but one explanation would be that Gorbachev's foreign policy agenda could only be carried out if America shared it and continued to be the dominant world power. As one of his Russian communist critics has pointed out, this was a strange policy for a Soviet leader to be pursuing.

The turning point in the relationship between James Baker, who had succeeded George Shultz as Secretary of State, and Edvard Shevardnadze, occurred in September 1989, when Shevardnadze accepted Baker's invitation to accompany him to his ranch at Jackson Hole, Wyoming. Before leaving Moscow, Shevardnadze had given vent to his frustration at the tardiness of Washington's response to Russian arms proposals. Shevardnadze stayed two weeks and developed as close a relationship with Baker as he had had with Shultz. On arrival the Soviet Foreign Minister was presented with a ten-gallon Stetson. Enquiries at the Soviet embassy in Washington had failed to elicit information about the size of Shevardnadze's head, so the Americans had worked it out for themselves. The dashing Georgian cut quite a figure in his ten-gallon hat, cowboy boots and three-piece suit.

To underline the economic crisis back home, Shevardnadze had brought along Nikolai Shmelev, a pro-market economist who had published some devastating analyses of the Soviet economy. The minister was desperate for a partnership with America, whatever the cost. Without gaining anything in return, he intimated that Moscow was willing to sign a START treaty. He confirmed that the giant Krasnoyarsk radar station contravened the ABM treaty. He had hinted at this in a speech to the UN in 1986, it was only now that action could be taken as the Soviet military were reluctant to give it up. Gorbachev was later to inform Bush that he had decommissioned Krasnoyarsk in order to 'make things easier for the President'. Krasnoyarsk was not a satellite-tracking station, as the Russians had been claiming for years, but a sophisticated battle management radar in a potentially anti-ballistic missile system. On his return to Moscow, he made other concessions. He accepted Washington's demand that it be permitted 880 submarine-launched Cruise missiles. Akhromeev, now an adviser to Gorbachev, and others berated him for not having gained reciprocity on this issue.

The Malta Summit, in December 1989, did not produce any tangible agreements but was a major step forward in Russian–American relations. In Washington in July 1989, Akhromeev was handed a note from Bush for Gorbachev suggesting a meeting in December. The proposal was not made known at the time as the administration was having difficulty in agreeing its policy on arms control.

Shevardnadze advised Gorbachev in November 1989 that it was very important to get Bush's 'public commitment to the reform programme' and warned him that Bush was an 'indecisive leader' [Dobrynin 1995, p. 634]. Bush made up his mind about perestroika before he arrived in Malta on 1 December: it was a good idea. He had a raft of proposals about economic cooperation. The Americans had warned Gorbachev about trying to outsmart Bush at their first meeting by launching a series of new initiatives. Reykjavik obviously still smarted.

Gorbachev understood Bush to be offering an economic partnership, although he soon demonstrated that he had a woolly understanding of a market economy. There were informal agreements on eastern Europe, Germany and the Baltic republics. Eastern Europe did not present a problem because Gorbachev and Shevardnadze had reiterated, on several occasions, that the Russians would not use military force to prevent the peoples there deciding their own fate. Gorbachev said he hoped the Warsaw Pact would continue. Bush countered by saying that as long as force was not used the USA would not seek to embarrass the Soviet Union in the region.

On Germany, Gorbachev counselled caution since no one in Russia favoured reunification in the short term. On the Baltic republics, he said he was willing to consider any form of association but not separation. Bush made it clear that the use of force there would be disastrous for their relationship, but otherwise the USA again promised not to make life difficult for Moscow there. Rumours circulated that a deal had been struck. Moscow would accept German reunification if the USA stayed out of eastern Europe and the Baltic. No such agreement was reached, much to the relief of these areas.

On arms, it was agreed to work towards the signing of a conventional forces in Europe (CFE) treaty, in 1990. A START treaty might be ready for signing at the next proposed summit, in Washington, in mid-1990. There were also sharp disagreements. Bush was critical of Soviet arms deliveries to Latin America and the behaviour of their ally, Cuba. Gorbachev retorted that he had kept his promise not to supply arms to Nicaragua. On Cuba, Gorbachev thought that the best solution was for the President to meet Fidel Castro face to face and offered to arrange a meeting. Bush brushed this aside contemptuously. Gorbachev took umbrage at Bush's assertion that western values were prevailing. This implied, responded Gorbachev, that Russia was caving in to western norms. He preferred the term 'universal, democratic values'. Eventually, they agreed to say democratic values. Malta was a watershed in Russian–American relations. Gorbachev assured Bush that he, as other Russians, did not consider America the enemy any more. Shevardnadze put it graphically. The superpowers had 'buried the Cold War at the bottom of the Mediterranean' [Beschloss and Talbott 1993, p. 165].

GORBACHEV AND EUROPE: OUR COMMON HOME

Gorbachev came up with the expression 'Europe is our common home' (the concept was elastic; it also included the USA and Canada) in Paris, in February 1986, during his first official visit to western Europe after taking office. He chose France because it was a nuclear power. It would be a feather in his cap if he could interest the French in a nuclear-free world, but President Mitterrand proved quite unresponsive. When Mitterrand visited Moscow in July 1986, he confided to Gorbachev that he opposed the whole idea of SDI, which he viewed as accelerating the arms race, whereas policy should be aimed at reducing arsenals. After the Reykjavik Summit, however, the French repeated their commitment to nuclear deterrence, disappointing Gorbachev.

In April 1987, in Prague, Gorbachev floated his pan-European idea but found little response from the leaders of western Europe. They preferred to take a lead from the Americans. When the British Prime Minister, Margaret Thatcher, visited Moscow in March 1987, she forcefully reiterated her commitment to nuclear deterrence (nuclear weapons have been invented, you cannot de-invent them) and her belief that the goal of the Soviet Union was to extend communism worldwide. Nevertheless, the two leaders got on extremely well as Mrs Thatcher enjoyed a good argument. As she had the ear of President Reagan, it was important for Gorbachev to attempt to win her over to his way of thinking. She was enthusiastic about something else: perestroika.

Although President Mitterrand regarded Reagan's belief in SDI as bordering on the mystical, he maintained a hard line on France's nuclear deterrent. It was non-negotiable. The French parliament even voted to upgrade their armed forces. In Moscow, in April 1987, Mrs Thatcher also confirmed her belief in the nuclear deterrent [*Doc. 15*]. In December 1987 Gorbachev dropped in on Mrs Thatcher en route to the Washington summit to sign the INF treaty. Geoffrey Howe, the British Foreign Secretary, was very impressed by their work rate. He compared them to two-star Stakhanovites (exemplary

Russian shock workers). Gorbachev's first extended official visit to Britain, in April 1989, found Mrs Thatcher passionately interested in the development of perestroika. When Gorbachev commented that many in the west were having their doubts about it, she brushed this aside and assured him that all in the west were enthusiastic about it.

After visiting France and Britain, the two west European nuclear states, it was time for Gorbachev to visit West Germany, in June 1989. The Germans had been feeling left out of the Soviet leader's diplomacy. When Kohl saw Gorbachev at Chernenko's funeral, the new Soviet leader enquired where the Federal Republic was drifting. He used the verb *driftovat*, to drift, which is not in any Russian dictionary. Kohl was probably the first western statesman to be treated to such neologisms – Gorbachev loved to pepper his remarks with newly mastered English expressions. Kohl found Gorbachev's communicative skills brilliant and attempted to pay him a compliment. Unfortunately, he likened him to Josef Goebbels, the silver-tongued Nazi propagandist. That soured relations for a while. In July, in Paris, Gorbachev told the French that the post-war era was over. At the Sorbonne he underlined that pure intellect without morality constituted a terrible danger. He was in Helsinki in October, then went to Italy in November. The reception he received in Milan was the most emotional of his career. Everywhere he was feted as if he were the first man from Mars. On 1 December he became the first Soviet leader to enter the Vatican and informed the Polish Pope John Paul II that democracy was not enough; morality was also essential.

GERMANY UNITES

When West German President Richard von Weizsäcker visited Moscow in June 1987, he touched on the question of German reunification very tactfully. Gorbachev made it clear to him that it was premature to consider such a thing and even harmful to raise the issue. Gorbachev's visit to East Berlin in October 1989 brought home to him the gravity of the situation in the GDR. On 1 November Egon Krenz, the new Party leader, met Gorbachev in the Kremlin to beg for aid. Krenz stated that if East German living standards had to rely exclusively on the GDR economy, they would drop by at least 30 per cent, a political impossibility. Gorbachev told him the Soviet Union could offer little aid as Soviet republics were demanding higher prices for their raw materials. Disappointed at hearing this, Krenz then touched on the common European home. He wanted to know what place in it Russia envisaged for the GDR. He pointed out that the Soviet Union was the father of the GDR and that 'paternity for the child had to be accepted'. Gorbachev explained that the Soviet Union was forging closer links with West Germany and Bonn expected Soviet backing for German unification. All he could advise was for the GDR to foster closer relations with Bonn.

After the Berlin Wall came down in November 1989, Chancellor Kohl launched a ten-point plan for German reunification. He did not consult his Foreign Minister, Hans-Dietrich Genscher, or even his allies. Genscher, in Moscow in December, had to defend a document, parts of which he disagreed with. The meeting was tense and painful for both Genscher and Gorbachev. When Hans Modrow, the GDR Prime Minister, saw Gorbachev in January 1990, he confessed that it would probably be impossible to save the GDR. Gorbachev and his advisers had reached the same conclusion a few days earlier. The Soviet Union would take the initiative to set up a group of six: the four victorious allies – Russia, America, Britain and France – and the two German states.

When James Baker met Gorbachev in February 1990, he was at pains to stress that the USA was not seeking any advantage from these developments. Next Gorbachev saw Kohl and told him that it was up to the Germans to decide things for themselves. Gorbachev hoped for a neutral, united Germany, but Kohl, now full of self-confidence, rejected this and proposed that Germany should join NATO. In March the Alliance for Germany, backed by Kohl's own party, won the East German elections. In April the new government proposed that unification be achieved according to the federal constitution. The GDR would simply be integrated into West Germany and thereby disappear. In May the GDR signed the state treaty with the Federal Republic on economic, monetary and social unity. The Deutsche Mark (DM) became the common currency on 1 July.

The reunification of Germany on 3 October 1990 resulted from the coming together of three factors: the Gorbachev revolution in the Soviet Union, the collapse of the GDR economy which led to large numbers of its citizens making for West Germany and George Bush's determination to make German unity one of the crowning achievements of his presidency. Gorbachev simply conceded everything the man in the White House wanted. On the important issue of whether a united Germany should be a member of NATO, pressure from Bush and Baker led eventually to Gorbachev giving in, orally, to the consternation of his officials. In his memoirs, Gorbachev claims that the decision to allow Germans to decide their own security arrangements – it was a foregone conclusion that they would vote for NATO – originated with him and not Bush. The White House sees it the other way round. One of the reasons for the acceptance of Germany in NATO was Kohl's close personal relationship with Gorbachev.

One striking example of this took place at Archys, in the north Caucasus, in July 1990. Here, in formal and informal meetings, the two leaders agreed many of the details of reunification. Without consulting Shevardnadze, who had done all the spadework on Soviet–German relations, Gorbachev abandoned all claims as an occupying power and any restriction on German sovereignty. He agreed to the withdrawal of Russian forces, with the Germans promising to build accommodation in the Soviet Union for the returning personnel. The Germans also paid for the troops to leave. Had Gorbachev not been so desperate for German financial aid, he could have struck a much more profitable bargain. German unification, and the Soviet terms for it, were not discussed in the Politburo. Shevardnadze was unhappy as he was aware that the ire of the military and the conservatives would descend upon him for 'losing' the GDR.

GORBACHEV AND EASTERN EUROPE

Gorbachev met the east European leaders after Chernenko's funeral, in March 1985, and explained that the Brezhnev doctrine was dead. Henceforth, they could choose their own leaders and policies. This was reiterated at a meeting of the Warsaw Pact in April 1985. Gorbachev assumed, of course, that east Europeans had made their choice. They had chosen socialism and would never go back on this. Reform, therefore, in these countries would be socialist and would enhance the appeal of socialism worldwide.

The Brezhnev leadership had ruled out military intervention in 1981, when the Polish military took over. This remained the Politburo's policy. It had invested too much in the peace process to throw it away by invading Poland. In March 1989, the Hungarian Party leader, Károly Grósz, in Moscow, explained why Hungary had introduced a multi-party system. There was not a murmur of protest as it was considered a Hungarian internal affair. In July 1989 the communists were defeated in Poland in elections and the way was clear for a non-communist Prime Minister to take office.

Also in July Gorbachev, at the Council of Europe, stated: 'Any interference in domestic affairs of any kind, any attempt to limit the sovereignty of states, both of friends and allies, no matter whose it is, is impermissible.' In October 1989, attending the 40th anniversary celebrations of the GDR, Gorbachev and the communist leader Erich Honecker did not see eye to eye. East Germans called on Gorbachev to save them. He told East Berliners that history punished those who are left behind. Honecker departed and was replaced by Egon Krenz, but the latter was quite incapable of coping with the disintegration of the GDR. Gorbachev was not the only one who believed that the East Germans would remain within the socialist camp: the West German Social Democratic Party (SPD) also advised him that this would happen. The SPD was taken aback by calls for reunification and most members opposed it. Only Willy Brandt, among SPD leaders, caught the public mood and sought the disappearance of the East German state. When the Berlin Wall came down on 9 November 1989, it marked the end of post-war politics. Revolution rolled over eastern Europe like an irresistible tide. It washed away four decades of communist rule as the people rejected Russian-style socialism. In Czechoslovakia, it was called the velvet revolution. No one had to die for freedom. Some blood was, however, spilt in Romania. Nicolae and Elena Ceausescu, the hated dictators, were summarily tried and shot on Christmas Day 1989.

GORBACHEV AND CHINA

Gorbachev's visit to China in May 1989 had tragic consequences. Soviet reforms had aroused great interest among Chinese youth and many of them dared to hope that democracy, unknown in China's history, could take root there. Economic success was breeding optimism. Gorbachev's visit was a triumph for him and he was feted as a hero by masses of Chinese demonstrators. However, this adulation of a foreign leader deeply embarrassed the ageing Chinese leadership. They and Gorbachev agreed to normalise relations between the two neighbours and not to interfere in one another's internal affairs. The Gorbachev visit added impetus to the democratic movement in China and led to the decision by Deng Xiaoping to use force in Tiananmen Square, in Beijing on 4 June. The Communist Party of China feared it was losing its grip on the country. Democracy to it meant anarchy and the possible break-up of the People's Republic. The world condemned the Chinese leadership and ostracised it for its action on 4 June. Trade, however, continued. The lesson was not lost on some Soviet and east European leaders. The GDR openly applauded the brutal suppression of unarmed civilians.

GORBACHEV'S DOMESTIC DIFFICULTIES CAUSE PROBLEMS FOR BUSH

Gorbachev and Bush maintained regular contact and the US ambassador, Jack Matlock, a fluent Russian speaker, saw the Soviet leader regularly. One of the most contentious issues was Gorbachev's nationality policy. The USA did not want to promote the break-up of the Soviet Union and made it clear to the republics, especially those in the Baltic – Estonia, Latvia and Lithuania – that it would not support their drive for independence. American policy was to support Gorbachev in his efforts to transform the Soviet Union into a democratic federation. Washington also made no secret about seeing a liberal market economy as the solution to the travails of the Russian command economy.

The Russian Federation posed a bigger problem for Washington. The American ambassador cultivated good relations with Boris Yeltsin and Russian democrats and official American policy was to encourage Gorbachev and Yeltsin to work closely together. A post-communist, democratic Soviet Union, headed by Gorbachev and Yeltsin, was the dream ticket. Unfortunately, Yeltsin had other ideas. Gorbachev found it very difficult to accept criticism, especially from Russian democrats.

Gorbachev and Yeltsin had fallen out in November 1987, when Yeltsin had been unceremoniously dumped as Party leader in the city of Moscow. When the Russian Supreme Soviet, the new parliament, was elected in the spring of 1990, he became chair or speaker, and this constitutionally made him head of the Russian Federation, an eventuality which Gorbachev had done his best to prevent.

When the US ambassador paid a courtesy visit on Ruslan Khasbulatov, Yeltsin's nomination as deputy speaker, in June 1990, he was astonished by what he heard. Khasbulatov informed him that the Russian Federation would soon be the successor state to the Soviet Union. There would be a union, a loose confederation, which would not need a constitution, as it would not be a state in international law. Economic decision making would rest with the republics. The Russian Federation wanted to move towards a market economy but the central Soviet bureaucracy was hindering this. It wanted its diplomats in Soviet embassies abroad and would eventually conduct its own foreign economic relations. Eventually Soviet embassies would become Russian embassies, as the Russian Federation would become the successor state. Conventional military forces would be under the command of the republics, nuclear forces would be run from the centre. This was an astonishing scenario, given that Yeltsin was always swearing allegiance to the federal or confederal goal proposed by Gorbachev. Now his deputy was informing the USA that his real goal was a very loose confederation, dominated by Russia. Since Gorbachev stood in the way, he would be destroyed. Since this is remarkably close to what actually did happen in December 1991, it is tempting to see Yeltsin playing a double game. However, had it not been for the attempted coup in August 1991, the plan might not have come to fruition.

Khasbulatov's vision of the future was not what the US administration wanted to hear. The Americans found Yeltsin difficult to deal with, mainly because he acted on instinct when taking some key decisions. He also lacked the charm and suave demeanour of Gorbachev. Since, presumably, Khasbulatov's office had been bugged by the KGB, Gorbachev was soon apprised of the conversation. On occasions when Bush encouraged Gorbachev to work more closely with Yeltsin, he would counter that he regarded Yeltsin as a 'destroyer'.

In the spring of 1990 the state planning commission, Gosplan, recommended that the country move towards a market economy, although there was considerable confusion about what a market economy entailed. However, many leading economic officials, especially in the military–industrial complex, quickly decided they were not in favour, as it would weaken their position. The battle raged during the summer but eventually a plan was proposed for the economy to move to the market in 500 days, the so-called 500-day programme, authored by Academician Shatalin and Grigory Yavlinsky. There was also a counter-variant, a much more modest approach, proposed by Prime Minister Nikolai Ryzhkov and Academician Abalkin. Gorbachev invited the two groups to negotiate a compromise but this was like mixing chalk and cheese. Gorbachev could not make up his mind and the radical proposal lapsed. As a consequence, he moved politically to the right from the autumn of 1990 to the spring of 1991.

It was during this period that the tragic events in Vilnius, in Lithuania, occurred. In January 1991 tension between Moscow and Vilnius escalated and Gorbachev sent the Lithuanians an ultimatum: either retreat from their goal of independence or face the consequences. Shortly thereafter Moscow's troops stormed the radio and TV centre and the TV tower, leaving 13 dead. Gorbachev denied he had given instructions to attack and shed blood. The USA deplored the deaths but accepted Gorbachev's assurances that he had not been the butcher. Washington appealed for a political solution and warned that the use of force would seriously jeopardise relations between the two states. A week later, Moscow's forces attacked the Latvian Ministry of Affairs' building in Riga, killing four people. Again Gorbachev denied complicity. It turned out that a local officer had acted on his own initiative. This brought into doubt Gorbachev's control of his military and police. The west took a lenient line because it was engaged in the Gulf War and needed Gorbachev on board.

THE GULF WAR LEADS TO JOINT SUPERPOWER POLICY

Saddam Hussein's invasion of Kuwait on 1 August 1990, and its incorporation in Iraq, was a severe test for the evolving Soviet–American relationship. Gorbachev faced a dilemma: Iraq was an ally and there were thousands of Russian troops in the country. James Baker and Edvard Shevardnadze met at Vnukovo 2 airport in Moscow and agreed on a statement condemning the Iraqi aggression – the precursor of joint votes in the UN. On 9 September Gorbachev and Bush met in Helsinki and talked most of the day. The Soviet leader wanted assurances on two points: that military pressure would be used against Saddam Hussein, without its escalating into war, and that US forces would leave Kuwait after it was liberated.

Gorbachev asked about the possibility of US financial aid for Russia. He was obliquely hinting that Kuwait and credits were linked. After the tragic events in Vilnius, Bush made it clear that further use of force would make it impossible for America to help economically. Gorbachev assured Bush he was aware of this but, in his judgement, the Soviet Union was on the brink of civil war. The Soviet leader kept his promise, made in Helsinki, that the Soviet Union would cooperate with the United States in ensuring that Iraqi aggression did not reap any rewards.

GORBACHEV'S PROBLEMS MOUNT

President Bush was due in Moscow for a summit in February 1991, but tension in the Baltic republics made it impossible to travel. There was also the fact that the Soviet military were not observing the conventional forces in Europe (CFE) treaty, agreed in Paris in November 1990. One ruse was to transfer tanks behind the Urals, in Asia, to prevent their being destroyed. Another was to arm the navy with some tanks. It appeared that Gorbachev would not or could not rein in his military. General Moiseev, Chief of the General Staff, was dispatched to Washington to iron out the misunderstandings.

In March 1991 James Baker dropped in to see Gorbachev in Moscow. The Soviet leader then informed him that he had received information from one of Yeltsin's associates: the Russian leader had approached the United States, wanting to know what the US reaction would be if he took power by unconstitutional means. This revelation was news to Baker and he managed to convince Gorbachev that no such approach had been made. How could Yeltsin take power with the KGB and the military on Gorbachev's side? It was disinformation, fabricated by the KGB. This was another instance of Gorbachev giving too much credence to KGB reporting. The KGB chief, Vladimir Kryuchkov, consistently argued that a state of emergency was needed to restore order. He also negatively assessed American initiatives, seeing them as a US attempt to undermine his country. The trouble about Kryuchkov was that he actually believed much of the disinformation he was showering on Gorbachev.

In May 1991 the US ambassador was surprised, during one of his meetings with Gorbachev, to be treated to a plaintive monologue. The gist of the flood of words was that the President feared that President Bush was preparing to change his policy towards the Soviet Union. It was quite clear that Gorbachev desperately needed Bush's support and he also needed money. The ambassador had asked for his tour of duty to end and Gorbachev pointedly asked him if he thought that the Soviet ship of state was about to sink. The next day Gorbachev met Rupert Murdoch, the media magnate. He was even more pessimistic and told him that Bush was risking a new cold war. This stung the President into action. He caressed Gorbachev with warm words of empathy and assured him that the thought of cooling their relationship had never entered his head. Progress was made on the CFE treaty and it could be sent to the Senate. In June Gorbachev was informed that America would grant the Soviet Union a much needed credit of US$1.5 billion to purchase grain.

This was fine but much more was needed. Every foreign statesman he met was informed that the Gulf War had cost US$100 billion. The money had been instantly found. Why could such a sum not be raised to support perestroika? After all, it was ten or a hundred times more important for the world than the Gulf War. The rich man's club was the group of Seven (G7). Could the Soviet Union possibly join? In order to get an invitation, he needed a financial plan.

The ideal person to draw one up was Grigory Yavlinsky. He went off to Harvard to work with Graham Allison. Yavlinsky called the joint effort the 'window of opportunity', Allison described it as the 'great design'. Gorbachev pulled out all the stops and invited Mrs Thatcher to his Moscow dacha. She was completely won over and instructed the US ambassador to send a message to the President: he was to lead the western initiative to save Gorbachev. When Matlock pointed out that this would be difficult since Gorbachev had yet to adopt market reforms, she brushed his words aside and told him to think like a statesman, not as a diplomat, trying to avoid doing anything.

On 17 June 1991 Valentin Pavlov, the Prime Minister, requested parliament to confer on him some extraordinary powers, mainly on economic policy. He had not cleared it first with the President. On 20 June Gavriil Popov, the newly elected Mayor of Moscow, paid a farewell visit to the US ambassador, who was soon to return to Washington. Popov scribbled on a piece of paper that a coup was being organised to remove Gorbachev. News about this had to be got to Yeltsin, at the time in America. Matlock asked for the names. They were Pavlov, Kryuchkov, Yazov, Lukyanov. (They turned out to be the attempted coup leaders in August 1991.) The ambassador then informed Gorbachev that President Bush had information about an attempt to remove him. Gorbachev thanked the President for his concern but said that he had everything under control. Bush then phoned Gorbachev and revealed that the source had been Popov. Now the KGB knew who had blown the whistle on them. Bush decided not to name the alleged conspirators but this may have been a mistake. Gorbachev, apparently, thought they were a group of conservative deputies in parliament.

Gorbachev's bid for G7 money was doomed from the outset. President Bush had thought that he had made it clear to the Soviet leader that only a programme which clearly mapped out the steps to a market economy would be likely to succeed in London, in July. On 31 May Bush and Baker met Vladimir Shcherbakov, Deputy Prime Minister, and Evgeny Primakov, head of foreign economic relations in the Security Council. The US President concluded that Gorbachev did not have a viable programme. Yavlinsky was not consulted. Gorbachev reasoned that, as the reform programme had to be implemented by the government, it should draft it. In London, everyone listened politely to Gorbachev and there was little reaction to his invitation to business leaders to invest in the Soviet Union, but no money was promised by the G7. Gorbachev asked for, and was granted, membership of the International Monetary Fund (IMF), an international body concerned with macro-economics. Gorbachev was dejected by his first major foreign policy failure since Soviet–American relations had become friendly.

He took out his ire on Bush on 17 July. In a long, rambling speech he complained about not knowing what the United States expected of the Soviet Union. How was the Soviet Union to develop? What did George Bush want from him? Again he mentioned US$100 million as the sum the Gulf War had cost and which had been found easily. Why could a similar amount not be found for the project of the century? President Bush was offended by these remarks and coldly apologised for not having made himself clear before. He reiterated the American wish that the Soviet Union become a democratic state with a market economy, integrated in the western world. Again he stated that America did not want the political and economic ruin of the Soviet Union. What is remarkable about Gorbachev's words is that Bush had repeated time and again what America wanted from the Soviet Union. He made a poor impression on Bush, who began wondering if Gorbachev was beginning to lose his grip on reality. The reason for his *faux pas* may have been his total inability to grasp what a market economy entailed and KGB analyses which stressed that America was trying to destroy Russia.

THE LAST SUMMIT

George Bush arrived in Moscow in July 1991 for his first Moscow summit as President. It was to be the fourth, and last, Bush–Gorbachev meeting. Ironically, it was the most rewarding for both leaders, on a purely personal basis. The START treaty was ready for signature, after ten years of hard negotiations; the CFE treaty was with the Senate for ratification; a bill was before Congress conferring on the Soviet Union most favoured nation status; and there was a tentative agreement on a Middle East peace conference. However, the realities of the domestic situation impinged on the meeting. A note was passed to Bush, informing him that six Lithuanian customs officials had been killed during the night. Gorbachev was embarrassed as this was the first he had heard of the incident. It appeared that the incident had been staged by the Minister of Internal Affairs to disrupt the summit. It also demonstrated that Bush was better informed about Soviet domestic events than President Gorbachev. He, it would appear, was not in full control of the police.

The growing influence of the republics was marked by Gorbachev's invitation to Boris Yeltsin and Nursultan Nazarbaev, the leader of Kazakhstan, to join him in a working lunch and to participate in some of the sessions. Yeltsin replied that he preferred to meet Bush face to face, president to president, in his office. He kept Bush waiting ten minutes and the meeting overran. The Americans were not amused. At the official dinner Yeltsin tried to upstage Gorbachev. When Barbara Bush entered he attempted to escort her to the top table, as if he were the host.

In planning his itinerary, Bush had been advised by American diplomats to visit Kiev, the capital of Ukraine. Initially, the Soviet Ministry of Foreign

Affairs raised no objection, but then it changed its mind and advised Bush against travelling to Kiev, given the tense situation there. Instead, he could spend time with Gorbachev in Stavropol krai. Evidently, Gorbachev was piqued by Bush's wish to visit Ukraine at a time when the Ukrainians were proving difficult during negotiations on a new Union treaty. In Kiev, President Bush was to meet the constitutional head of the republic, Leonid Kravchuk. All toasts were to be in Ukrainian and English. No Russian was to be used. Bush advised the Ukrainians to concentrate on developing democracy before aiming for independence and to avoid the pitfalls of nationalism. Their future lay as part of the new Union Gorbachev was forging. They turned a deaf ear to this advice. Bush's words were dubbed, disrespectfully, his chicken Kiev speech.

THE ATTEMPTED COUP AND AFTER

The attempted coup in August 1991 was a devastating blow for Gorbachev. He felt betrayed since the coup leaders were all his own men. President Bush, when he met the press, was defensive and gave the impression that the coup had been successful and that he would have to deal with the coup leaders. They seized upon this and broadcast it repeatedly on the Soviet media. Bush declined to phone Yeltsin. One of the reasons for the lack of clarity in the US position was that Jack Matlock, the very able ambassador, had returned to Washington. He was not consulted but on television declared that the coup was bound to fail. President Mitterrand began to refer to the 'new leaders' of the Soviet Union.

The failed coup transformed the Gorbachev–Yeltsin relationship. The Russian leader was now in the driving seat and unsophisticated in driving this home to the Soviet President. He displayed a nice turn of phrase when he telephoned Gorbachev, in Crimea, at the end of the coup; he enquired if the Soviet leader were still alive. He then told him that George and Barbara Bush had been in contact and that they sent their greetings. The couple had been praying for everyone for three days.

America and the west hoped that Gorbachev would salvage a Union of Sovereign States from the wreckage of the Soviet Union. They preferred to deal with one central authority with control over nuclear weapons rather than four nuclear powers: Russia, Belarus, Ukraine and Kazakhstan. The G7 went through the motions of arranging a loan to the Soviet Union. America and the west recognised the independence of the Soviet republics, such as Estonia, Latvia and Lithuania. The Gorbachevian world was finally shattered in December 1991, when the leaders of Russia, Belarus and Ukraine met outside Minsk, Belarus, to dissolve the Soviet Union and give birth to the Commonwealth of Independent States (CIS), a loose confederation of states. Their first move was to inform President Bush, before telling Gorbachev.

The Cold War was over and the United States had won. It was the only superpower left standing. In the shadows, China was growing and will, eventually challenge American dominance. Eastern Europe, long regarded as absolutely essential to Soviet security, just withered away. The Soviet command economy simply caved in before the capitalist economy of the west. Yet the United States was not economically and socially healthy. The huge budget deficits of the Reagan years had weakened the country and the government simply did not have the resources to deal with crime, poverty, health care and unemployment. Washington was not rich enough to pay for the Gulf War alone. Saudi Arabia and other rich Arab states had to contribute. Yet US arms proved invincible. Domestically, there was a feeling of pessimism and malaise. Some commentators talked about the imperial burden slowly breaking the back of America.

The reaction to crises in the Soviet Union and the United States could not have been more different. In the former, there was a lack of willingness to face up to the problems and this rendered solutions ineffective. Money making was frowned on. In the latter, crises were treated as challenges and stimulated great creativity. Rampant materialism held sway. Whereas in 1991 America seemed as if it could cede economic primacy eventually to Japan, by the late 1990s this appeared absurd. The budget deficit was down, employment was up. Russia, the successor state to the Soviet Union, was still struggling to turn its economy round.

CHAPTER EIGHT

THE JUDGEMENT

INTRODUCTION

Europe dominated the world in 1900 but two civil wars, World Wars I and II, destroyed that hegemony. In 1945 Russia was the major military force but America dominated the world in the same vein as Europe in 1900. The USA, in 1945, was both an economic and military power. This combination made it possible for the American political leadership to begin dreaming of a new world order which would mirror American values. Russia and America were isolationist powers until 1945, the former by force of circumstances and the latter by choice.

Russia began as an expansionist power under Lenin but the defeat of revolution in Germany in 1921 ended that dream. Afterwards, the young Soviet state concentrated on building up its domestic strength. First and foremost, this meant developing a strong industrial base. This, in turn, would make it possible to produce the armaments that would make the country secure from outside attack. Stalin's misreading of Hitler almost cost him and the Soviet Union their existence. His near fatal pact with Hitler taught him a lesson he never forgot: do not trust to alliances to guarantee Russia's security. As far as Stalin was concerned, it was once bitten twice shy. This was to have unfortunate consequences in and after 1945 when America attempted to draw the Soviet Union into a mutually enriching relationship to guarantee the peace of the world.

The period from 1900 to 1991 can be divided into two neat halves. The first half, to May 1945, saw Russia and America never pose a threat to one another's security. America did intervene in the Russian Civil War (1918–20) but balanced this by forcing the Japanese to leave the Russian Far East afterwards. American communists did contribute to the construction of the Soviet Union, but then Henry Ford built much more: for instance, the tractor plant at Stalingrad, now Volgograd.

The second half, from May 1945 to December 1991, was full of hostility and almost erupted into nuclear war. The Cold War got under way in earnest in 1947 and lasted until the late Gorbachev era. The first two years and the last two years of this period were the most relaxed and hopeful. The 1950s, 1960s, 1970s and the first half of the 1980s, contrariwise, saw a violent ideological conflict between two empires competing for world dominance.

The world outside Europe, later to become known as the Third World, was dominated by European empires during the first half of the century. The largest was the British, then came the French, Dutch, Belgian, Portuguese, Spanish and Italian. The Japanese came on to the scene in the 1930s when they penetrated China. All these empires collapsed after 1945. In their place appeared a plethora of new states, many of them appearing on the world stage for the first time. Most of them were not nation states but groupings of tribes or clans. They all wanted their place in the sun and to escape from imperial influence. To America, this caused some alarm. Since most of these new states were unstable, they were fertile soil for the spread of communism. To the Soviet Union, these new states presented an unprecedented opportunity. If they adopted the Leninist brand of socialism, this would serve as the demonstration effect. It would also subtract other countries from the sum of capitalist states in the world. The Third World, the periphery for the superpowers, was to pay a high price for the Cold War. Russia and America intervened in their own interests, not those of the locals [*Doc. 6*].

In 1945, economically, America and Russia not only led the world, they dominated it. In 1991 the US economy was still the largest, but other countries, the oil states of the Gulf and Japan, for instance, were in front as regards wealth per head of the population. Russia was in freefall and about to embark on a bumpy ride from the command to a market economy. Japan, under the US nuclear umbrella and consequently able to devote little to defence, was the outstanding success story. Hong Kong, South Korea, Taiwan, Indonesia, Malaysia, Singapore and Thailand also expanded rapidly.

The great surprise was the People's Republic of China, long the victim of Mao Zedong's wrong turnings in economic policy. The great leap forward (dubbed the great leap backward by his critics), the Cultural Revolution, the promotion of communes as the route to agricultural growth (and disastrous espousals of the Russian Lysenko's crazy theories, such as killing all insect-eating birds) dragged China down. Fortunately for China, Deng Xiaoping won the succession struggle and market reforms began in the late 1970s. By 1991 China had registered the greatest economic expansion of any state in history, in physical terms. The Tiananmen Square massacre, in June 1989, led to recentralisation and a rapid drop in growth rates in 1990–91. This experience discredited those who had advocated greater central control of the economy and led China to declare that its goal was a full market economy.

In Europe, West Germany was the star performer and by 1991 the European Union (EU) had become a major economic power in its own right. In 1996 the EU accounted for about 31 per cent of world output and 20 per cent of world trade. The USA provided about 27 per cent of global production and 18 per cent of world trade. However, in 1996 the US dollar had between 40 and 60 per cent of world finance, far exceeding the economic weight of the USA. Contrariwise, in the 15 years to 1996, the USA had been running current account deficits. Its net foreign debt exceeded US$1 trillion, and it was rising at 15 to 20 per cent annually. Only the euro can challenge the dollar as a world currency in the twenty-first century.

Until the late 1970s one-third of the world placed their faith in centrally planned economies. To nervous Americans it was not certain that market economies, which entailed some level of democracy, would prevail. The tide then turned and by 1991 the command economy model had been completely discredited. The fear of communism dissipated in the 1980s, when it became evident that the economic battle had been won. The decline of the Soviet Union in the 1980s rendered its subventioning of client states in eastern Europe and the Third World economically impossible. All collapsed except Cuba and North Korea. By the late 1990s these two states were among the poorest in the world.

Post-war economic prosperity in the west (western Europe, North America and Japan) was based on the Bretton Woods agreement of 1944. The main currency became the US dollar and it was placed on the gold standard. All other convertible currencies fluctuated against the US dollar. Market economies functioned in the knowledge that there was always a fallback currency, the dollar, and a state that would not allow them to collapse, America. If one major capitalist country collapsed, the communists could take over and this could start a chain reaction which could undermine capitalism worldwide. The main loser would be the United States. Market economies accepted US dominance as the affordable price for their own well-being. The willingness of the USA to open its markets to foreign goods was a major factor in the rapid expansion of the EU and Japan.

In the nuclear world, only the USA could guarantee the nuclear security of the west. This arrangement was to the liking of the west European powers since it meant that they could cut their defence budgets and prevail on Washington to keep its troops and war matériel in Europe. But not all Europeans welcomed American dominance. France was the outstanding exception. General de Gaulle took France out of the military aspect of NATO but relied on NATO to make France secure. West European socialists bridled at the irresistible tide of American capitalism but, when in office, sought American loans.

Russia took the decision to remain outside the Bretton Woods agreement and declined to join its institutions, the IMF and World Bank. It also stayed outside the General Agreement on Tariffs and Trade (GATT). The Stalin leadership did not rate the opportunity of obtaining loans from the IMF and World Bank very highly. Trade was not of much consequence either.

These decisions were, presumably, defensive. Western loans would require the divulgence of foreign currency and gold reserves and economic growth rates, data which were treated in Moscow as state secrets. In 1945 self-confidence was high as victory over Germany appeared to have confirmed the superiority of the Soviet model over the capitalist model. The Soviet empire was expanding and the correlation of forces appeared to be moving in Moscow's favour. This was not only the view of the Stalin leadership, it was shared by anti-communist intellectuals in eastern Europe who became extremely pessimistic about the future. Once Leninist socialism descended on them, the likelihood of its being overthrown was viewed as extremely remote.

The contrast between the opportunities facing Stalin in 1945 to become a member of the world club and the desperate efforts of Gorbachev to break down its doors is extreme. Whereas Stalin did not regard the club as capable of contributing to Soviet growth, Gorbachev saw it as the last-chance saloon. Only its largesse could save the Soviet Union. Perceptions of the market changed rapidly over time. If Stalin had introduced elements of the market into the Soviet economy, arguably it would have made it more effective, but he equated the market economy with capitalism, therefore a cancer.

The Chinese leadership, by way of contrast, in the late 1970s, regarded the market and capitalism as separate entities. It viewed the market and socialism as quite compatible. The main reason may be that the Chinese, in the late 1970s, were in dire economic straits and adopted the only other successful model available – capitalism. Hong Kong may have been the catalyst. In the late 1970s, the British colony was prosperous, but Britain did not permit any democracy at that time. The Hong Kong Chinese appeared to prove that a flourishing market economy could develop under authoritarian rule. The Russians had nothing similar to contemplate at the end of the war. In 1945 Stalin wished to impose his authority again over the Soviet Union in order to rebuild it quickly. The most effective way of doing this, he reasoned, was to have strong central government and central planning.

The Vietnam War weakened the USA economically. It came off the gold standard and began to run up larger and larger budget deficits. The latter were financed, increasingly, by selling government bonds to the Japanese and anyone who would buy them. The Japanese began to run up huge trade surpluses with the USA. Washington tried to cope with this unsettling phenomenon by appealing to the Japanese to restrict their exports and to open up their market to US exports. However, Japanese consumers preferred Japanese goods. The budget deficits, the largest in history, meant the USA could not finance the Gulf War out of its own resources. It had to prevail on the Saudis and other rich Arab states to help to foot the bill. This graphically underlined the transformation of America's fortunes. Paradoxically, at a time when it was struggling economically, it was militarily dominant. This was not due to the number of troops or military vehicles but the advanced technological equipment it was able to deploy. Militarily, the US was pre-eminent in 1991, but politically and economically, it was losing ground. The bipolar world of 1945 had become the multipolar world of 1991.

SOURCES OF HOSTILITY BETWEEN THE SUPERPOWERS

What are the sources of the hostility which marked relations between Russia and America from the mid-1940s to the mid-1980s?

- The decision of the US administration to play a global role after 1945, for the first time. The wealth and power of America permitted it to contemplate this role. It would make the world safe for democracy by establishing a new world order.
- The ideological drive of both states; both regarded their destiny as shaping the world in their image.
- The imperative of security.

If the USA had decided, in 1945, to retreat to the Americas and leave the rest of the world to its own devices, as in 1919, the Cold War would not have emerged. There would have been no competition and tension between Russia and America. The USA, secure in the knowledge that it would be extremely difficult for any power to invade and conquer the country, would have been content merely to trade with the rest of the world.

The reason it decided to play a world role was due to the politicians and diplomats who held sway at the time. They were European specialists and they concluded that it was America's withdrawal from Europe after World War I that prepared the ground for the rise of Hitler and fascism. The same applied to the Far East, with the rise of Japanese military imperialism. European economic weakness in the 1920s had contributed to the Great Depression, beginning in 1929. There was a real chance that capitalism would not survive the 1930s. Roosevelt's New Deal saved America but it meant that Washington had no time or energy for the rest of the world. It paid a heavy price for this insouciance. A major reason why the European economies did not prosper were the barriers to trade. Each state concentrated on autarchy, to husband its foreign and gold reserves and, in so doing, exacerbated the general economic situation. For instance, the British practised imperial preference, trading with the empire at the expense of comparable goods.

The Bretton Woods agreement signified that the USA was willing to take on the role of the world's banker. As America was the leading world economy, it naturally favoured free trade and stable foreign exchange rates. This made risk management easier. The states of the United States had the same currency and traded freely with one another. However, the USA did not always observe free trade. Prohibition is an example, but that disastrous attempt at regulating alcohol intake had proved the point. The Americans were convinced that they had arrived at the most successful political and economic model of all time – American democracy.

All the rest of the world needed to do in order to become as rich as America was to copy it. This implied a liberal political and economic order. Since the USA was a strong state and was rich, it needed weak (small may be a better term) government. But it needed a strong state to project its influence abroad. Hence, the USA was against empires, imperial preference, closed clubs, military rule, indeed rule by small elites. Americans believed that the benefits of the market economy would not ripen without democracy. Time has revealed, however, that strong economic growth can be achieved without democracy. Some American policy makers felt a moral responsibility to bring the gifts of the American experience to the great unwashed. Those with religious convictions also felt morally bound to help the needy.

Roosevelt and Truman were against zones of influence as they undermined this scenario for world development. However, in practice, they were willing to concede that the Soviets had a right to protect their security on their western borders. East European governments should not engage in anti-Russian policies. Had Russian occupation policy been as benign in eastern Europe as in Finland then the tensions might have been resolved. As Soviet suspiciousness grew, to them the new world order meant their political demise and they took measures to increase their country's security in eastern Europe. This, in turn, made the Americans anxious. A vicious circle came into existence: every move to enhance one side's security was perceived as a threat by the other. This, inevitably, led to counter-measures and snowballed into the Cold War. Each side presented its moves as defensive but these moves were perceived by the other side as offensive. This underlines the fact that mutual trust had evaporated. This phenomenon can also be called the security dilemma.

WHY DID AMERICA COME TO GUARANTEE WEST EUROPEAN SECURITY?

West European political parties (except in Britain) felt insecure when faced with communist parties. The authority of the Soviet Union was great and communists argued that German fascism had buried capitalism. Private ownership of the means of production had led to war; public ownership was more equitable and would prevent war. It would also guarantee a rising standard of living for working people. Free elections could bring communists to power. The dilemma was more severe for Britain. Economically, it could no longer play its imperial role and appealed to the United States to take over the burden in Greece and the Middle East. West European government needed large loans from Washington. If the Americans were not generous, they could be faced with a rapidly expanding communist sphere of influence and the military budget would then have to rise.

The Truman administration sympathised with the west Europeans but Congress would not foot the bill. The tactic adopted was to exaggerate the threat of Soviet expansionism. Washington was aware that Moscow had no intention of invading western Europe but had to frighten legislators with the prospect. The Marshall Plan and the Truman doctrine were the result. Funds were provided for Greece, Turkey and western Europe. Washington learnt two lessons from this experience. The first was that the President, to get his way, needed to summon up a crisis by exaggerating the Soviet threat. Second, since Congress would always jib at increasing budget spending, covert means had to be developed to raise funds. The communist takeover in Czechoslovakia in February 1948, and the Berlin blockade which began in June 1948, were like self-fulfilling prophesies to the Truman administration. In reality, there were no Soviet troops in Czechoslovakia and the Czechoslovak communists took power themselves, partly due to the lack of political skill of the social democrats. The west, however, saw the whole episode as being manipulated by the Kremlin.

The Berlin blockade was to prevent the introduction of the Deutsche Mark and the inevitable West German state. It was defensive but Stalin revealed a startling lack of finesse in his handling of the situation. Early on, he could have secured an agreement on terms favourable to himself but declined. The astonishing thing is that the longer the blockade lasted the more likely a West German state was to come into existence. It also gave credence to Truman's analysis of Soviet intentions. Stalin was very slow to react to this. The formation of the Federal Republic in 1949, and, as a counter, the GDR, divided Germany and Europe until 1989. Stalin's policies had led to his worst case scenario coming into existence – a divided Germany in the western camp which would eventually join NATO.

Access to Soviet archives since 1991 has thrown little light on Stalin's maladroit diplomacy. But they have revealed that Stalin's advisers in Germany had not anticipated the airlift and, once it was underway, thought that it would fail. The Berlin blockade made east–west relations adversarial and poisoned Berlin relations until 1990. Time and again Khrushchev returned to the Berlin problem in an effort to make up for Stalin's failure in 1948–49. The Berlin blockade also promoted the establishment of NATO. West Europeans felt insecure and appealed to the Americans to retain their military presence and to guarantee the security of the region. Only the USA could do this, as it was a nuclear power. The Marshall Plan and the Truman doctrine were tangible successes for west European lobbying. It was the weakness of the region which led to the Americans playing a vital role in the economic development and security. The Marshall Plan kick-started the west European economies and an extraordinary growth of the region got under way until the 1970s. Britain obtained the largest share of Marshall Aid, but it was West Germany which benefited most, as it retooled its industries.

The US nuclear monopoly lasted four years, until 1949, when the Russians successfully tested their first atomic bomb. Now Soviet capabilities, rather than merely their intentions, had to be considered very seriously. Truman was obliged to give the go-ahead for the development of a US hydrogen bomb. The adoption of NSC-68 underlined the American determination to retain their ascendancy. This then became the pattern for the next 40 years between the superpowers. A technical advance by one side had to be countered by the other and this promoted the spiral of arms production. It was also a period of considerable anxiety as neither side could rest assured that it had achieved security. This can be called the spiral of angst. The Russians were always very concerned about Germany. Their policies directly contributed to the establishment of a West German state, its rearmament and integration in NATO. West Germany, with nuclear weapons, was a nightmare which never materialised. Given the proximity of the Soviet Union to western Europe and the distance between it and the United States, it was inevitable that the Americans would come to depend more and more on the nuclear deterrent. Conventional superiority over time was conceded to the Russians but high technology and nuclear weapons rendered this of less and less significance. The Middle East wars were useful testing grounds for Soviet equipment and it was often found wanting. This was an added reason for prudence on the Soviet side.

WHY DID RUSSIA AND AMERICA GRADUALLY BECOME SYSTEMIC RIVALS?

Russia and America competed with one another as systems. The systems can be perceived as communism and capitalism, freedom and tyranny, the command economy versus the market economy, individualism and collectivism and the 'red' world versus the free world. Both dominant ideologies were utopian.

In the Soviet Union, Marxism claimed to have discovered the laws of human existence, in which the conflict between capital and labour, between management and workers, was conceived of as a drama in which the actors play preordained roles which they are powerless to change. The dénouement, revolution, is inevitable and therefore certain. Marxists inhabited the kingdom of certainty. This had great benefits but also great disadvantages. It provided a map of the world and the conviction that history was moving in the right direction. The Soviet Union would one day be the leading world power and America, which appeared to be so powerful and threatening, would become socialist. The downside was that once Marxism had been codified into a ruling ideology, it became inflexible. There was always a gap between the party line and reality. The Soviet leadership revealed no interest in critical Marxism, a Marxism that would be consistently revised to take changes in the world into consideration.

Only Gorbachev was capable of escaping from orthodox Marxism but he acted too late. The command economy, regarded as the cornerstone of a communist society, failed to generate the economic growth to satisfy the population. This presaged economic collapse. Elements of the market could have been introduced, but this would have resulted in greater inequality in Russia and the ruling Party elite would not have exercised the influence it did. Russia's aim was a strong state and its leaders believed this could only be achieved through strong or big government. The country concentrated on the internal market and, hence, foreign trade was not considered important. Economic growth did not depend on the expansion of foreign trade. Hence, the Soviet Union did not need to learn much about the thought patterns and ways of foreigners. Knowing and understanding other nations is critically important to trading nations. Also, the latter are more acutely aware of changes in technology, culture and taste in the outside world.

America also had a utopian ideology. It was articulated by Woodrow Wilson and was born of the conviction that Americans had the right and duty to enlighten the world. America had discovered the laws of human existence and was willing to enlighten others. To become rich, happy and free other nations had just to copy the United States. This meant acknowledging American hegemony throughout the world. Other terms can be used – universalism, internationalism, the new world order – to describe this phenomenon. It was almost inevitable that Russia and America, given their utopianism, would construct empires. The number of countries in the respective zone of imperial influence would be used as a benchmark to determine which was gaining the upper hand. This was the essence of zero-sum diplomacy. By the 1970s superpower rivalry, beginning in Europe in 1945, had encompassed the globe. The American outreach was called the Pax Americana, the American peace or peace brought about by America. The Soviet version was dubbed the Pax Sovietica, or Soviet peace. Both were mutually exclusive and neither regarded the other as legitimate.

The negative evaluation of the Soviet Union by the Americans emerged during the Stalin period. The image of Russia as expansionist, aggressive, totalitarian, consolidated in the late 1940s and remained until the late 1980s. Mutual respect and trust disappeared at the same time and only returned under Gorbachev. The Cold War also damaged the American political system. Presidents, believing that it was their duty to intervene worldwide and faced with a Congress and people who were very sceptical, circumvented the legislature and the law to achieve their ends. This applied especially to Johnson, Nixon, Reagan and Bush, who became as deceitful as any Russian ruler. Another tactic was to exaggerate the danger so as to frighten everyone into following the president. Truman was the master of this manoeuvre. In this way the concept of the communist threat took root in America.

A HARD LESSON FOR THE SUPERPOWERS: EMPIRES ARE LIABILITIES

The lesson of the 1990s was that empires are liabilities, not assets. The greatest European empires, measured in terms of the magnitude of the territory acquired in relation to the size of the mother country, were Portugal, Spain, France, the Netherlands, Great Britain and Russia. None appears to have gained lasting benefit from their vast territories overseas. The so-called glittering prizes of imperial power deflected attention from domestic concerns and distorted economic life. The United States followed in the footsteps of the European empires and paid a very heavy price for its lack of historical awareness. America in 1945 was an anti-imperial power which desired to see the great European empires buried. By the 1980s, it was acting in the same manner as the nineteenth-century European imperialists.

The conflict in Britain at the turn of the century was between liberalism and imperialism. The former argued that the wealth, prosperity and well-being of a nation was not related to its political power. Smaller nations, exercising little political influence, were often the most prosperous. The imperialists countered that war and the extension of empire were the way of the world and therefore good. If Britain did not seize a territory, its competitor could do so and place London at a disadvantage. This is an earlier example of zero-sum diplomacy. The liberals thought that free trade was of fundamental significance. Openness to trade enhances prosperity and makes it possible for small states to become richer, in per capita terms, than large states. The imperialists preferred imperial preference. A common market was created to promote trade among the various parts of the empire and tariffs were set to prevent outsiders competing effectively in the imperial market. This arrangement benefited the large British companies but penalised others. The rest of the empire would have been better off with free trade, allowing all suppliers to come into the market. Unfortunately for Britain and the world, the imperialists won the argument in 1914.

IS THERE A LINK BETWEEN GOOD GOVERNMENT AND ECONOMIC PROSPERITY?

There is also a correlation between countries enjoying good governance and sound policies and economic prosperity. In these, real income per capita grew by 3 per cent annually between 1964 and 1993. In countries where there was poor government but reasonable policies, annual growth was down to 1.4 per cent. In countries where there was neither good governance nor good policies, growth was 0.4 per cent annually. There is also a direct relationship between the size of a country and economic growth.

In 1997 ten countries had populations over 100 million. Only two, the USA and Japan, were rich. The others, China, India, Indonesia, Brazil, Russia,

Pakistan, Bangladesh and Nigeria, were remarkable for their modest per capita incomes and the difficulties their governments faced in achieving control and ruling effectively. The USA and Japan were exceptions to the rule that large states are not wealthy and special reasons appear to apply. The rule is that a small state encounters less difficulty in achieving good government and sound economic policies. But the USA and Japan are market economies and dedicated to expanding exports. All communist states faced enormous problems in achieving economic growth and neglected exports.

How does all this apply to the superpowers? Both became expanding empires and the lesson of history is that all empires are eventually a burden. Another lesson is that a state cannot develop economically without sound government and policies. The post-1945 era was special, it was the era of decolonialisation. This meant that many new states came into existence without indigenous leaderships. Often, tribes or clans competed for power as the territory they inherited had not previously been ruled as an entity in pre-imperial days. Unfortunately, good government has to be learnt and takes time.

The United States came to accept authoritarian government in South Korea as a bulwark to communism. It did the same in south east Asia where fighting the communists took precedence. In Vietnam, the United States deluded itself into thinking that the first priority was military victory. Good government could then follow. In Africa in the 1970s the USA again gave priority to military victory as the prelude to a better life. In the Middle East, America concerned itself little with social problems. In Guatemala and El Salvador, Washington ignored the social context and concentrated on military force.

The Soviet Union fared no better. It was mindful of the social context but equated good government and sound policies with Party leadership and a planned economy. It helped the Vietnamese to power but did not control them. Castro was not willing to heed Moscow's advice on many occasions. In Angola and Ethiopia, the Russians and Cubans fought alongside their clients. Moscow and Washington were fighting a losing battle in Africa. Angola was too large and diverse, as was Congo (Zaire). Ethiopia itself was an empire. Afghanistan was too large and ethnically divided to permit Moscow's will to be done.

Both superpowers poured vast sums into their empires and most of it was wasted. Much of it was military and this fuelled conflict. One estimate of the number of military-related deaths in the Third World is 21.8 million. Another lesson of the 1990s is that only a market economy generates rising prosperity over decades. Expanding trade is needed as the internal market is soon exhausted.

It was asking too much of the Americans, although they were convinced of the accuracy of these maxims, to have taken a relaxed view of communist expansion. The greatest difficulty in moving to good government and policies promoting economic growth and trade is being encountered by those states, notably Russia and Vietnam, in which the military were or are strong. Resistance to expanding trade, which involves attracting foreign direct investment, is linked to retaining a traditional way of life. Interest groups in the USA still resist free trade but the global economy is becoming a reality. China flirted with empire for a short period in the 1970s, especially in Angola and Tanzania, but quickly decided it was not worth the effort. The conflicts with Russia, India and Vietnam were not geared to acquiring influence but forcing neighbours to respect Beijing.

WAS THE GROWTH OF NUCLEAR ARSENALS INEVITABLE?

The imperative of security was fuelled by the perceptions of both sides that incremental growth in their nuclear arsenals served peace and was defensive. Neither superpower, until the late Gorbachev era, was willing to concede that each innovation was perceived by the other as a new and more ominous threat. Stalin was usually prudent and always drew back from directly challenging the United States. That could be done by others, for example North Korea. Truman and Eisenhower enjoyed nuclear superiority and were not adverse to using blackmail against the Russians and Chinese. Eisenhower, as a military man, knew that the supposed Russian superiority, of which Khrushchev was bragging, was a fiction. He even decided to allow the Soviets to be first in space. He was confident of America's power and restricted the military budget.

Kennedy was more confrontational and less secure about US superiority. Khrushchev pushed him to the limit in Berlin and Cuba. Neither wished to use nuclear weapons but there was always the risk that a conflict could have occurred. Just as the reasons for the outbreak of World War I are not fully understood, so it was possible for nuclear war to occur by accident. Cuba was the last nuclear confrontation between the superpowers. It introduced realism and the desire to reach arms control agreements.

WHY DID THE COLD WAR END?

The Cold War came to an end because it was impossible for two powers to divide and rule the world. The willpower had drained away. The burden was so great that the Soviet Union buckled and then disintegrated. By 1991 the United States was no longer able to intervene at will and was immensely relieved when the need to do so, the communist threat, melted away. The vast resources poured into imperial wars and the arms race exacerbated tensions in American society. Kennedy and Johnson's great society remained a utopia.

The Cold War internationalised local conflicts, most tragically in Indochina and Angola. Had it not been deemed necessary to support anti-communist rulers, it is unlikely the USA would have bothered about the Third World.

Americans had realised that trade was a more effective way to become rich than an expanding empire. The non-aligned movement, led by Yugoslavia, and consisting mainly of Third World states, was pro-Soviet. Moscow advertised itself as anti-imperialist, anti-colonialist and the friend of the Third World. Afghanistan ruined all that. Countries such as India developed close ties with Russia. Fabian socialism and the desire to regulate almost everything inclined India to follow Russia. In 1949 per capita income in India and China was about the same. In 1997 China's was about double that of India. Delhi's policies have not served its people well.

AMERICA'S CHANGING DOCTRINE

America's response to regional conflicts changed over time. Beginning with Korea, it was willing to send its own troops to fight in wars in foreign fields. Many presidents gave their names to doctrines:

- the Truman doctrine, which protected Greece, Turkey and, indirectly, other states
- the Eisenhower doctrine, which identified the Middle East as of great strategic importance to the USA
- the Nixon doctrine, which envisaged the building up of regional allies to resist communist subversion; America would supply the technology but the locals would do the fighting
- the Carter doctrine, in the wake of the Soviet invasion of Afghanistan, envisaged America intervening with its own troops if the Persian Gulf region were threatened
- the end of the Cold War meant that Bush, in countering Iraqi aggression in 1990, did not give his name to a new doctrine. He merely referred to Iraq as an 'outside force'. He could engage militarily in Kuwait with the blessing of the UN Security Council, for the first time since 1950. Instead of a doctrine, he proclaimed the new world order, with the UN playing the role originally intended for it.

The present level of prosperity in the world is inconceivable without the Bretton Woods agreement. It established the US dollar as the world's trading currency. The generosity of the Americans kick-started west European economic recovery (although there is a revisionist view which claims it was not really necessary). The willingness of Washington to open its doors to imports led to western Europe and Japan flourishing. This then encompassed Hong Kong, South Korea, Taiwan, Indonesia, Malaysia, Singapore and Thailand. Another factor was the US willingness to export high technology to friendly states. The GDP of EU states in the mid-1990s was higher than that of the USA.

It is striking that of the countries which benefited most, the USA only intervened militarily and fought a war in South Korea. Without the Cold War,

America almost certainly would not have been so generous. The best defence against the spread of communist influence was affluence. GATT played an important role in expanding trade and was followed by the more ambitious World Trade Agreement (WTA). By the same token, some of the countries in which the USA intervened were and have remained the poorest in the world: Angola, Cambodia, Congo (Zaire), El Salvador, Guatemala, Laos, Somalia and Vietnam.

WAS THE USA AN IMPERIALIST POWER?

The USA was an imperialist power after 1944, but it was benign imperialism. The world is now richer and more secure because of it. Had it not been for the arms race, the Soviet Union might still be a communist state. It had to devote about two-thirds of its scientists and about one-third of its economy to its military effort. Whereas there was a spin-off in the USA from military research and development, there was almost none in Russia.

The end of the Cold War has resulted in greater disarray in Russia than in the United States. It is still searching for its role in the world. China has benefited greatly. Its most difficult task is to manage political change, which is inevitable given the rapid economic growth. Wars, now, are rarely between states, and never between developed states, but within countries. Marxism is very rarely an issue nowadays. Nationalism and ethnic or clan loyalties are much more likely to be the genesis of conflict. The world was relatively simple to understand during the Cold War. It is now extremely complex. The threat of a nuclear holocaust is no longer real. Wars have reverted to being conventional. The greatest threat to life on this planet is no longer war but the destruction of the environment. There are now two camps: those who pollute most, led again by the USA, and the rest. The world is always divided.

PART FOUR　　DOCUMENTS

1.　KHRUSHCHEV AND DIVERSIONARY TACTICS

2.　KHRUSHCHEV AND CHINA

3.　KENNEDY AND VIETNAM

4.　KENNEDY, KHRUSHCHEV AND CUBA

5.　KISSINGER, BREZHNEV AND DÉTENTE

6.　THE KGB

7.　THE KGB AND ITALY

8.　THE RUSSIANS AND THE PALESTINIANS

9.　AFGHANISTAN

10.　POLAND

11.　A TOP ADVISER'S WITHERING CRITICISM OF SOVIET FOREIGN POLICY

12.　GORBACHEV'S NEW THINKING

13.　THE REYKJAVIK SUMMIT

14.　GORBACHEV, REAGAN AND SDI

15.　GORBACHEV AND MRS THATCHER

16.　MOSCOW AND FRATERNAL PARTIES

Khrushchev, four days before he was elected Party leader, in September 1953, signed this order to the Ministry of Internal Affairs (MVD), making the ministry responsible for certain espionage and other activities.

Central Committee, Communist Party	Secret Confidential
of the Soviet Union	Special Dossier
Resolution	

On the organisation of the 12th section (special) in the 2nd principal directorate (espionage), USSR

MVD
Moscow

1) The USSR Minister of the Interior [Kruglov] is to organise in the 2nd principal directorate of the MVD (espionage) a 12th section (special) to engage in diversionary operations against important strategic military targets and communications routes in the leading aggressor states, the United States and Great Britain, and also in other capitalist states being used as the main aggressors against the USSR. Terror attacks [crossed out and corrected by hand, 'active operations'] are justified against the most active and the most bitter enemies of the Soviet Union in capitalist states, the most dangerous foreign spies, the leaders of anti-Soviet émigré organisations and traitors.
2) Arrange for all enterprises [gulag] of the USSR MVD under section 12 to be inspected and approved by the Presidium [Politburo] of the CC, CPSU.
3) Register the statute, the structure and the personnel of the 12th section (special) of the 2nd principal directorate (espionage) of the USSR MVD.

Secretary of the CC, CPSU
N. Khrushchev

Boukovsky, Vladimir, *Jugement à Moscou. Un Dissident dans les Archives du Kremlin*, Robert Laffont, Paris, 1995, pp. 114–115.

(a) Mao felt insulted when he visited Moscow for the first time, in 1950, as head of the People's Republic of China. He asked for substantial aid but was only given a modest loan, on which he was required to pay interest. When Stalin died Mao regarded himself as the doyen of world communist leaders and expected to be consulted on all major issues. However, Khrushchev had no intention of treating Mao in this fashion, in 1957, and

wanted to demonstrate that the Soviet Union was dominant, but found Mao unfathomable.

'If there is an attack on the Soviet Union, I would recommend that you do not offer resistance.'

I was immediately on my guard. The imperialist states attack the Soviet union, and we must not offer resistance? How could this be? What were we supposed to do?

Mao Zedong explained: 'Retreat for a year, or two or three. Force your enemy to stretch out his lines of communications. That will weaken him. Then, with our combined strength, we will go for the enemy together and smash him.'

I said: 'Comrade Mao, I don't know what to say. What you are saying is out of the question. Can you imagine us retreating for a year? Would the war go on for a year? Think about what can happen in a year!'

Mao answered: 'But in World War II you retreated to Stalingrad for two years. Why can't you retreat for three years now? If you retreat to the Urals, China is nearby. We'll use our resources and territory to smash the enemy.'

I said: 'Comrade Mao, we see things differently. We believe in immediate retaliation, with all the weapons at our disposal. Our ability to do that is what deters our enemy. We can keep him from committing aggression in the first place.'

'No,' said Mao, 'I don't think that's right.'

Later, I often wondered how to argue against such reasoning. Mao is a clever man. How could he think this way? Could it have been a provocation? I can't believe Mao would try something so stupid with us. Could he really have believed that what he was saying made military sense?

Khrushchev, Nikita, *Khrushchev Remembers*, with an introduction,
commentary and notes by Edward Chankshaw, trans. by Strobe Talbott,
Sphere Books, London, 1971, pp. 147–50.

(b) This extract is by Shmuel Mikunis, then leader of the Israeli Communist Party. It captures nicely Mao's vanity.

In the way he spoke and held himself, and in the way he replied to questions, [Mao Zedong] resembled a sage of ancient China. He gave me the impression, at any rate, when I saw him for the first time in St George's Hall [in the Kremlin]. He had trouble with his legs and usually spoke sitting down. His favourite theme, to which he kept returning, was World War III. He regarded it as an absolutely inevitable event, for which one must be ready at any moment. I would even go so far as to say he lived and thought in terms of this war, as though it had already begun. I well remember how he sat there, surrounded by Soviet delegates, and philosophised aloud: 'Nehru and I,' he said, 'are at present discussing the question of how many people would perish in an atomic war. Nehru says we'll lose a billion and a half, but I say only a billion and a quarter.'

Palmiro Togliatti then asked him: 'But what would become of Italy as a result of such a war?' Mao Zedong looked at him in a thoughtful way and replied, quite coolly: 'But who told you that Italy must survive? Three hundred million Chinese will be left, and that will be enough for the human race to continue.' . . . He talked a lot, but in an absolutely peremptory way: he did not really talk but insist.

Shmuel Mikunis, *Vremya i My* (Tel Aviv), no. 48, 1979, pp. 164–5.

DOCUMENT 3   **KENNEDY AND VIETNAM**

In January 1961, ten days before his inauguration, President-Elect Kennedy, at his request, met the evangelist Billy Graham for a game of golf in Florida. Among the things they discussed was foreign policy. Here, Kennedy reveals that he was an adherent of the domino theory, if one country falls to the communists then its neighbours will as well. He already has firm ideas about Vietnam.

In the clubhouse afterward, we got into a lively discussion. Kennedy aired his view that the sixties would be filled with challenges, promises, and problems. As we sat relaxing with soft drinks, he began to talk about Vietnam. Kennedy agreed with Eisenhower's domino theory. 'If Laos goes,' he said, 'all of Southeast Asia will go. Then India. We're going to have to do something about it. Eisenhower's got a number of people over there. We can't allow Vietnam to fall to the Communists.'

That was the first time I heard that Vietnam – that far-off country in the Orient – was such a problem. It all sounded so remote to me.

Graham, Billy, *Just as I Am*, Harper, San Francisco, 1997, p. 395.

DOCUMENT 4   **KENNEDY, KHRUSHCHEV AND CUBA**

(a) President John F. Kennedy wanted to improve relations with the Soviet Union, but in this extract from a conversation in July 1959 he reveals his pessimism. However, he is prescient about the desire of Soviet-dominated countries, especially in eastern Europe, and also non-Russian nationalities in the Soviet Union, to be free.

You have to first decide what is the motive force of the Soviet Union. Is it merely to provide security for them, and in order to provide security for the Russian mainland, do they have to have friendly countries on the borders? . . . Or is it evangelical, that communists can, by continuing to press on us, weaken us so that eventually they can [achieve] world revolution?

I guess, probably, obviously, a combination of the two. So therefore, I don't think there is any button that you press that reaches an accommodation with the Soviet Union which is hard and fast . . . What it is is a constant day-to-day struggle with an enemy who is constantly attempting to expand his power . . . You have two people, neither of whom – who are both of good will, but neither of whom can communicate because of a language difference . . .

I don't think there's any magic solution to solve or really ease East–West [tension] at the present time. Now maybe a successor to Khrushchev – or even Khrushchev himself . . . It's like those ads you see in the *Sunday* [*New York*] *Times* . . . about some fellow in a beard about 'he releases the magic power within you' . . . The magic power really is the desire of everyone to be independent and every nation to be independent. That's the basic force which is really, I think, the strong force on our side. That's the magic power, and that's what's going to screw the Russians ultimately.

Beschloss, Michael R., *Kennedy v. Khrushchev, The Crisis Years 1960–63*, Faber and Faber, London, 1991, p. 20.

(b) On Wednesday 24 October 1962, during the Cuban missile crisis, President Kennedy received the rudest letter from a Soviet leader to an American President since the days of Stalin. The Americans had just imposed a quarantine around Cuba to prevent any more nuclear missiles or warheads being delivered.

Imagine, Mr. President, that we had presented you with the conditions of ultimatum that you have presented us by your action. How would you have reacted to this? . . . Who asked you to do this? You, Mr. President are not declaring quarantines but advancing an ultimatum and threatening that unless we subordinate ourselves to your demands, you will use force.

Consider what you are saying! . . . You are no longer appealing to reason, but wish to intimidate us . . . And all this not only out of hatred for the Cuban people and their government, but also because of considerations having to do with the election campaign in the USA . . . The actions of the USA toward Cuba are outright banditry or, if you like, the folly of degenerate imperialism.

Unfortunately such folly can bring grave suffering to the peoples of all countries, not least the American people, since with the advent of modern types of armament, the USA has fully lost its invulnerability . . . If someone had tried to dictate these kinds of conditions to you, you would have rejected them. And we also say – no . . . We shall not be simply observers of the pirate-like actions of American ships on the high seas. We will be forced to take measures which we deem necessary and adequate to protect our rights.

Beschloss, Michael R., *Kennedy v. Khrushchev, The Crisis Years 1960–63*,
Faber and Faber, London, 1991, p. 501.

(c) On Friday 26 October 1962, President Kennedy received a letter from Khrushchev. It contained corrections of the original text by Khrushchev himself. It had clearly been put together in a hurry and had not been sent from the Kremlin to the Ministry of Foreign Affairs for the official seal to be attached. Khrushchev's assurance that Soviet ships, en route to Cuba, were not carrying weapons was false. They were transporting nuclear war heads.

In the name of the Soviet government and the Soviet people, I assure you that your conclusions regarding offensive weapons in Cuba are groundless . . . You are a military man and, I hope, will understand me . . .

You are mistaken if you think that any of our weapons on Cuba are offensive. However, let us not quarrel now. It is apparent that I will not be able to convince you of this. But I say to you – you, Mr. President, are a military man and should understand – can one attack if one has on one's territory even an enormous quantity of missiles of various effective radiuses and various power, but using only these means. These missiles are a means of extermination and destruction. But one cannot attack with these missiles – even nuclear missiles of a power of a hundred megatonnes, because only people, troops, can attack. Without people, any weapons, however powerful, cannot be offensive.

Therefore how can one give such a completely incorrect interpretation as you are now giving, to the effect that some sort of weapons on Cuba are offensive? All the weapons located there, and I assure you of this, have a defensive character, are on Cuba solely for the purpose of defence, and we have sent them to Cuba at the request of the Cuban government. You, however, say that these are offensive weapons.

Mr. President, do you seriously think that Cuba can attack the United States and that even we together with Cuba can attack you from Cuban territory? . . . I assure you that on those ships, which are bound for Cuba, there are no weapons at all. The weapons necessary for the defence of Cuba are already there . . . I propose: we, for our part, will declare that our ships bound for Cuba will not carry any kind of armaments. You will declare that the United States will not invade Cuba with its forces and will not support any kind of forces that might intend to carry out an invasion of Cuba. Then the necessity for the presence of our military specialists in Cuba will disappear.

Beschloss, Michael R., *Kennedy v. Khrushchev, The Crisis Years 1960–63*,
Faber and Faber, London, 1991, pp. 517–20.

(d) On Sunday 28 October 1962, Radio Moscow broadcast the tenth message between Khrushchev and Kennedy.

I very well understand your anxiety and that of the American people about the fact that the weapons you describe as offensive are formidable weapons indeed . . .

In order to eliminate as rapidly as possible the conflict which endangers the cause of peace . . . the Soviet government, in addition to previously issued instructions to cease further work on weapons construction sites, has issued a new order to dismantle the weapons which you describe as offensive, and to crate and return them to the Soviet Union . . .

Mr. President . . . I respect and trust the statement you have made in your message . . . that there would be no attack or invasion against Cuba, not only by the United States but other countries of the Western Hemisphere . . . Therefore the motives which induced us to give aid of this kind to Cuba have disappeared . . .

We are prepared to reach an agreement to enable United Nations representatives to verify the dismantling of these weapons.

Beschloss, Michael R., *Kennedy v. Khrushchev, The Crisis Years 1960–63*,
Faber and Faber, London, 1991, p. 541.

DOCUMENT 5   **KISSINGER, BREZHNEV AND DÉTENTE**

(a) Henry Kissinger visited the Soviet Union in early May 1973 to prepare the ground for a summit between Brezhnev and Nixon. He gives a caustic account of Brezhnev and his milieu.

The American party was housed in an East German-built villa resembling an oversized Swiss chalet blown out of scale by the heavy stolidity that in the Communist world denotes status. The exterior looked vaguely Alpine; the inside was all velvet-covered Victorian opulence.

The largest private residence in the compound belonged to Brezhnev. It was a two-storey chalet built in the same style as my residence, though on an even grander scale . . .

Brezhnev came to my residence soon after my arrival and greeted me boisterously. A little later he invited my colleagues and me to dinner at his villa, which he first showed off with all the pride of a self-made entrepreneur. He asked me how much such an establishment would cost in the United States. I guessed tactlessly and mistakenly at four hundred thousand dollars. Brezhnev's face fell. My associate, Helmut Sonnenfeldt, was psychologically more adept: two million, he corrected – probably much closer to the truth. Brezhnev, vastly reassured, beamed and resumed his private tour . . .

Brezhnev conducted almost all the negotiations for the Soviets; only highly technical subjects, such as the European Security Conference, were left to Foreign Minister Andrei Gromyko. Brezhnev's repertory of jokes seemed as inexhaustible as the previous year's, now spiced with a new familiarity that probably went further than he intended. His drinking was less restrained . . .

The timetable was, as usual, enigmatic. No schedule or advance indication of subjects was ever given, even though Brezhnev had no other visible program . . . Twice, when our conversation did not come up to Brezhnev's hopes – on the Middle East, and on some dispute over the nuclear agreement – he sulked in his villa and refused to schedule another session. . . . When I maintained my position – simply by putting forward no additional thoughts – Brezhnev suddenly materialized again as if nothing had happened. His ploy having failed, he would then do the best with what he had and set about to restore an atmosphere of ebullient goodwill . . .

Brezhnev could not hear often enough my avowal that we were proceeding on the premise of equality – an attitude inconceivable in Peking, whose leaders thought of themselves as culturally superior whatever the statistics showed about relative material strength. Brezhnev endlessly sought reassurance that he would be courteously received in America, that he would not be exposed to hostile demonstrations, and that he would have the chance to meet 'ordinary' people . . .

One day he called for me in the black Cadillac sedan that Dobrynin had suggested might be a suitable state gift for Nixon to bring the year before . . . With Brezhnev at the wheel, we took off along winding country roads at speeds that made one pray hopelessly for some policeman's intervention, unlikely as it was that a traffic cop – if indeed they existed in the countryside – would dare halt the General Secretary. Thus propelled to a boat landing, Brezhnev bundled me off onto a hydrofoil – mercifully not driven by him – which nevertheless seemed determined to break the speed record established by the General Secretary in getting me there. My brain being addled by these multiple jolts, I lack a precise recollection of this excursion . . .

One afternoon I returned to my villa and found hunting attire . . . It was an elegant, military-looking olive drab, with high boots, for which I am unlikely to have any further use. Brezhnev, similarly attired, collected me in a jeep driven, I was grateful to notice, by a game warden. Since I hate the killing of animals for sport, I told Brezhnev that I would come along in my capacity as adviser. He said some wild boars had already been earmarked for me. Given my marksmanship, I replied, the cause of death would have to be heart failure . . .

All was absolutely still. Only Brezhnev's voice could be heard, whispering tales of hunting adventures: of his courage when a boar had once attacked his jeep; of the bison that stuffed itself with the grain and potatoes laid out as bait and then fell contentedly asleep on the steps of the hunting tower, trapping

Soviet Defense Minister Marshal Rodion Malinovski in the tower until a
search party rescued him . . .

Kissinger, Henry, *The White House Years*,
Weidenfeld and Nicolson, London, 1979, pp. 229–32.

*(b) Brezhnev took the Chinese threat very seriously and here warns the United
States against aiding China militarily.*

Brezhnev's split personality – alternatively boastful and insecure, belligerent
and mellow – was in plain view . . . The truculence appeared in his discussion
of China. He began describing the experiences of his brother who had worked
there as an engineer before Khrushchev removed all Soviet advisers. He had
found the Chinese treacherous, arrogant, beyond the human pale. They were
cannibalistic in the way they destroyed their top leaders (an amazing comment
from a man who had launched his career during Stalin's purges); they might
well, in fact, be cannibals. Now China was acquiring a nuclear arsenal. The
Soviet Union could not accept this passively; something would have to be
done. He did not say what.

   Brezhnev was clearly fishing for some hint of American acquiescence in a
Soviet preemptive attack. I gave no encouragement; my bland response was
that the growth of China was one of those problems that underlined the
importance of settling disputes peacefully. Brezhnev contemptuously ignored
this high-minded theory and returned to his preoccupation. China's growing
military might was a threat to everybody. Any military assistance to it by the
United States would lead to war . . . the next day Dobrynin took me aside to
stress that the China portion of the discussion in the hunting blind was not to
be treated as social. Brezhnev had meant every word of it.

Kissinger, Henry, *The White House Years*,
Weidenfeld and Nicolson, London, 1979, p. 233.

*(c) Here Henry Kissinger defends his policy of détente and ruminates on the
loss of American hegemony.*

Détente did not prevent resistance to Soviet expansion: on the contrary, it
fostered the only psychologically possible framework for such resistance.
[President] Nixon knew where to draw the line against Soviet adventure
whether it occurred directly or through proxy, as in Cienfuegos, Jordan,
along the Suez Canal, and during the Indian–Pakistan war . . . If the Vietnam
war had taught us anything, it was that a military confrontation could be
sustained only if the American people were convinced there was no other
choice . . .

The United States and the Soviet Union are ideological rivals. Détente cannot change that. The nuclear age compels us to coexist. Rhetorical crusades cannot change that, either.

Our age must learn the lessons of World War II, brought about when the democracies failed to understand the designs of a totalitarian aggressor, sought foolishly to appease him, and permitted him to achieve a military superiority. This must never happen again . . . An American President thus has a dual responsibility: He must resist Soviet expansionism. And he must be conscious of the profound risks of global confrontation. His policy must embrace both deterrence and coexistence, both containment and an effort to relax tensions . . . Yet if we pursue the ideological conflict divorced from strategy, if confrontation turns into an end in itself, we will lose the cohesion of our alliances and ultimately the confidence of our people. That was what the Nixon Administration understood by détente . . .

The late 1960s had marked the end of the period of American predominance based on overwhelming nuclear and economic supremacy. The Soviet nuclear stockpile was inevitably approaching parity. The economic strength of Japan and Europe was bound to lead them to seek larger political influence. The new, developing nations pressed their claims to greater power and participation. The United States would have to learn to base its foreign policy on premises analogous to those by which other nations historically had conducted theirs. The percentage of the world's Gross National Product represented by our economy was sinking by 10 per cent with every decade: from 52 per cent in 1950 to 40 per cent in 1960, to some 30 per cent in 1970 (and 22 per cent now – 1982) . . . Still the strongest nation but no longer preeminent, we would have to take seriously the world balance of power, for if it tilted against us, it might prove irreversible . . .

The strategy of the Nixon Administration presupposed a decisive President willing to stake American power to resist Soviet expansionism and ready to negotiate seriously if the Soviets would accept coexistence on this basis. But both of these courses of action were being destroyed by our domestic passion play . . . I am convinced, for a long range policy that avoids either confrontation for its own sake or acquiescence in Soviet expansion, we must resist marginal accretions of Soviet power even when the issues seem ambiguous.

Kissinger, Henry, *The White House Years*,
Weidenfeld and Nicolson, London, 1979, pp. 237–8.

(d) Kissinger explains the reasons for the failure of his foreign policy.

Still, I reflect with melancholy on the way America consumed its unity in 1973–1974 . . .

There is no question in my mind that one of the casualties of the period was a balanced, careful, thoughtful approach to East–West relations. The sober teaching of the 1973–1974 period is that idealism did not, in the end, enhance the human rights of Jews in the Soviet Union (the emigration figure for 1975 was less than 40 per cent of that of 1973); that the undermining of SALT did not improve our military posture . . . The approach being legislated did not deter Soviet expansion. That increased, and the same domestic divisions that had spawned the confrontation prevented an effective response. The Soviet Union was not induced to behave in a more reasonable manner. The Administration had no illusions about Soviet purposes, but the domestic debate confused, instead of illuminated, the nation's understanding of the complexity of our challenge.

Kissinger, Henry, *The White House Years*,
Weidenfeld and Nicolson, London, 1979, p. 1030.

DOCUMENT 6   **THE KGB**

These Party documents reveal the wide-ranging activities of the Soviet author-ities in their never-ending struggle to undermine American power in the United States and Central America.

(a)

KGB,	Secret Confidential
USSR Council of Ministers,	Special Dossier
28 April 1970	
No. 1128–A	
Moscow	

CPSU Central Committee

Lately, the radical black organisation, the Black Panthers, has been sub-jected to ferocious repression by the US authorities, under the command of the FBI, which regards the Black Panthers as a serious threat to national security.

As the Black Panthers is an organisation representing blacks, dynamic and dangerous for the ruling classes of the United States, the Communist Party [of the USA] is attempting to influence it, in a positive manner. This policy of the Communist Party is beginning to bear fruit. Since the growth of the Negro protest movement will create difficulties for the ruling circles of the United States, and will lead the Nixon administration to develop an active foreign policy, we think it advisable to implement a series of measures to strengthen and enlarge this organisation. Hence we propose, based on the capabilities of the KGB in the countries of Africa, to encourage politicians and popular figures, youth organisations, trade unions and nationalist groups to forward petitions, statements and declarations, supporting the rights of Negroes in America, to the UN, to representatives of the US in those countries and to the government of the United States. Publish in the press of several African states articles and letters accusing the American government of genocide. Make use of the facilities of the KGB in New York and Washington to influence the Black Panthers to forward to the UN and other organisations petitions requesting their help to end the policy of genocide being conducted by American authorities against American Negroes. It is correct to assume that, after the above measures have been set in motion, it will be possible to mobilise public opinion in the United States and in third countries to support American Negroes and also to encourage the Black Panthers to step up their campaign.

Chair of the KGB
Andropov

Boukovsky, Vladimir, *Jugement à Moscou. Un Dissident dans les Archives du Kremlin*, Robert Laffont, Paris, 1995, pp. 35–6.

(b)

To be returned within three days to the   Secret Confidential
Central Committee, CPSU (general service, 2nd section)   Special Dossier
No. St–37 gs
27 December 1976

Extract from the minutes no. 37, para. 37 gs, CC Secretariat

For the attention of the international department, CC, CPSU

Responding to the request of the leadership of the Communist Party of Argentina, the Popular Party of Panama, the Communist Party of El Salvador and the Communist Party of Uruguay, welcome to the USSR *for training in the techniques of Party security, espionage and counter-espionage, 10 Argentinian communists, three Panamanians, three Salvadorans, three Uruguayans, for a period of six months.*

The organisation of their training is to be the responsibility of the KGB, USSR Council of Ministers; welcome, services and assistance will be the duty of the international department and the administration of affairs of the CC, CPSU. The travel expenses of the 10 Argentinian comrades from Buenos to Moscow and return, of the three Panamanians from Panama to Moscow and return, of the three Salvadorans from San Salvador to Moscow and return, and the three Uruguayans from Montevideo to Moscow and return will be charged to the Party budget.

Secretary of the CC
For: comrades Andropov, Ponomarev, Pavlov

Boukovsky, Vladimir, *Jugement à Moscou. Un Dissident dans les Archives du Kremlin,*
Robert Laffont, Paris, 1995, p. 37.

(c)
No. St–224/71 gs   Secret Confidential
18 August 1980   Special Dossier

Resolution of the CC Secretariat, CPSU

For the attention of the international department, CC, CPSU

Responding to the request of the leadership of the Communist Party of El Salvador, admit, in 1980, thirty Salvadoran communists, already in the USSR, *for military training for a period of six months.* Welcome, services, material assistance, *organisation of the training* of the thirty Salvadoran communists, as well as their travel expenses from Moscow to Salvador will be *charged to the budget of the Ministry of Defence.*

[Signed: A. Chernyaev]

Those who voted: (signatures) Kirilenko, Zimyanin, Gorbachev, Kapitonov, Dolgikh
Copies to: comrades Ustinov, Ponomarev
Distributed on 18 August 1980

Boukovsky, Vladimir, *Jugement à Moscou. Un Dissident dans les Archives du Kremlin,*
Robert Laffont, Paris, 1995, p. 38.

(d)

Secret Confidential
(Translated from Spanish)

To the CC, CPSU

Dear comrades,

I request you to welcome thirty members of our young communists living in Moscow *for military training* for four or five months in the following branches:
1) six comrades in *military espionage*
2) eight comrades to be specially trained as *commanders of guerrilla detachments*
3) five comrades as *artillery commanders*

4) five comrades as *diversionary tactics commanders*
5) six comrades in *communications*

I thank you for the help the CPSU has extended our Party.

Shafik Handal
General secretary of the CC, Communist Party of El Salvador
23 July 1980, Moscow
Translation: V. Tikhmenev

Boukovsky, Vladimir, *Jugement à Moscou. Un Dissident dans les Archives du Kremlin*,
Robert Laffont, Paris, 1995, p. 38.

(e)
No. St–225/5 gs   Secret Confidential
20 August 1980   Special Dossier

Resolution of the CC Secretariat, CPSU

For the attention of the leadership of the Communist Party of El Salvador

1) Responding to the request of the leadership of the Communist Party of
    El Salvador, the Ministry of Civil Transport Aviation, during September–
    October of this year, is to transport *fire arms and western produced
    munitions*, weighing 60 to 80 tonnes, from Hanoi [Vietnam] to Havana
    [Cuba], to be forwarded by our Cuban comrades to our friends in Salvador.
        The costs of transporting the *arms* from Hanoi to Havana will be
    charged to the state aid budget and not any foreign state.
2) The texts of the telegrams to the Soviet ambassadors to Cuba and Vietnam
    (enclosed) are confirmed.

[Signed: Chernyaev]

Those who voted: Kirilenko, Russakov, Gorbachev,
Dolgikh, Zimyanin, Kapitonov
Copies to: comrades Gromyko, Ponomarev
to comrades: Bugaev, Garbuzov (without the enclosed)

Boukovsky, Vladimir, *Jugement à Moscou. Un Dissident dans les Archives du Kremlin*,
Robert Laffont, Paris, 1995, p. 39.

(f)
Havana   Secret Confidential
                                                          Special Dossier
                                       Addendum no. 1 of the PV 5 gs pr. 225
                                                                   Urgent

To the Soviet Ambassador

662. *Inform Shafik Handal, general secretary of the CC, Communist Party
of El Salvador, or, if he is absent, a member of the leadership of the*

Communist Party of El Salvador, that his request for the transport of western manufactured arms from Vietnam to Cuba has been considered by our authorities and is granted. Inform our Cuban friends also and add that we have taken this decision in the light of the provisional agreement which has already been reached by comrades F. Castro and S. Handal.

For your information: the delivery of the *arms* will be by Aeroflot planes. Ensure the indispensable cooperation necessary for the organisation of these deliveries to our Cuban friends in Havana for onward transfer to our Salvadoran friends.
Report on the implementation of the above.

[Signed: Chernyaev, Russakov]

Boukovsky, Vladimir, *Jugement à Moscou. Un Dissident dans les Archives du Kremlin*, Robert Laffont, Paris, 1995, pp. 39–40.

DOCUMENT 7   **THE KGB AND ITALY**

In 1974 the Italian Communist Party became concerned about a lurch to the right in Italy and began to fear for the safety of members. The following document is the CPSU's response to a request by the Italian communists for documents which would allow 50 comrades to cross France, in wigs and false beards, carrying French passports supplied by the KGB!

Proletarians of the World Unite!

To be returned within 24 hours to the CC, CPSU   Secret Confidential
(general service, 2nd section)
Communist Party of the Soviet Union: Central Committee   Secret Dossier

P136/53

5 May 1974

To comrades Andropov, Ponomarev complete; paragraph 2 to Pavlov

Special assistance to the Italian Communist Party

1) Meet the request of the leadership of the Italian Communist Party (PCI) and welcome to the Soviet Union, for special training, nineteen Italian communists of which six are to study radio transmissions, work on the BR–3Y broadcasting stations and codes (for three months), two instructors for training radio telegraphers and encoders (three months), nine on Party techniques (two months), two for *altering the external appearance* (two weeks) and one

specialist for discussions on the organisation of particular types of internal radio broadcasting (one week). Meet the request of the leadership of the PCI and provide 500 blank and 50 completed (reserved for personnel and cadres of the PCI) Italian documents, for internal and external use, and 50 complete sets of documents of this type, French and Swiss, as well as wigs and the equipment for altering one's *external appearance*. The manufacture of the identity documents and the equipment for altering one's *external appearance* will be the responsibility of the international department of the CC, CPSU and the KGB, USSR Council of Ministers . . .

The text of the telegram to the KGB *rezident* (head) in Italy is approved.

CC Secretary

Boukovsky, Vladimir, *Jugement à Moscou. Un Dissident dans les Archives du Kremlin*, Robert Laffont, Paris, 1995, pp. 42–3.

DOCUMENT 8   THE RUSSIANS AND THE PALESTINIANS

The KGB supplied weapons on a regular basis to the Palestinians.

USSR KGB,	Very Important
USSR Council of Ministers	Special Dossier

16 May 1975
No. 1218–A/ov
Moscow
To Comrade L. I. Brezhnev

Following the decision of the CC, CPSU, the KGB delivered to Uadia Haddad, the person agreed by the KGB espionage services and the chief of the department for foreign affairs of the National Front for the Liberation of Palestine, a consignment of foreign manufactured arms and the necessary equipment (53 machine guns, 50 pistols of which 10 had silencers), 34,000 cartridges and bullets.

   This delivery of these arms, which was illegal, was carried out in neutral waters in the gulf of Aden, at night, with as little contact as possible, in extreme secrecy, using a patrol vessel of the USSR Navy.

   Haddad is the only foreigner aware that the above mentioned arms were delivered by us.

Chair of the KGB
Andropov

Boukovsky, Vladimir, *Jugement à Moscou. Un Dissident dans les Archives du Kremlin*, Robert Laffont, Paris, 1995, p. 46.

DOCUMENT 9 AFGHANISTAN

(a) The Soviet decision to intervene in Afghanistan was taken by the Politburo on 12 December 1979, with the following present: Leonid Brezhnev, Party General Secretary; Yury Andropov, chair of the KGB; Dmitry Ustinov, Minister of Defence; Konstantin Chernenko; Arvid Pelshe; Mikhail Suslov; Andrei Kirilenko; Viktor Grishin; Nikolai Tikhonov. Boris Ponomarev was also present, but as a candidate member did not have the right to vote. Those who were absent but who signed the document later were: Dinmukhamed Kunaev, who signed on 25 December, and Grigory Romanov and Vladimir Shcherbitsky, on 26 December. The document itself, in Chernenko's handwriting, does not reveal the significance of the decision.

On the Situation in Afghanistan

1) Approve the views and measures outlined by comrades Andropov, Ustinov, Gromyko.

    Changes may be made during the implementation of these measures but they may not undermine the principles laid down.

    Submit in due course to the Politburo those decisions which require the approval of the Central Committee.

    Comrades Andropov, Ustinov and Gromyko are responsible for implementing all these measures.

2) Comrades Andropov, Ustinov, Gromyko are to keep the Politburo informed about the implementation of the above measures.

L. Brezhnev
Secretary of the Central Committee
P176/125, 12 December 1979

Boukovsky, Vladimir, *Jugement à Moscou. Un Dissident dans les Archives du Kremlin*,
Robert Laffont, Paris, 1995, p. 383.

(b) A battalion of Spetsnaz (special forces), consisting of Central Asians, but commanded by a Russian, Lieutenant Colonel Kolesnik, had been forming since May 1979. The battalion, consisting of 500 men, was flown to Bahram, Afghanistan, in Afghan uniforms, and moved to Kabul, on 21 December. Two KGB units joined them. On 25 December, at 1500 hours Moscow time, Soviet troops crossed the border into Afghanistan. Most troops came by air. There were 343 flights spread over 47 hours, involving 7,700 men, 894 pieces of military equipment and 1,062 tonnes of supplies.

The immediate target for the KGB units was the palace in Kabul where Hafizullah Amin, the Afghan communist leader, was hiding (he thought the Russians were coming to save him). Amin and his personal guard (100 to 150 men) were to be killed and no survivors left alive.

On 27 December 1979 the Politburo informed foreign communist and workers' parties that the intervention in Afghanistan was 'provisional' and 'limited'. It provided more information, but only to its own officials throughout the Soviet Union: Afghanistan was of great strategic importance to Russian security, China was dangerously near, the capitalists would make a lot of the intervention, and then instructions were issued.

Any insinuation that there we have interfered in the internal affairs of Afghanistan is to be resolutely rebutted . . . When commenting on the domestic changes which have occurred in Afghanistan, underline firmly that these are the domestic concerns of the Afghan people and support this with reference to the public statements of the Revolutionary Council and the speeches of the chair of the Revolutionary Council of Afghanistan, Babrak Karmal [appointed by Moscow to succeed Amin].

Boukovsky, Vladimir, *Jugement à Moscou. Un Dissident dans les Archives du Kremlin*, Robert Laffont, Paris, 1995, p. 384.

(c) The Soviet leadership did not grasp the catastrophe which had befallen them. They thought the west would protest, make some noise and then forget about the whole episode. They also did not grasp the damage they were doing to their relations with the Muslim world. At a Party Central Committee plenum, on 23 June 1980, Gromyko spoke eloquently of the growing power of the Soviet Union.

It is not possible to perceive correctly this or that tendency if one does not give due consideration to the most important factor in international affairs, the constant strengthening of the position of socialism on the international stage.

The world map bears eloquent testimony to this.

In the western hemisphere, there is glorious Cuba.

In south-east Asia, Vietnam is building a new life.

The large family of fraternal parties has welcomed Laos and the People's Republic of Kampuchea.

A form of socialist development is evident in different countries, in various continents: Angola, Ethiopia, South Yemen, and a short time ago, Afghanistan. We can also recall the example of Nicaragua and certain countries which have turned towards socialism . . .

Despite the apparent solidarity of the NATO countries, class contradictions cannot fail to emerge. The United States embargo is not supported unanimously and many countries are dragging their feet: France, West Germany, Italy . . .

Even England, which, despite the blow which has befallen it, in the person of Mrs. Thatcher, does not agree with Washington on everything. (Laughter in the hall.)

The plenum approved the 'various types of aid' *extended to Afghanistan to prevent* 'attacks and interventions', *the aim of which was to* 'suffocate the Afghan revolution and to transform Afghanistan into a base of military aggression on the southern frontiers of the Soviet Union'. *It also called on the Politburo to* 'strengthen the fraternal union of the socialist states, peaceful co-existence, support the just struggle of peoples for their freedom and independence, the slowing down of the arms race, the maintenance and development of international détente, mutual economic, scientific and cultural cooperation . . .'

Boukovsky, Vladimir, *Jugement à Moscou. Un Dissident dans les Archives du Kremlin*, Robert Laffont, Paris, 1995, pp. 391–2.

DOCUMENT 10   POLAND

(a) Poland was an important country from Russia's point of view. Strategically, lines of communication to East Germany ran through Poland. Khrushchev, in 1956, was alarmed by events, and he and other members of the Soviet leadership visited Poland. He took it for granted that Russia had the right to ensure that Poland stayed in the socialist camp. A Politburo meeting on 22 January 1981 discussed the situation and how to cope with Solidarity, the trade union movement.

Brezhnev: We are all very alarmed by the recent turn of events in Poland. The worst thing is that our friends listen to us, agree with our recommendations but do nothing. Counter-revolution has been progressing on all fronts recently. Kania [Party leader] informed me on the telephone that the leadership had been criticised at the plenum. I replied that that was alright. 'It is not enough just to criticise you, but to wave the rubber truncheon. This would have made you understand.' These are literally my words. Comrade Kania has recognised that he has been acting too softly, that he has to be much harder. I told him: 'How often have we tried to explain to you that you have to take more energetic measures, that you cannot keep on making concessions to Solidarity? You only talk about the "peaceful way" without understanding or wanting to understand that the peaceful way which you are adopting can cost you blood' . . . Perhaps we should send Andropov and Ustinov to Brest [on Belorussian–Polish border] to talk with comrades Kania and Jaruzelski.
Andropov: Leonid Ilich's [Brezhnev] proposals are absolutely correct. We have to increase our influence, our pressure on our friends.
Gromyko: Of course, American and east European information on the Polish situation is presented in a tendentious way. It spells out the 'justification' for the demands of Solidarity and the anti-social forces in Poland and the inability of the Polish leadership to cope with the domestic situation. We are being advised not to intervene militarily in the internal situation in Poland.

I have to inform you that the state of mind of Kania and Jaruzelski is not encouraging. Certain hints point to the fact that Jaruzelski is beaten and does not know what to do . . . The Poles must realise that any new retreat on their part is unacceptable, that they must not retreat any further.

Andropov: Jaruzelski has been getting everything off his chest and Kania, lately, has been hitting the bottle. It is all very sad . . . The situation in Poland is influencing the western regions of our country. In Belorussia, in particular, where many villages can pick up Polish radio and TV. It should also be added that in some other regions, such as Georgia, there have been spontaneous demonstrations, groups of loudmouths have assembled in the street, as recently in Tbilisi [capital of Georgia], and shouted anti-Soviet slogans. Here as well, domestically, we shall have to take severe measures.

Boukovsky, Vladimir, *Jugement à Moscou. Un Dissident dans les Archives du Kremlin*, Robert Laffont, Paris, 1995, pp. 442–4.

(b) By the end of 1981, Moscow had changed its mind. It was up to the Poles to decide for themselves what to do. Under no circumstances would Moscow intervene militarily in Poland. At a meeting on 10 December 1981, the Politburo was unclear what Jaruzelski had in mind, only three days before he proclaimed martial law in Poland.

Andropov: Our position, formulated at the previous meeting of the Politburo and expressed many times by L. I. Brezhnev, is absolutely correct and we may not deviate from it. In other words, we have adopted the position of international aid, we are disturbed by the situation which has arisen in Poland, but, as regards operation X [military measures], this is absolutely and completely the responsibility of our Polish comrades, whatever they decide will be fine. We shall not insist on anything and not dissuade them from doing anything . . .

If comrade Kulikov [Warsaw Pact commander, a Russian] has actually spoken of the sending of troops, I think that he has acted incorrectly. We cannot take any risks. We are not inclined to send troops to Poland. This is a correct attitude, and we need to hold to it. I do not know what will happen in Poland, but even if it falls to a Solidarity coup, that would be something. Otherwise the capitalist countries would hurl themselves at the Soviet Union, and they have already reached all types of agreements to impose all kinds of economic and political sanctions on our country. This would be very painful for us. We have to look after our own country and strengthen the Soviet Union . . . As regards the lines of communications between the Soviet Union and east Germany across Polish territory, of course, we must do something to protect them.

Boukovsky, Vladimir, *Jugement à Moscou. Un Dissident dans les Archives du Kremlin*, Robert Laffont, Paris, 1995, p. 454.

(c)

Jaruzelski kept on requesting all kinds of aid and there were those in the Politburo who thought he was playing a tactical game. If he failed to get aid, he could blame the Russians for the shortages in Poland. However, some meat was being sent. Baibakov, chair of Gosplan, reports, on 10 December 1981, about the fate of the Polish meat. Poland was expensive. One estimate put the cost to Russia, in 1981 alone, at US$2.9 billion. This extract reveals that the Poles no longer feared the Russians. They enjoyed baiting the Russian bear. This is a prelude to the collapse of the Soviet empire in eastern Europe at the end of the 1980s.

As you know, according to the instructions of the Politburo and the request of our Polish comrades, we had to deliver 30,000 tonnes of meat to them. 16,000 tonnes of this has already crossed the frontier. It should be pointed out that . . . the meat has been delivered in dirty wagons, wagons which had previously carried ore, and had not been cleaned, and that it looked rather pathetic. Sabotage occurred during the unloading of this meat at Polish stations. The Poles expressed themselves in the most inappropriate manner about the Soviet Union and its inhabitants, they refused to unload the wagons, etc. It would be impossible to count the number of insults which showered down on us.

Boukovsky, Vladimir, *Jugement à Moscou. Un Dissident dans les Archives du Kremlin*, Robert Laffont, Paris, 1995, pp. 459–60.

DOCUMENT 11   A TOP ADVISER'S WITHERING CRITICISM OF SOVIET FOREIGN POLICY

(a) Vyacheslav Dashichev, the leading German specialist in the Academy of Sciences, provided situation papers on various aspects of Soviet foreign policy. On 22 April 1982 his institute submitted the following document by him, 'An Analysis of the Present State of East–West Relations', to the Party Central Committee. As he later wrote, the 'dangerous and irresponsible' policies undertaken by the Brezhnev leadership 'shocked' him. Brezhnev, as far as is known, did not react to this report.

The intervention of our troops in Afghanistan, without any doubt, over-stepped the permissible limits of the east–west confrontation in the Third World. The advantages of such a move are nothing compared to the disadvantages:

•   The Soviet Union created a dangerous, third front – after that in [eastern] Europe against [western] Europe and in east Asia against China – on its southern flank under very unfavourable geographical and socio-political conditions. Here we shall have to contend with the combined resources of the USA, NATO and China as well and the Islamic countries and the Afghan feudal-clerical insurgent army, which has imposed great pressure on the Afghan people. We face, for the first time since the Second World War, the possibility of a local military conflict, in which we, in contrast to the Korean, Vietnamese and other wars, will have to fight with our own troops. As a result, the threat of a military escalation increases.

- The number of anti-Soviet states has significantly increased and consolidated.
- The influence of the USSR on the non-aligned movement, especially the Islamic world, has sharply fallen.
- Détente has been blocked and the prerequisites for arms control are no longer present.
- The economic and technological pressure on the Soviet Union has risen sharply.
- Western and Chinese propaganda have been presented with great opportunities to step up the campaign to undermine the standing of the Soviet Union in the west, the Third World and socialist states.
- The events in Afghanistan, coupled with those in Cambodia, have nullified the possible normalisation of Sino-Soviet relations.
- These events could act as a catalyst to overcome the crisis in relations between Iran and the USA and for their reconciliation.
- Mistrust of Soviet policy has increased and Yugoslavia, China and Romania have become more distant. For the first time, the Hungarian and Polish mass media have been less than supportive of Soviet policy in Afghanistan. This is manifested by the mood of the public and the fear of the leaderships of these countries that they could become involved in the world-wide policies of the Soviet Union. Our partners, due to the limitations of their resources, are not equipped for such a struggle.
- The western powers are increasingly adopting differing policies. They have adopted a new tactic, that of interfering actively in Soviet relations with socialist countries and of concentrating on conflicts and their different interests.
- The Soviet Union faces a new economic burden. The escalation of the conflict between the Soviet Union and the west, and China in the Third World, brought into question, at the end of the 1970s, the most important achievements of détente. The continued expansion of our military-political offensive in the Third World will be countered by the west by moving more and more towards a 'cold' or 'semi-cold' war and increasing pressure on the Soviet Union in the political, economic, military-strategic and propaganda-psychological spheres. A gradual return to détente could be achieved by abandoning our military commitments in the Third

World, but only if the crisis does not spread to other regions, in particular, eastern Europe.

Jahrbuch für Historische Kommunismusforschung,
Akademie Verlag, Berlin, 1997, pp. 219–21.

(b) Dashichev knew Andropov quite well and their children were friends. He felt, for the first time, that he could speak his mind about the follies of Soviet foreign policy and submitted the following situation report to the new General Secretary on 10 January 1983. It is a devastating indictment of Soviet policy and warns of the risks of nuclear war. Some of the concepts were later adopted by Gorbachev.

If a great power sets out to expand rapidly its influence and its sphere of hegemonic power, what would be the consequences for the world community? Weak countries would be forced to submit to the dominance of the great power. It would thereby become stronger and would oblige larger and larger states to accept its rule until the whole world had become one super state or be ruled by this super state. But this has yet to occur. The reason for this is that in the world community there is the law of the 'automatic repercussions [or reactions]', which acts to contain the expansion of the great power and opposes the extension of its dominance. This occurs when its power oversteps certain limits and begins to threaten the interests of other states, especially those of the great powers.

The result of the 'automatic repercussions' promotes the formation of a 'counter-coalition' of powerful states to oppose the potential or actual strongest state. The level of the 'repercussions' is the result of its appropriateness or its over-reaction, i.e. the growth of an expansionist great power at a particular time will either be blocked, or through the setting up of a stronger coalition, will be decisively weakened. The latter results in practice from a growth in power, the consequence of new states joining the 'counter-coalition' and mobilising their whole material, spiritual and human resources . . .

Events have underlined the invalidity of the assertion that countries which have embarked on the road of socialist development would recognise the leading role of the Soviet Union. Also that relations between the Soviet Union and other socialist states could be based, on the international level, on the intra-party principle of democratic centralism. It transpired that the hegemonic role [of the Soviet Union] – irrespective of whatever slogan was chosen – provoked a reaction from the capitalist but also – in no less extent – from socialist countries. In the immediate post-war years it was difficult to conceive of some socialist states opposing the Soviet Union. These turned out to be Yugoslavia, China, Albania, and to a certain extent, North Korea and Romania. It was even more unlikely that socialist China would cooperate with the 'counter-coalition' . . .

Détente presented the Soviet Union with rare opportunities:

- To demonstrate its determination to reduce the conflict with the west to the barest minimum so as to prevent the strengthening of the 'counter-coalition'.
- To direct all its energy and resources to the development of the socio-economic potential of the country, to switch the economy to intensive development, which would reduce the level of the 'automatic repercussions' and weaken the 'counter-coalition'.
- To build up the hinterland and strengthen the whole system of relations and cooperation within Comecon and the Warsaw Pact, based on a socialist partnership.
- To seek new ways and forms of support for national liberation movements which would not undermine détente.

Unfortunately, these chances were missed and the Soviet Union was subjected to an unprecedented attack by the imperialists. This policy turn will cost [the USSR], in the five years 1981–6, (only to be compared with the military budget of the USA), US$1.5 trillion, if not more. This has resulted in a dangerous growth of military tension . . .

From the western point of view, the expansion of the Soviet zone of influence in the post-war period reached a critical point with the invasion of Afghanistan by Soviet troops. Previously that could have led to the 'counter-coalition' beginning a war. However the danger of mutual annihilation prevented the west from launching a full frontal attack on the Soviet Union. Since nuclear war was not a rational means of attaining political goals, the 'counter-coalition' adopted other means of pressure. The massive expansion in defence spending, the maximum damage to the Soviet economy, the goal of military-strategic superiority and the concentration of the spiritual and material resources of the capitalist world, are among the most important.

The contemporary policy of the USA and its allies can be labelled 'excessive repercussions [or overreactions]'. This means that the world is now in an extremely dangerous, critical period which can lead to a new world war. The hopes of nuclear deterrence and certain nuclear annihilation serving as factors to prevent war may prove to be fatal illusions . . .

The Soviet Union is now in an extremely difficult position. Almost all the great powers of the world, except India, have lined up against it. Resisting their vastly greater potential is dangerously way beyond the potential of the Soviet Union.

Ways of reducing the 'excessive' pressure of the 'counter-coalition' on the Soviet Union is the main concern at present of Soviet foreign policy. It is perfectly clear that this task can only be achieved by gradual self-limitation and careful behaviour on the world stage by the Soviet Union.

Under present circumstances, the Soviet Union can no longer act as the guarantor and protector of the revolutionary and national liberation movements. This mission is beyond the Soviet Union. A fundamental reorientation of our behaviour on the international stage is now necessary . . . this is the only possibility to arrest and neutralise the processes which, if they get out of control, will inevitably result in a nuclear war . . .

It is also clear that it is impossible to solve the problem of restraining the arms race and reducing the risk of war by merely engaging in military negotiations without fundamentally changing political relations between the USSR and the west. The key question is not, at the end of the day, about the quantity and quality of the weapons one side has but to what extent a political modus vivendi is possible between the Soviet Union and the western powers. Precisely here, in the political sphere, is to be found the key to solving the problem of disarmament and the reduction of the risk of war.

Jahrbuch für Historische Kommunismusforschung,
Akademie Verlag, Berlin, 1997, pp. 224–32.

DOCUMENT 12   GORBACHEV'S NEW THINKING

Gorbachev's astonishing innovations in foreign policy transformed the world. Here he admits that the Soviet Union had been going up a blind ally for decades. The time was ripe for Moscow to emerge from its self-imposed isolation and join the rest of the world. This momentous decision meant the end of a class-based foreign policy. Henceforth, the common interests of mankind would take preference over the interests of the working class. This was very controversial and Ligachev, for one, strongly opposed this policy change.

In late May 1986, we discussed the new role of Soviet diplomacy at a conference held at the Ministry of Foreign Affairs . . . The Minister of Foreign Affairs [Shevardnadze] made a speech which was then discussed by the participants, and I later addressed the conference. The gist of my speech was the lagging behind of our international agencies, which did not keep up with the policies and practical steps undertaken by the country's political leadership. Today I consider this meeting the starting point for the full scale implementation of our 'new thinking'.

We realised it was vitally necessary to correct the distorted ideas we had about other nations. These misconceptions had made us oppose the rest of the world for many decades, which had negative effects on our economy as well as on the public consciousness, science, culture and the intellectual potential of our country.

We understand that in today's world of mutual interdependence, progress is unthinkable for any society which is fenced off from the world by impenetrable state frontiers and ideological barriers. A country can develop its full potential by interacting with other societies, yet without giving up its own identity.

We realised that we could not ensure our country's security without reckoning with the interests of other countries, and that, in our nuclear age, you could not build a safe security system based solely on military means. This prompted us to propose an entirely new concept of global security, which included all aspects of international relations, including the human dimension.

Gorbachev, Mikhail, *Memoirs*, Doubleday, London, 1996, pp. 402–3.

DOCUMENT 13   **THE REYKJAVIK SUMMIT**

Gorbachev and Reagan almost achieved a sensational breakthrough in arms control at the summit. It foundered on SDI, on which Reagan would not budge. At a Politburo meeting on 22 October 1986 Gorbachev gives vent to his frustrations.

Gorbachev: We have to alter our views on the measures connected to the latest hostile behaviour by the American administration. The turn of events since Reykjavik reveals that our 'friends' in the United States lack any positive programme and are doing everything to increase pressure on us. And into the bargain, with extreme brutality, and are conducting themselves like true bandits.

Solomentsev: Yes, they are behaving like really big bandits.

Gorbachev: It is quite impossible to expect the American administration to do anything or come up with anything constructive. At present, we have to score propaganda points, continue our media offensive directed at American and international public opinion. The leaders in Washington are afraid of that. Customs have blocked for three days my statements for Reykjavik and Soviet TV.

Yakovlev: Comrade Bugaev telephoned me to say that these texts are still being held up by the American customs.

Gorbachev: We have to keep on applying pressure on the American administration by explaining our positions to the public and demonstrate that the responsibility for the failure to agree on the limitation and liquidation of nuclear armaments rests fairly and squarely with the Americans.

Boukovsky, Vladimir, *Jugement à Moscou. Un Dissident dans les Archives du Kremlin*, Robert Laffont, Paris, 1995, pp. 482–3.

DOCUMENT 14   GORBACHEV, REAGAN AND SDI

President Reagan was a strong believer in SDI, and Gorbachev did his best, at Geneva, to wean him away from it.

Ronald Reagan's advocacy of the Strategic Defence Initiative struck me as bizarre. Was it science fiction, a trick to make the Soviet Union more forth-coming, or merely a crude attempt to lull us in order to carry out the mad enterprise – the creation of a shield which would allow a first strike without fear of retaliation? Yet I had consulted scientists on the issue beforehand, and the volley of arguments which President Reagan launched at me did not catch me unprepared. My answer was sharp and strong. I said that Mr. Reagan's words simply proved that the Americans mistrusted us. Why should we trust them any more than they trusted us?

'SDI is the continuation of the arms race into a different, more dangerous sphere,' I continued. 'It will only foment mistrust and suspicion, with each side fearing the other is overtaking it. The Soviet Union strongly opposes an arms race in space . . . I think you should know that we have already developed a response. It will be effective and far less expensive than your project, and be ready for use in less time.' . . . I can assure you that we were not bluffing. Our studies had proved that the potential answer to SDI could meet the requirements I had mentioned.

Gorbachev, Mikhail, *Memoirs*, Doubleday, London, 1996, p. 407.

DOCUMENT 15   GORBACHEV AND MRS THATCHER

Gorbachev's first meeting with Mrs Thatcher, the British Prime Minister, in December 1984, had been a success. The two were to develop a special relationship during the perestroika years.

Mrs. Thatcher came to Moscow in late March 1987 . . . Stressing the signific-ance of her visit, I remarked that the last high-level visit to the Soviet Union by a British Prime Minister had taken place more than twelve years earlier. She corrected me immediately, saying that the last time a British Conservative Prime Minister had visited the Soviet Union had been more than twenty years before . . .

Mrs. Thatcher had maintained that the Soviet Union aspired to 'establish communism and domination worldwide' and that 'Moscow's hand' could be seen in virtually every conflict in the world. Obviously I could not leave it at that and replied that much of her speech in Torquay [a week before] as well as most of the accusations she had made were conservative stereotypes going back to the 1940s and 1950s. But Mrs. Thatcher stood her ground. 'You are supplying weapons to the Third World countries,' she rejoined, 'while the West supplies them with food and aid in addition to helping establish democratic institutions.' The discussion became very heated.

Our discussion had reached a point where I considered it necessary to say: 'We have frankly expressed our respective views on the world in which we live. But we have not succeeded in bringing the standpoints any closer. It seems to me that our disagreements have not become less after this conversation.'

My partner struck a more conciliatory note. Suddenly changing the course of our conversation, she said: 'We follow your activity with great interest and we fully appreciate your attempts to improve the life of your people. I acknowledge your right to have your own system and security, just as we have the right to ours, and we suggest taking this as a basis for our debate.

'In spite of all the differences between our systems,' she added, 'we can exchange some useful experiences. We are deeply impressed by the vigorous policy of reform you are trying to implement. We have a common problem here – how to manage change.'

Mrs. Thatcher advanced the familiar argument that nuclear weapons represented the best guarantee for peace and that there could be no other guarantee in present conditions. 'We believe in nuclear deterrence,' she continued, 'and we do not consider the elimination of nuclear weapons practicable.'

In reply I delivered quite a long harangue . . . 'Today, we are closer than ever before to making a first step towards genuine disarmament. But the moment we were given this opportunity, you hit the panic button . . .'

Mrs. Thatcher seemed somewhat taken aback by my tirade. 'That's what I call a speech!,' she exclaimed, 'I don't even know where to start.'

Gorbachev, Mikhail, *Memoirs*, Doubleday, London, 1996, pp. 434–5.

DOCUMENT 16   **MOSCOW AND FRATERNAL PARTIES**

(a) The CC Secretariat, on 18 January 1989, discussed a request from Colonel Qadaffi, the Libyan leader. It resolved that the Ministry of Defence was to receive, in 1990, 20 Libyan terrorists for 'special military training'. In April 1989 a CC document revealed the extent of the training of comrades from non-socialist countries.

Secret Confidential
Special Dossier

No. St–99/248 gs
10 April 1989

Resolution of the CC Secretariat, CPSU

The leadership of several fraternal parties in non-socialist countries every year request the CC to accept their activists for special training. During the last ten years, over 500 full time Party officials from 40 communist and workers' parties (including members of their Politburos and CC) have received instruction. According to the decision of the CC, the international department has been responsible for welcoming and looking after them, and the KGB for providing their training.

[Signed: [Aleksandr] Yakovlev]

Boukovsky, Vladimir, *Jugement à Moscou. Un Dissident dans les Archives du Kremlin*, Robert Laffont, Paris, 1995, p. 495.

(b) Despite the espousal of universal human values, Gorbachev's Soviet Union continued to fund communist parties around the globe until 1990. A hilarious episode, at least to the outsider, was the case of Luis Corvalán, the former leader of the Communist Party of Chile, who had been living illegally in Chile since 1983, 'with a different face', while conducting the communist struggle against General Pinochet. Corvalán requested the CC to help him to become legal again. There was no need to stay in hiding since Pinochet had called elections and lost them. However, there was a problem. Corvalán had undergone plastic surgery so as to go unrecognised in Chile. He needed to return clandestinely to the Soviet Union, have plastic surgery to restore his original face, and obtain a legal passport. The Communist Party of Chile requested the CC to arrange for comrade Corvalán to be eased into a western country where he could go to the Chilean embassy to obtain a valid passport. While waiting, he had to leave Chile unrecognised, so he needed another new face to leave!

Secret Confidential
Special Dossier

No. St–112/27 gs
14 February 1990

Resolution of the CC Secretariat, CPSU

1) Partially fulfil the request of the leaderships of the Communist Parties of Argentina and Chile and welcome to the Soviet Union, in 1990, for a period of up to three months, five members of the Communist Party of Argentina and four members of the Communist Party of Chile, seeking instruction in the security of the Party and its leaders, based particularly on technical means.

2) Reception and maintenance of these comrades will be the responsibility of the international department of the CC, CPSU. Their training, provision of documents and special equipment will be the duty of the KGB.

Boukovsky, Vladimir, *Jugement à Moscou. Un Dissident dans les Archives du Kremlin*, Robert Laffont, Paris, 1995, p. 494.

GLOSSARY

CONFERENCES AND SUMMITS

Bandung Conference, 18–24 April 1955   The first international meeting of developing states and provided a forum for anti-colonialism and non-alignment. It laid the foundations for the Third World movement. It took place in the former Dutch colony of Indonesia and was attended by 29 Afro-Asian states. Nehru, India's leader, played a major role at the conference and the meeting adopted his five principles of cooperation. Western states were sharply criticised. This paved the way for Khrushchev and Bulganin's tour of Afghanistan, Burma and India in November 1955. They discovered that courting the Third World could pay dividends and thus began a policy which was only abandoned by Gorbachev.

Beijing Summit, 15–18 May 1989   Relations between the Soviet Union and China had deteriorated after 1959 when Kosygin had met Mao Zedong. The Chinese listed three conditions for the improvement of Sino-Soviet relations: a Soviet withdrawal from Afghanistan, the end of Vietnamese dominance over Kampuchea (Cambodia) and a reduction in Soviet forces along the Sino-Soviet border. Gorbachev addressed all these after 1985. His main objective in meeting Deng Xiaoping was to normalise relations with China and establish personal contact. Gorbachev confirmed Soviet force reductions along the frontier. The visit deeply embarrassed the Chinese leaders as Gorbachev was mobbed as a hero of democracy. This forced changes in the itinerary. The student demonstrations had begun on 18 April, three days after the death of Hu Yaobang, the General Secretary of the Communist Party of China. The Party leadership was deeply split over its reaction to the demonstrations and Gorbachev's presence exacerbated the situation. Shortly after Gorbachev's departure martial law was proclaimed and on 3–4 June 1989 the students, demonstrating for democracy, were mown down.

Camp David Summit, 26–27 September 1959   This was the first Soviet–American summit without any other great powers being present. In August 1959, in the wake of tension over Berlin, President Eisenhower suddenly invited Nikita Khrushchev, the Soviet leader, to America. Eisenhower hoped that Khrushchev would moderate his hostility to all things American if he were exposed to a dose of the American way of life. The trip was the first by a Soviet leader to America and impressed Khrushchev greatly. He picked up some useful tips on growing maize and was so taken by overnight sleeper trains that they were introduced widely afterwards in the Soviet Union. The two leaders met at Camp David after a previous meeting in Washington and agreed that a great power summit should take place in 1960. Khrushchev backed away from his ultimatum on Berlin and it was agreed that problems should be solved by peaceful means. There was no agreement, however, on Germany or disarmament.

Geneva Conference, 26 April–21 July 1954   The death of Stalin breathed new life into east–west relations as the new Soviet leaders competed with one another for supremacy. One of the by-products of this was a search for a less confrontational foreign policy and this was the first meeting of Soviet and Allied foreign ministers since 1949. The main goal was a peace treaty with Germany but the window of opportunity did not open and no agreement was reached. Had Beria won the power struggle in 1953 he might have moved towards a unified, neutral Germany but Khrushchev revealed little appetite for this approach. The Soviets wished to preserve East Germany in a united Germany, thereby hoping to expand communist influence and exert Soviet pressure on the evolution of the new German state. This was as vain a hope in 1954 as it proved in 1990. The summit also discussed the draft Austrian peace treaty, Korea and Indochina. It was agreed to meet in April 1954 to discuss the last two issues.

Geneva Summit, 18–23 July 1955   Khrushchev's first meeting with President Eisenhower and his first summit in the west. It is the first meeting of the victorious allies since the Potsdam Conference in July–August 1945. It is attended by Khrushchev and Bulganin (Khrushchev was still sharing power at this time), Eisenhower, Anthony Eden (later Lord Avon) and Edgar Faure (France) as well as their foreign ministers. In his memoirs, Khrushchev relates that the Soviet delegation felt somewhat inferior on arrival. The leaders get on well and the spirit of Geneva is born. An Austrian peace treaty, providing for Austrian neutrality, had been signed in May 1955 and Moscow would have liked a similar agreement on Germany. The major Russian fear is that a united Germany would fall into the western camp and become a threat to the Soviet Union. The west, especially German Chancellor Konrad Adenauer, are concerned lest a neutral Germany break away from its pro-western moorings with Germany playing off the east against the west. The Soviets do not alter their views on how a united Germany should come about: East and West Germany agreeing and then elections. The west wants elections and then an all-German government. Moscow proposes that NATO and the Warsaw Pact be abolished and replaced by a collective security system. This finds no favour with the west. On disarmament Eisenhower proposes an open skies policy of allowing the US and USSR to collect aerial photographs of the other's territory to verify any arms deal. Moscow shies away from this.

Geneva Summit, 19–20 November 1985   The first summit for six years and the first between President Ronald Reagan and Mikhail Gorbachev. The main goal of the meeting was to establish personal contact and improve the dismal state of Soviet–American relations. They hit it off after they retired to have a fireside chat and agreed to meet again. Various agreements were signed on the landing rights of civilian aircraft, cultural exchanges and the opening of new consulates.

Glassboro', New Jersey, mini-summit, 23–25 June 1967   This was the only top-level meeting between the Soviets and the Americans between 1961 and 1972. Prime Minister Aleksei Kosygin, in the USA for a meeting of the UN on the Arab–Israeli war just ended, met President Lyndon Johnson on 23 and 25 June. They discussed the Middle East and Vietnam but there was no meeting of minds. At this time Kosygin spoke for the Soviet Union on foreign affairs but was pushed aside after the Warsaw Pact invasion of Czechoslovakia in August 1968 by Brezhnev.

Helsinki Summit, 9 September 1990   The third Gorbachev–Bush summit took place as a result of Saddam Hussein's invasion of Iraq. It was referred to as the first post-Cold War summit. The two Presidents demanded that Saddam withdraw from

Kuwait and agreed that economic sanctions be applied to Iraq. Gorbachev was keen to prevent a military confrontation with a former ally of the Soviet Union and wanted more time for talks. The USA proposed military action. Gorbachev was concerned about Soviet military advisers in Iraq and whether the USA would withdraw militarily from Saudi Arabia when the crisis was over.

Malta Summit, 2–3 December 1989   Gorbachev was concerned about the long delay in arranging a summit with the new US President George Bush. The President needed time to reassess American foreign policy but US public opinion was becoming restive as the Soviet leader enjoyed wide popularity among ordinary Americans. The summit took place after the opening of the Berlin Wall and the collapse of communism in eastern and south-eastern Europe. The weather was dreadful and this epitomised Gorbachev's prospects in the Soviet Union. No agreements were signed and there was no communiqué issued but the two leaders got on well. Both declared the Cold War was over.

Moscow Summit, 22–26 May 1972   The first summit between Leonid Brezhnev and President Richard Nixon which was marked by the signing of the strategic arms limitation treaty (SALT I). Besides SALT, agreements were signed on health, a joint space adventure (the 1975 Apollo–Soyuz mission), an agreement on avoiding accidents at sea and the setting up of a commercial commission. The two sides also agreed on certain basic principles regulating their relations, including restraint during times of crisis and the avoidance of confrontation. This marked the high point of Soviet power and the Soviets viewed it as America conceding nuclear parity with them.

Moscow Summit, 27 June–3 July 1974   Watergate overshadowed the third and final Brezhnev–Nixon summit. They reached agreement on one nuclear arms question: both sides were to restrict themselves to one anti-ballistic missile field instead of the two agreed in the 1972 ABM treaty. There was also an agreement on energy research, a ban on small nuclear tests and discussion of the SALT II treaty.

Moscow Summit, 29 May–2 June 1988   This was the last of the Gorbachev–Reagan summits and was marked by the exchange, on 1 June, of the instruments of ratification which implemented the INF treaty. The two superpowers agreed to apprise one another of nuclear missile launches. They began to lay the ground for a reduction in strategic nuclear arms.

Moscow Summit, 30 July–1 August 1991   The centrepiece of the fourth and last Gorbachev–Bush summit was the signing of the START treaty. Gorbachev had returned empty-handed from the G7 meeting in London earlier in July, having failed to obtain any firm promises of credits from the west, and was under great pressure at home. Bush pressed for a more liberal policy towards the Baltic republics and advised that the Soviet economy should move more rapidly towards the market. There was a tentative agreement on a Middle East peace conference. The summit was a great success personally for the two leaders and developed further the cooperation between the superpowers. President and Mrs Bush were made aware of the demands of President Yeltsin of Russia when he ignored protocol at an official dinner. Yeltsin made it clear he objected to not being seated at the top table.

New York Summit, December 1988   On 7 December, Gorbachev, at the UN, announces that the Soviet Union will reduce its armed forces by 500,000 within two years without requiring reciprocal moves by the USA or its allies. He also stresses that the common interests of mankind and freedom of choice are universal human principles. Later he meets President Reagan and President-Elect Bush on Governors Island. He has to cut his visit short after receiving news of an earthquake in Armenia.

Paris Summit, May 1960 The summit was proposed at the Camp David meeting of the US and Soviet leaders in September 1959. However Chancellor Adenauer and French President de Gaulle had doubts about the advisability of such a meeting, presumably fearing that America might make concessions to Khrushchev on Germany and other matters. On 1 May 1960 a US U2 spy plane was shot down over Sverdlovsk and the pilot, Gary Powers, captured alive. Khrushchev used the incident to demand an apology from Eisenhower who had initially denied the existence of such an aircraft over the Soviet Union. The British Prime Minister, Harold Macmillan, pointed out to Khrushchev that the President of the United States could not make such an apology. Khrushchev used the incident to scupper the summit. The leaders arrived in Paris on 11 May but the meeting was cancelled within less than 48 hours.

Reykjavik Summit, 11–12 October 1986 Gorbachev proposed the summit in September and since neither leader was willing to go to the other's capital, Reykjavik, the Icelandic capital, seemed an ideal half-way house. The summit was preceded by Soviet–American tension which began with the arrest of a Soviet intelligence officer with the Soviets responding by arresting Nicholas Daniloff, a US journalist. Various US and Soviet personnel were then expelled from the respective countries. The two men were exchanged on 29 September. Gorbachev made dramatic proposals for nuclear weapons reductions but agreement eluded them as the USA would not give up its strategic defence initiative (SDI). The US regarded the summit as a failure until Gorbachev, at a press briefing afterwards, portrayed it as quite a success. The Americans then concurred.

Vienna Summit, 3–4 June 1961 The only meeting between President Kennedy and Khrushchev was marked by the Soviet leader's heavy-handed treatment of the US President. Khrushchev thought that Kennedy's youth and lack of political experience would permit him to gain the upper hand. Kennedy was on the defensive after the Bay of Pigs fiasco when Cuban exiles had invaded and been trounced by Castro's Cuban forces. Khrushchev demanded that the USA recognise East Germany but they did agree that there should be a neutral and independent Laos. Kennedy kept his head. Khrushchev misjudged him and this was revealed during the Cuban Missile Crisis.

Vienna Summit, 15–18 June 1979 The only summit between President Jimmy Carter and Leonid Brezhnev was marked by the signature of the SALT II treaty. There was considerable opposition in the USA to the treaty with some commentators seeing détente as a one-way street – all the benefits to the USSR and none to the USA – and the Soviets were nervous about Sino-American collaboration. By this time Brezhnev's physical faculties were failing him and he was not capable of establishing a rapport with the American President. The Soviet invasion of Afghanistan in December 1979 killed détente and a new Cold War descended on Soviet–American relations.

Vladivostok Summit, 23–24 November 1974 The only summit between President Gerald Ford and Leonid Brezhnev and followed a tour by President Ford of East Asia. The meeting had been arranged by Henry Kissinger to provide the two leaders an opportunity to become acquainted. The meeting produced a 'base agreement' on the SALT II treaty, with both sides accepting a limit of 2,400 strategic missiles and bombers, of which 1,320 could have multiple warheads. The Chinese took umbrage at the summit and slowed the Sino-American rapprochement. The expected visit to America by Brezhnev in 1975 did not materialise.

Washington Summit, 16–24 June 1973   This was the second Brezhnev–Nixon summit and the Soviet leader's first trip to America. It took place during the Watergate hearings which were suspended for the summit. The first meeting was in Washington, the next in Camp David and the two leaders also met in San Clemente, California. There were agreements on agriculture, transport and cultural exchanges and the framework for SALT II talks and a treaty and both countries promised to consult one another if nuclear war ever threatened to involve one or both of them. It could not match the first Moscow summit for drama but it helped to establish the fact that superpower summits were becoming normal.

Washington Summit, 7–10 December 1987   Talks on reducing intermediate-range nuclear forces (INF) in Europe between George Shultz, the US Secretary of State, and Edvard Shevardnadze, the Soviet Foreign Minister, 15–18 September 1987, progressed well and produced a framework for an INF treaty. The treaty was signed at the summit, the first signed by the US and Soviet leaders on arms since 1979. It was a highly successful summit with Americans taking to Gorbachev, indeed one can say that Gorbymania was born there. Gorbachev had been warned, in a KGB briefing, that Americans were reserved towards him and the Soviet Union. He grasped the opportunity to stop his car, get out and meet and talk to ordinary Americans. This experience had quite an impact on him.

Washington Summit, 30 May–4 June 1990   The second Bush–Gorbachev summit was conducted in a friendly atmosphere, symbolising that the two superpowers were now partners and not adversaries and major strategic arms reductions were agreed in principle. There were also discussions about conventional arms cuts in Europe and the control of chemical weapons. Gorbachev held to the Soviet view that the reunification of Germany was premature; if it did occur the new Germany should not be in NATO. He was irritated by US criticism of Soviet policy in the Baltic republics (there were diasporas in the USA). The Soviet leader continued his efforts to secure US loans to bail out the Soviet economy.

TREATIES AND AGREEMENTS

ABM Treaty, 1972   The American–Soviet summit in Moscow in May 1972 completed the drafting and the signature of two treaties. First, an anti-ballistic missile treaty which restricted both sides to building two ABM fields, of 100 missiles each, one around their capital city and one to protect their ICBM sites. The ABM treaty was ratified by the US Senate on 3 August 1972. Second, there was an interim agreement on offensive missiles, with a freeze on existing numbers of strategic (long-range or intercontinental) weapons as follows: 1,054 intercontinental ballistic missiles (ICBMs) for the USA and 1,618 for the Soviet Union; 656 submarine-launched ballistic missiles (SLBMs) for the USA and 740 for the Soviet Union; 455 strategic (capable of reaching the Soviet Union) bombers for the USA and 140 for the Soviet Union. The treaty was to cover five years. These two treaties form the

Strategic Arms Limitation Treaty (SALT I). They were important advances in nuclear arms control but attracted criticism from several quarters. They did not involve new strategic systems, such as the multiple independent re-entry vehicles (MIRVs). The USA had a sizeable lead in the number of nuclear warheads. The Soviet Union, by way of contrast, had more ICBMs and SLBMs. The treaty did not cover the Soviet deployment of new heavy missiles, such as the SS-19. In 1973 the Soviet Union tested its own MIRV, an event that surprised the Americans.

Austrian Peace Treaty, May 1955   The *Anschluss* (union of Austria and Germany in 1938) was declared null and void by the allies in 1943. The same arrangement as for Germany (four occupation zones (USA, USSR, Britain and France) and Vienna, the capital, divided into four sectors) was agreed. Vienna, just like Berlin, was inside the Soviet zone. The Soviets set up a provisional government, under the social democrat Karl Renner, in April 1945 and the allies recognised this government in October. A similar government for Germany could not be agreed. Under Stalin Soviet policy on Germany and Austria was similar, neutral and united with communists maintaining influence. Khrushchev gauged that Moscow had much to gain from a united Austria in the western camp. NATO's lines of communications between West Germany and Italy ran through Austria and Austrian neutrality would cut this link. A peace treaty was signed and this provided for the withdrawal of all foreign troops. This was the first occasion after 1945 that Soviet troops had left any part of Europe willingly.

Comecon (or CMEA)   The Council for Mutual Economic Assistance was set up on 25 January 1949 and the founding members were the Soviet Union, Bulgaria, Hungary, Poland, Romania and Czechoslovakia. Albania joined on 23 February 1949 (left 1962) and the GDR on 29 September 1950. Vietnam, China (until 1966), North Vietnam and Cuba acquired observer status. Mongolia became a member on 6–7 July 1962 and thus was the first non-European state to join. Cuba joined in July 1972 and Vietnam in June 1978. On 17 September 1964 Yugoslavia became an associate member. In East Berlin in October 1983 Afghanistan, Angola, Ethiopia, North Yemen, Laos, Mozambique and Nicaragua attended as observers. Comecon grew out of the Soviet desire to wean eastern European states away from economic relations with the west and to offer a substitute for the Marshall Plan. Comecon languished until 1959 when goals and principles were laid down. Comecon was to serve socialist economic integration and became an economic organisation to enable governments to coordinate their economic plans with other governments. The Soviet Union dominated, producing about two-thirds of the social product but in terms of per capita social product, the GDR was at the top with Mongolia, Vietnam and Cuba at the bottom. The secretariat was in Moscow and in addition to the meetings, there was an executive committee, four special committees and 21 permanent commissions on various sectors of the economy. In the 1980s about 60% of trade turnover of member states was through Comecon. The highest proportion was 96% of trade turnover by Mongolia in 1984 and the lowest in 1984 was 46.6% by Romania. As member states rejected communism and moved to the market economy Comecon became less and less relevant. It dissolved itself at its 46th council meeting on 28 June 1991.

Cominform   The Communist Information Bureau was established in September 1947 at a conference of nine Communist Parties (the CPSU, the Polish, Czechoslovak, Hungarian, Bulgarian, Romanian, Yugoslav, French and Italian parties) in Szklarska Poreba, Poland. The tasks of the Cominform were more limited than those of the

Comintern and it was restricted to Europe and formally only facilitated the transfer of information and coordinated the activities of its member parties. Its headquarters were in Belgrade and after the expulsion of Yugoslavia in June 1948, in Bucharest. It had its own newspaper, *For a Lasting Peace, for People's Democracy*. The Cominform was to promote the integration of the people's democracies in the interests of the Soviet Union and oppose the Marshall Plan. The conflict between Stalin and Tito in 1948 seriously undermined the viability of the organisation and it declined in prestige from 1949 onwards. Tito informed Khrushchev that the dissolution of the Cominform was a necessary part of the normalisation of relations between the two countries. On 17 April 1957 the Cominform was officially dissolved.

Commonwealth of Independent States (CIS)   The leaders of Russia, Ukraine and Belarus met in Belovezh forest near Minsk, Belarus, on 7–8 December 1991 and decided to dissolve the Soviet Union and replace it with the CIS. They claimed they were entitled to take this action as they were founder members of the USSR in 1922. On 12 December the Central Asian leaders, meeting in Ashkhabad (Ashghabat), Turkmenistan, requested membership of the CIS as founding members. On 21–22 December 1991 in Almaty these three were joined by another eight former Soviet republics and the CIS was expanded (Estonia, Latvia, Lithuania and Georgia did not attend). Gorbachev resigned as USSR President on 25 December and the Soviet Union ceased to exist on 31 December 1991. The Soviet Union could not cope with its ethnic problems and the elections of 1990 produced parliaments in the Baltic republics and elsewhere which were legitimate and could speak for the population. Republics and regions claimed sovereignty but it was the declaration of sovereignty by Russia in June 1990 which was the decisive moment. Gorbachev attempted to broker a new Union of Sovereign States at Novo-Ogarevo, his dacha outside Moscow but in vain. A Union of Sovereign States, a confederation, was negotiated in the USSR State Council but Yeltsin and Shushkevich (Belarus) refused to initial it on 25 November and this indicated that they had decided to break up the Soviet Union. Minsk was declared the capital of the CIS and its secretariat was also to be there. Meetings of members would take place in the various capitals, in rotation. Yeltsin's attempted coup of August 1991 accelerated the break-up of the Soviet Union as republics sought to leave before another possible coup succeeded.

Conventional Forces in Europe (CFE) Treaty, 1990   In January 1989 a Conference on Security and Co-operation in Europe meeting in Vienna agreed to reconvene conventional (non-nuclear) stability talks. These became the Conventional Forces in Europe (CFE) talks, when they opened, in March 1989, in Vienna, between NATO and the Warsaw Pact. Simultaneously, all CSCE members convened in a Conference on Disarmament in Europe to discuss confidence and security building in Europe. While they were underway the Berlin Wall was breached and communist regimes in eastern and south eastern Europe collapsed. This increased the significance of NATO to the west in a rapidly changing security environment.

Gorbachev, however, mindful of the declining power of the Soviet Union, the disintegration of the Warsaw Pact, and withdrawal of Soviet forces from eastern and south eastern Europe and the reunification of Germany, wanted the CSCE to assume greater responsibility for the security of Europe. This meant the downgrading of NATO. In Paris, in November 1990, two major agreements were signed:

1. The CFE treaty between NATO and the Warsaw Pact, signed on 19 November, was tilted in favour of NATO and promised to end the Soviet superiority in holdings of conventional weapons in Europe. Numbers of soldiers were not negotiated but there were limits on the amount of armament to be held by signatory states. For example, each alliance could have 20,000 tanks with no single state having more than 13,300. The Soviet military evaded their strict limits by transferring tanks and other equipment east of the Urals and hence to Asia. Some tanks were likewise transferred to the navy.

2. CSCE states signed a declaration on individual rights and guaranteed democratic freedoms, including private property. A CSCE secretariat was established and a Conflict Prevention Centre was established in Vienna.

Cuban Missile Crisis   A confrontation between the Soviet Union and the United States which brought the world to the brink of nuclear war in October 1962. Khrushchev judged John F. Kennedy to be a young, cautious president after their meeting in Vienna in June 1961and the erection of the Berlin Wall in August 1961. There was, however, the danger that the Americans might permit the Cuban exiles to try again after the fiasco of April 1961 at the Bay of Pigs. In order to prevent this and also to overcome the lack of Soviet intercontinental nuclear missiles, Khrushchev began placing intermediate-range nuclear missiles on Cuba. At the 22nd Party Congress, in October 1961, Marshal Malinovsky claimed military superiority for the USSR but it was not true that the Soviets had more missiles than the Americans. The USA discovered the Cuban missiles on 18 October 1962 and on 22 October President Kennedy warned Khrushchev that any attack from Cuba would be treated in the same way as an attack from the Soviet Union. He then imposed a naval blockade to prevent any more missiles being delivered to Cuba. In reality, all the missiles were already in place. Between 23 and 28 October Khrushchev and Kennedy exchanged letters. With the situation very tense Khrushchev, without consulting Castro, accepted the solution proposed by President Kennedy. Soviet missiles would be removed from Cuba in return for a promise by the USA and its allies that they would not invade Cuba. The USA would withdraw its Jupiter missiles from Turkey.

Helsinki Final Act   NATO and the western allies always treated Soviet proposals for a European security conference – the first proposal for which had been made in 1954 – with suspicion. It was perceived as a tactic to separate the USA from western Europe and undermine NATO. Contrariwise, Moscow never made up its mind whether it would be better off with the USA out of Europe or with the USA in Europe as a brake on German policy. In December 1971 the Atlantic Council accepted a proposal by the Warsaw Pact for a security conference on Europe. Preparatory talks got under way in November 1972 and in July 1973 a conference convened in Helsinki which was attended by 33 states, including NATO, the Warsaw Pact, non-aligned and neutral states. The only European state of any significance which boycotted the proceedings was Albania. NATO participation led to the USA and Canada also being present. On 30 July–1 August 1975 the Helsinki Final Act was discussed and signed by President Gerald Ford, Leonid Brezhnev (as General Secretary of the CPSU he was technically not a head of state or prime minister. In 1977 he assumed the role of Soviet head of state) and other leaders. There were three baskets:

1. On security issues, principles such as sovereignty and non-interference in the domestic affairs of states were underlined and European borders were referred to as inviolable. They could be changed, but only through negotiations. This was one of the goals of the Soviet Union which wished to have the post-1945 frontiers, including the division of Germany, confirmed.
2. Cooperation was to develop in trade, technology and cultural exchanges.
3. The Soviet Union accepted for the first time that human rights were of a universal character and that there was to be a free exchange of ideas and people across Europe.

Moscow made this concession in order to get the rest to accept basket one and the inviolability of post-war frontiers. Brezhnev lived to regret this concession as it opened the door to Helsinki monitoring groups in the Soviet Union and the flowering of human rights groups. Moscow had accepted that human rights in the Soviet Union were the legitimate concern of other states. This was then used by the west to criticise the Soviet record on human rights and to request improvements. A Conference on Security and Co-operation in Europe was to convene in follow-up meetings to monitor progress and promote further developments. The next meeting in Belgrade, in 1978, took place at a time of increasing east–west tension and there was no meeting of minds on human rights. The CSCE process was revived under Gorbachev and after the collapse of the Soviet Union the CSCE became the Organisation for Security and Co-operation in Europe (OSCE).

INF Treaty, 1987   The intermediate-range nuclear forces treaty was signed in Moscow between the Soviet Union and the USA on 8 December 1987. It provided for the destruction of about 2,600 missiles stationed in Europe with a range of between 500 and 5,500km, within 36 months. The treaty was the first major disarmament treaty between the superpowers since 1945, while the ABM treaty of 1972 and the SALT I treaty of 1973 merely set ceilings for further arms production. A 1974 treaty covered the conditional ending of atomic tests and SALT II was signed in 1979 but these two treaties were not ratified by the US Senate because of the stationing of new Soviet middle-range missiles (SS-20s) and the Soviet invasion of Afghanistan. The USA offered the USSR talks in 1981 about removing the SS-20s and NATO not placing Cruise and Pershing missiles in western Europe. This was the double-track policy which involved NATO negotiating with the Soviet Union to remove the SS-20s and if this failed the Cruise and Pershings would be put in place. No progress was made until the advent of Gorbachev who was willing to make concessions on the vexed problem of verification. The INF treaty resulted from the new START talks and was the first tangible fruit of the new political thinking.

Moscow Treaty, 12 August 1970   The usual name of the Soviet–West German treaty of 12 August 1970 which laid the foundation for the political normalisation of relations between the Warsaw Pact countries and the Federal Republic of Germany and prepared the way for the Polish–West German and GDR–West German treaties. It also produced the Four-Power Agreement on Berlin. After the Cuban Missile Crisis, the Soviet-led intervention in Czechoslovakia and the Sino-American rapprochement, beginning in 1969, the Soviet Union was interested in a relaxation of tension in the German question. Bonn was prepared to normalise relations with the GDR and recognise the status quo in eastern Europe. The treaty acknowledged the existing states and the inviolability of all European frontiers, including the

Oder–Neisse Line (the eastern border between the GDR and Poland) and the inner-German border (between East and West Germany). It did not, however, recognise the GDR in international law but it did confirm the existence of two German states. Bonn never recognised the GDR as a foreign state. The Moscow treaty was overtaken by the 2 (East and West German) + 4 (the USSR, USA, France and Great Britain) agreement of 1990 which permitted the unification of Germany on 3 October 1990 within the terms of the Federal constitution.

Nuclear Non-proliferation Treaty, 1 July 1968   The major nuclear powers had an interest in preventing the spread of nuclear weapons and this treaty was signed in Geneva by many countries. Nuclear powers were bound not to help any other state to acquire nuclear devises. Moscow thereby ensured that the USA would not provide West Germany with nuclear weapons. However, the impact of the treaty was limited by the fact that many states refused to sign it, including Argentina, Brazil, Israel, India, Pakistan and South Africa, all capable of developing their own nuclear weapons. At the signing ceremony, the USA and USSR announced that they were to begin strategic arms limitation talks (SALT).

Sino-Soviet Treaty, February 1950   Stalin would have preferred the communist victory in China to have been postponed until he was in a position to exercise major influence over the Communist Party of China. Mao Zedong went for power against the advice of Stalin. Mao came to Moscow in December 1949, two months after the proclamation of the People's Republic of China. As such he acknowledged the leading role of the Soviet Union but wanted aid from Moscow to develop China rapidly. Stalin attempted to demonstrate to Mao that he was master and the negotiations were long and arduous. It was much easier to agree on foreign policy than on economic policy. China and the Soviet Union agreed to assist one another if Japan, or countries allied to it, began acting aggressively. Mao wanted to end the Soviet Union's right to control Port Arthur, Dairen and the railways in Manchuria and Stalin had to concede this in principle. Mao wanted generous economic aid; Stalin did not want to become a competitor and only agreed to a small loan. He even insisted the Chinese paid interest on it. Stalin forced Mao to agree to Soviet participation in Chinese companies (as in eastern and south eastern Europe) as a way of monitoring and benefiting from Chinese industrial expansion. The treaty was to last 30 years. Hence Sino-Soviet tension existed from the very inception of the People's Republic of China. The Soviet Union and its east European allies unilaterally withdrew their specialists from China in 1959 and this, to all intents and purposes, ended this treaty.

Strategic Arms Limitation Treaty (SALT I), 1972   Strategic arms limitation talks, first proposed by President Lyndon B. Johnson, in 1967, were accepted by the Soviet Union in the summer of 1968. Full-scale negotiations began in November 1969. The SALT I agreements were signed by President Richard Nixon and Leonid Brezhnev, in Moscow, on 26 May 1972. SALT I consisted of various agreements, the most important of which were the Anti-Ballistic Missile (ABM) Treaty and the Interim Agreement and Protocol on the Limitation of Strategic Offensive Weapons.

Strategic Arms Limitation Treaty (SALT II), 1979   Negotiations began in late 1972 and lasted seven years. A major problem for the negotiators was the asymmetry between the strategic forces of the two superpowers. The Soviet Union concentrated on missiles with large warheads while the USA had developed smaller missiles of greater accuracy. Technological advance was another problem, as was the thorny question of verification, including on site verification. A draft SALT II agreement was floated at the Vladivostok Summit between President Ford and Leonid Brezhnev in November 1974: there should be equal ceilings of 2,400 long-range weapons (missile launchers – missiles which can be equipped with multiple independently targetable re-entry vehicles (MIRVs) – and bombers) for the Soviet Union and the USA, of which 1,320 could have a MIRV capability. Détente came under attack in the USA for allegedly conceding too much to the Soviet Union and this slowed progress on SALT II. Superpower relations were subject to some tension as the United States normalised its relations with China in December 1978. SALT II was signed in Vienna by President Jimmy Carter and Leonid Brezhnev on 18 June 1979. The Soviet invasion of Afghanistan in December 1979 led to President Carter withdrawing the treaty for ratification in the Senate in January 1980. However, both signatories pledged themselves to observe the treaty limits voluntarily. The next stage in disarmament talks, which opened in Geneva in June 1982, assumed the name of strategic arms reduction talks or START.

Strategic Arms Reduction Treaty (START), 1991   Relations between the superpowers deteriorated after the Soviet invasion of Afghanistan in December 1979 and when President Reagan took over in 1981 he renamed the strategic nuclear weapons talks START, emphasising that they were about reducing the nuclear arsenals not merely limiting them. When they began, in June 1982, in Geneva, estimates of the strategic arsenals were as follows:

- The USA had 1,052 intercontinental, land-based missiles; 576 submarine-launched missiles; and 316 long-range bombers (with multiple warheads, about 9,000 warheads in all).
- The Soviet Union had 1,398 intercontinental, land-based missiles; 989 submarine-launched missiles; and 150 long-range bombers (about 8,400 warheads in all).

One major stumbling block to START was the strategic defence initiative (SDI or Star Wars), announced by President Reagan in March 1983. The talks were broken off in December 1983 after NATO's deployment of Cruise and Pershing missiles and only got under way again after Mikhail Gorbachev became Soviet leader. However, American interest was then focused on an Intermediate Nuclear Forces Treaty and it was signed in 1987. Star Wars was a constant theme during the talks and also at the Bush–Gorbachev summits. In 1989–90 attention tended to be concentrated on the Conventional Forces in Europe (CFE) Treaty. START problems were finally ironed out and Presidents Bush and Gorbachev met in Moscow on 31 July 1991 to sign the agreement. The main features of the treaty were:

- Ceilings were placed on launchers (ICBMs, SLBMs and bombers) at 1,600 each and warheads at 6,000 each.
- Overall, strategic arsenals were to be reduced by about 30%. The total US missile and bomb arsenal was to be cut from 12,000 to about 9,000, that of the Soviet Union from 11,000 to about 7,000.
- Submarine-launched Cruise missiles were limited to 880 each under a separate agreement.
- The Soviet Union agreed to reduce warheads on heavy SS-18s by 50%.

- Limits were to be implemented over eight years, accompanied by verification, including on-site verification.
- Nuclear technology should not be passed to third parties (except for US sales of Trident missiles to Britain).

The collapse of the Soviet Union on 31 December 1991 resulted in four successor states becoming nuclear powers, Russia, Belarus, Ukraine and Kazakhstan. Negotiations of these states with the United States resulted in a supplementary agreement, signed on 23 May 1992, by which the parties agreed to adhere to the 1991 treaty. In addition, Belarus, Ukraine and Kazakhstan agreed either to destroy their nuclear warheads or transfer them to Russia.

Test Ban Treaty, August 1963   Public concern about the negative effects of nuclear tests surfaced in 1954 after a Japanese fishing boat suffered radiation from a US test. The Campaign for Nuclear Disarmament in Britain formed and became influential. In March 1958 the Soviet Union announced a moratorium on tests. In July 1958 the Soviet Union, USA and Britain began discussing controls on nuclear tests in Geneva. In October, Washington and Moscow announced they would observe a voluntary moratorium. A sticking point was the refusal of the Soviets to permit on-site inspection of underground nuclear tests. In August 1961 Moscow began a series of tests in the atmosphere again. President Kennedy followed suit but also engaged in underground tests. The Cuban Missile Crisis was a sobering experience for all sides and a treaty was negotiated between the Soviet Union, the USA and Britain which banned them from nuclear tests in the atmosphere, underwater and in space.

Union of Sovereign States   A USSR Congress of People's Deputies was convened immediately after the failure of the August 1991 attempted coup and it resolved to speed up the transition of the Soviet Union to a Union of Sovereign States. The new Union was to be based on the principles of independence and territorial integrity, human and civil rights, social justice and democracy. The desire of the states to be recognised in international law and to join the UN was to be supported. The USSR State Council formally recognised the independence of Estonia, Latvia and Lithuania and supported their application to join the UN on 6 September 1991. Yeltsin and other republican leaders in the USSR State Council agreed that the new Union should be a confederation on 14 November. However, on 25 November Yeltsin and Shushkevich (Belarus) refused to initial the treaty on the confederation which had been negotiated. When Yeltsin, Shushkevich and Kravchuk (Ukraine) met in the Belovezh Forest, outside Minsk, on 7–8 December 1991 and agreed to leave the Soviet Union and establish the Commonwealth of Independent states, the Union treaty became a dead letter.

Warsaw Pact   The name used in the west to describe the Soviet-led counter to NATO. It was set up by the treaty on friendship, cooperation and mutual assistance, signed in Warsaw on 14 May 1955. It followed the admission of West Germany to NATO on 23 October 1954 and thereby fully integrated the Federal Republic into the western alliance system. The Soviets argued that the pact was necessary since the west had declined to reach an understanding with them on the future of Germany and Europe. However, if a system of collective security in Europe was achieved, the pact would dissolve. The original signatories were the Soviet Union, Poland, Czechoslovakia, the GDR, Romania, Bulgaria and Albania (which left in 1968).

These states recognised the principle of equal sovereignty and were obliged to consult one another when international crises arose. They had to come to the aid of a member state when necessary, were not permitted to interfere in the domestic affairs of member states and were not permitted to join other alliance systems. A united supreme command and a political consultative committee were to be established. The treaty was for 20 years and, if not annulled, to be extended for another ten years. For the Soviet Union, the pact performed functions which the Cominform and Comecon did not. However, Moscow revealed little interest in developing the consultative political committee into a body which could contribute to the further integration of the east and south east European communist states. It met at infrequent intervals. The supreme command was a different matter. It was always in Moscow and the commander-in-chief of the pact was always a Soviet marshal and, ex officio, a deputy USSR Minister of Defence. Military cooperation between the Soviet Union and its allies had been laid down in the bilateral treaties signed between 1944 and 1947 and renewed in the 1960s. The pact required agreements on the stationing of Soviet troops and these were concluded in 1956–7. The agreement with the GDR permitted Soviet troops to enter and leave the country without reference to the GDR authorities. There were no Soviet troops stationed in Czechoslovakia, but there were in Poland, Hungary and Romania (the Romanians, however, managed to convince them to leave). The Warsaw Pact intervention in Czechoslovakia in August 1968 was based on the perception that socialism was in danger and thus required assistance. This became known as the Brezhnev doctrine and limited the sovereignty of member states. Gorbachev abandoned the Brezhnev doctrine and refused to permit the use of Soviet forces to shore up the national communist parties. This ensured that the revolutions in eastern and south eastern Europe in 1989 were bloodless. The GDR left the pact when Germany reunited in October 1990 and other post-communist regimes were also concerned to leave. The pact was dissolved on 1 July 1991.

WHO'S WHO

Akhromeev, Marshal Sergei Fedorovich (1923–91)   He ended his brilliant military career by hanging himself in his Kremlin office after the failed coup against Gorbachev in August 1991. He accompanied Gorbachev to various summits but was regarded as more conservative than the Soviet leader. His view of the USA remained adversarial and when Gorbachev announced unilateral defence cuts at the United Nations, December 1988, Akhromeev resigned as Chief of the General Staff. However, he remained an adviser to Gorbachev and addressed the US Congress in July 1989. Held in high regard by western specialists, Akhromeev, however, could not move with the political times. He became one of the ringleaders of the attempted August coup against Gorbachev and then, shortly afterwards, one of the few top conspirators to commit suicide.

Arbatov, Georgy Arkadevich (1923–)   One of the most influential academics and journalists in the Soviet Union and the leading specialist on the USA, especially in the Gorbachev era. He became an academician of the USSR Academy of Sciences. His institute blossomed under Gorbachev and was a major centre of the New Political Thinking but it gradually lost its commanding position on policy towards the USA. Gorbachev's gifts in foreign policy presentation lessened his reliance on any one adviser and Arbatov's glory days were almost over. He continued to advise President Yeltsin after 1991.

Brezhnev, Leonid Ilyich (1906–82)   Vain and an excellent mimic, Brezhnev was leader of the Soviet Union at the apogee of its powers and influence but presided over its precipitate decline. In October 1964 Brezhnev became First Secretary (renamed General Secretary in 1966) of the Party and by 1969 he was top dog. Soviet intervention in Czechoslovakia gave rise to the Brezhnev doctrine: the right of Moscow to intervene in any socialist country where it deemed communist power was under threat. In the early 1970s, Brezhnev took the lead in articulating Soviet foreign policy and made many visits abroad, including going to Washington in June 1973 and receiving two US Presidents, Nixon and Ford, in Moscow and Vladivostok. Various agreements were reached and the Americans accepted, for the first time, the concept of nuclear parity between the two superpowers. In Europe, Brezhnev searched for increased security and signed the Helsinki Final Act, 1975, which accepted that the post-1945 frontiers could only be changed by negotiation. Brezhnev once remarked that his strength was in cadres' policy: finding the right men and a few women for important posts. He was not a man of bold initiatives and innovative thinking – one of the reasons why his comrades had chosen him to follow the quixotic Khrushchev. He rarely met a problem head on, preferring to wait his chance to deal with the person who was criticising him. He appears to have become dependent on drugs in the mid-1970s, once remarking that the more he took the better he slept. The Soviet Union also went into physical decline. The tragedy for the Soviet Union was that at a crucial point in its decline, it was being run by a man who could only function part of the time from the late 1970s. Brezhnev became the butt of many cruel jokes. Brezhnev instructs a clever assistant to write him a ten-minute speech. The next day Brezhnev is livid and abuses the unfortunate scribe: 'I told you to prepare me a ten-minute speech and it took me twenty minutes to deliver it. You idiot!' The assistant, in an embarrassed tone rejoins: 'But comrade Brezhnev, I gave you two copies!'

Bush, George Herbert Walker, Sr. (1924–) President of the United States from 1989 to 1993 and Vice-President from 1981 to 1989 under President Reagan. He served as a pilot on aircraft carriers in the Pacific during World War II. He went into business in the oil industry in Texas and moved into Republican politics there in 1959. He was elected to the US House of Representatives in 1966. He served as US ambassador to the UN (1971–2) and defended President Nixon until August 1974 when he called on him to resign. He headed the CIA in 1976–7. He abandoned a campaign to gain the Republican nomination ahead of Ronald Reagan in 1980 and became his nomination for the vice-presidency. In 1988 he easily defeated the Democratic candidate Michael Dukakis. In December 1989 he sanctioned the invasion of Panama to topple the incumbent President Noriega. In August 1990, when Iraq invaded Kuwait, Bush led an international coalition to oust Iraq. In January 1991 a US-led air offensive devastated the Iraqi forces and a ground offensive in February expelled them from Kuwait. The decision was taken not to continue the war into Iraq and to leave Saddam Hussein in power. Bush was to regret this decision later. The Soviet Union dropped its traditional support of Iraq and went along with the war. Presidents Bush and Gorbachev struck up a good working relationship and one of the fruits was the Malta Summit in December 1989 at which they declared that the Cold War had been buried at the bottom of the Mediterranean. Bush would have preferred a post-Soviet state headed by Gorbachev but this was not to be. It took the Americans some time to realise that President Yeltsin of Russia was the coming man.

Carter, James Earl, Jr. (Jimmy) (1924–) President of the United States from 1977 to 1981. A submariner, he worked on the submarine nuclear programme, but resigned his commission in 1953 on the death of his father. He returned to Georgia to take over the management of the family peanut farm. He was elected Governor of Georgia in 1970. He was nominated the Democratic presidential candidate in July 1976. He defeated the Republican President Gerald Ford in November 1976. In international affairs he championed human rights. In January 1979 Carter established diplomatic relations with the People's Republic of China and broke official ties with Taiwan. In 1978 Carter brought the Egyptian and Israeli leaders together at Camp David and they signed the Camp David Accords thus ending the state of war which had existed between the two countries since the founding of Israel in 1948. In 1979 Presidents Carter and Brezhnev, in Vienna, signed the SALT II agreement which would have established nuclear parity between the superpowers. Carter did not seek Senate approval after the Soviet invasion of Afghanistan in December 1979. He came under attack in the USA for continuing with détente since it was not restraining the Soviet Union from supporting revolutionary regimes in Africa and the Middle East. He conceded lamely that the Soviet invasion of Afghanistan had opened his eyes. In November 1979, a mob in Teheran stormed the US embassy and took the diplomatic staff hostage. Carter tried to negotiate their release but failed. A secret US mission in April 1980 failed to liberate them and the President was blamed. The USA and many other states declined to attend the Olympic Games in Moscow in 1980. He lost the presidential election to Republican Ronald Reagan whose anti-communism struck a responsive chord among the US electorate.

Chernenko, Konstantin Ustinovich (1911–85)   He contradicted the rule that losers never made a political comeback in the Soviet Union. He failed in his attempt to acquire the top prize after Brezhnev's death, being edged out by Andropov, but managed to push Gorbachev aside in 1984, when Andropov favoured Gorbachev as his successor. If the American political dream was to move from log cabin to the White House, Chernenko actually did move from an *izba* (cottage) to the Kremlin. Some have unkindly said that the reason why he did get to the top was because he carried Brezhnev's briefcase, in other words, his patron made him. Despite Andropov's favouring Gorbachev, Chernenko got the nod from the ageing Politburo, mindful of the fact that the 'young' man, Gorbachev might sweep them all away. At Andropov's funeral, Chernenko cut a poor figure. He attempted to salute the dead leader and failed to get his arm above his shoulder. When it came to his oration, he could hardly get the words out, he was clearly suffering from emphysema. When he died, after 13 months in office, the baton then passed to Mikhail Gorbachev but Chernenko passed the baton to Gorbachev at a time when the race was already lost.

Chuikov, Marshal Vasily Ivanovich (1900–82)   He became famous at the battle of Stalingrad and afterwards occupied many high posts. He was appointed commander of the 62nd Army at Stalingrad. His army was the mainstay of the defence of the city. It was honoured by being renamed the 8th Guards Army and he remained its commander until the end of the war, taking part in the battle for Berlin. He was deputy commander, then in 1949 commander of the Soviet occupation forces in (East) Germany. As such he played a role in suppressing the Berlin uprising of June 1953. His memoirs of the battle for Stalingrad, *The Beginning of the Road*, are a graphic and incisive account of that epic battle, one of the turning points of World War II.

Dulles, John Foster (1888–1959)   US Secretary of State under President Eisenhower between 1953 and 1959, he played a leading role in shaping American policy towards the Soviet Union during the unpredictable years of Nikita Khrushchev. A brilliant student and lawyer, he was US counsel to the US delegation at the Versailles Peace Conference at the end of World War I. He helped to draft the UN charter and attended the San Francisco UN conference as a senior adviser. Deciding that a peace treaty with Japan could not be negotiated if the Soviet Union were included, President Truman gave Dulles the task of negotiating it with interested states. It was signed in San Francisco by Japan and 48 other states. He became Secretary of State in January 1953 and became very active in foreign policy formation. Concluding that NATO could only protect western Europe, he proposed the Manila Conference in 1954 which resulted in the formation of the South East Asia Treaty Organisation (SEATO). This was followed by the Baghdad Pact in 1955, later renamed the Central Treaty Organisation (CENTO), which linked Turkey, Iraq, Iran and Pakistan in a defence organisation. Dulles played an important role in the Austrian State Treaty in 1955 which made Austria a neutral state. He fell out with the Egyptian leader, Nasser, refusing to contemplate a loan to build the Aswan dam. Khrushchev stepped in and Egypt became pro-Soviet. He always carried a copy of Stalin's *Problems of Leninism* with him as a reminder of the Soviet Union's world ambitions. However, Andrei Gromyko could always negotiate with him because he knew the limits beyond which the USA could not go.

Eisenhower, Dwight David (1890–1969) A professional soldier, he came from a modest background and excelled as a military planner and strategist. In December 1943, he became Supreme Commander of the Allied Expeditionary Forces and as such planned the D-Day landings of 6 June 1944. Germany surrendered on 7 May 1945. He was given a hero's welcome when he returned to the United States in June 1945. President Truman asked him to succeed General George Marshall as Chief of Staff in November 1945. He became President of Columbia University in May 1948 but was like a fish out of water. In early 1951 he became Supreme Commander of NATO. A Republican, he was elected President in 1953 with Senator Richard M. Nixon as his Vice-President. He did not favour strong executive leadership of the federal government and delegated much to his associates. He and his Secretary of State, John Foster Dulles, worked hard to fashion collective defence agreements to stem the advance of communism. Dulles was respected by Khrushchev as someone who knew the limits beyond which the United States could not go. He moved quickly after Stalin's death to secure an end to the Korean war. Eisenhower spoke of 'liberating' captive peoples but limited himself to protests during the uprising in East Germany in 1953 and the Hungarian revolution in 1956. He declined to provide troops to help the French in Indochina. In 1956 Eisenhower's failure to support the British and French attack against Egypt after the latter had seized the Suez Canal led to their defeat. However, threats by the Soviet Union to come to Egypt's aid led to the Eisenhower doctrine. Washington would come to the aid of any Middle East power facing a communist threat. He was reelected in 1957 in a landslide victory. The launch of Sputnik, in October 1957, was a wake-up call to America and many Americans blamed Eisenhower for small military budgets and a limited space programme. One result was that NASA was created in July 1958. To improve relations with the Soviet Union, Eisenhower invited Khrushchev to tour America in 1959 and the visit was a great success. When the U2 spy plane was shot down, in May 1960, over the Soviet Union, Khrushchev used the incident to scupper the Geneva summit and withdrew his invitation to Eisenhower to visit the Soviet Union. In January 1961, just before he left office, the USA severed diplomatic relations with Fidel Castro's Cuba. Castro immediately sought protection from the Soviet Union and the result was the Cuban Missile Crisis the following year.

Ford, Gerald Rudolph, Jr. (né Leslie Lynch King, Jr.) (1913–) As Vice-President to Richard M. Nixon, he succeeded to the Presidency when Nixon resigned in August 1974. He was nominated Vice-President in October 1973 after the resignation of Vice-President Spiro T. Agnew. Ford thus became the first President in US history who had not been elected either president or vice-president. He became minority leader of the US House of Representatives in 1965. In April 1975 he ordered the evacuation of 237,000 anti-communist Vietnamese refugees, most of whom settled in the United States. Confronted by the Democrat Jimmy Carter, he lost the presidential election and stepped down in January 1977.

Gerasimov, Gennady Ivanovich (1930–) One of the most colourful representatives of glasnost under Gorbachev as head of the press department of the USSR Ministry of Foreign Affairs. Very tall for a Russian, Gerasimov, a professional journalist, was always looking for the quotable phrase. He turned Frank Sinatra to good use by saying the Soviet Union was doing things its way. Once, when he fell off the podium, he scrambled back and quipped: 'Now for my next trick!' In 1986 Gerasimov moved to the foreign ministry and remained as principal press spokesman until 1990. His removal was an indication that more conservative forces were becoming influential in Moscow. He went off to Lisbon as Soviet ambassador to Portugal and in 1992 became Russian ambassador there. In Lisbon he felt isolated and missed the contact with the world's press. An American organisation once named him communicator of the year, something which gratified him deeply.

Gorbachev, Mikhail Sergeevich (1931–)   If Lenin was the father of the Soviet Union, Gorbachev was its gravedigger. A remarkable man for the Party to produce and then elect leader, he perceived that Stalinist socialism was doomed and set about democratising the system, including ending the Party's monopoly on power. He remains convinced that had it not been for the attempted coup in August 1991 he could have fashioned a Union of Sovereign States out of the moribund Soviet Union. The key to the Soviet Union's fate after August 1991 rested not with Gorbachev but with Boris Yeltsin of Russia and Leonid Kravchuk of Ukraine. If Russia decided it was in its interests to go it alone, no successor state to the Soviet Union was viable. If Ukraine also sided with Russia, no Gorbachev-inspired solution was feasible. Yeltsin's desire to be boss in the Kremlin doomed Gorbachev to political oblivion. Gorbachev made himself Executive President in 1990 in an effort to overcome conservative opposition to reform. Even more contentiously, the Party lost its monopoly on political power, enshrined in article 6 of the Constitution. The period 1990–1 saw the gradual breakdown of the economy and government as Gorbachev desperately searched for a successor state to the Soviet Union. Glasnost fuelled rising nationalism and republican elections in 1990, especially in the Baltic States, producing parliaments dominated by national fronts whose objective became independence. The draft agreement on a Union of Sovereign States was ready for signing when the coup plotters struck. He stood for Russian president in June 1996 but only received about 1% of the votes. Abroad he continued to weave his magic and his *Memoirs*, published in English in 1996, served as a focus for an international tour which was hugely successful. A prophet abroad but not in his own country, this is now his fate.

Gordievsky, Oleg Antonovich (1939–)   He was probably the most successful double agent ever recruited by British Intelligence until his cover was blown by a CIA agent in 1985. As a KGB officer he was responsible for Great Britain and Scandinavia, specialising in 'illegals', KGB agents infiltrated in foreign countries to operate under cover. He was posted to Copenhagen in 1966 as a press attaché at the Soviet Embassy and it was probably during his time there that he was recruited. In June 1982 he moved to the Soviet Embassy in London and in 1984 became *rezident*, or head of the KGB there. When his cover was blown by a CIA agent he was recalled to Moscow but managed to escape back to Britain. He provided much information on Soviet agents but, more importantly, on how the KGB operated. After the collapse of the Soviet Union he abandoned his habit of appearing on TV in disguise and made a good living commenting on spying and crime.

Gromyko, Andrei Andreevich (1909–89)   Known as 'grim Grom' (he always looked as if he had toothache) and 'Mr Nyet' (he was wont to say no), Gromyko personified Soviet foreign policy for almost three decades. When Mikhail Gorbachev became Party leader in 1985 he wanted to implement his new political thinking and

Gromyko became the unacceptable face of Soviet foreign policy. He was replaced in July 1985 by the Georgian, Edvard Shevardnadze, a more compliant, flexible official. He headed the Soviet mission at the UN, 1946–8, and in 1949 became first deputy USSR Minister of Foreign Affairs. He was downgraded in 1952 to become Soviet ambassador at the Court of St James in London. He returned to Moscow after Stalin's death to become First Deputy Foreign Minister again. Gromyko succeeded Molotov in 1957 when the latter (a leading member of the Anti-Party group) took on Khrushchev but lost. Khrushchev treated Gromyko with scant respect and once told de Gaulle, in Gromyko's presence, that if he asked Andrei Andreevich to take off his trousers and sit on a block of ice he would obey. Would de Gaulle's foreign minister, Couve de Murville, do the same? Gromyko became a member of the Politburo in 1973 and gradually dominated decision making in foreign policy. He cannot be classified as a successful foreign minister became tension increased between the superpowers and the arms race accelerated. He was much taken by Gorbachev and enthusiastically proposed him for the Party leadership in March 1985. He stated that Gorbachev had a nice smile but teeth of steel. Gromyko overlooked that he might be bitten and he was moved upstairs in July 1985 to become Soviet President. In 1988 Gorbachev decided to become President himself. So Gromyko had to go. Gromyko spoke beautiful Russian and enjoyed a wide culture, being especially well read in English literature. A British ambassador on one occasion was taken aback, after delivering a protest note from the British government, to hear Gromyko's response – he recited a Kipling poem flawlessly. Gromyko also had a sense of humour but he never practised this particular gift in public.

Johnson, Lyndon Baines (1908–73) A Democrat and a dynamic US Senate leader, he was Kennedy's Vice-President and succeeded him in November 1963. A brilliant politician, he ensured the passage of radical civil rights legislation and important social security programmes. He won re-election, in 1965, with a huge majority and this emboldened him to push ahead with his vision of the 'great society'. He inherited a poisoned chalice from the Kennedy administration: US involvement in Vietnam. He steadily increased the US presence in the light of communist success. In 1968 he admitted defeat and announced on television an end to the bombing of North Vietnam and the offer of peace talks. He would not serve as president beyond his present term. It was a tragedy for American social reform that Vietnam destroyed Johnson. He died of a heart attack shortly before the signing of an agreement to end the Vietnam war. He was thus spared the ignominious American exit from Saigon in 1975.

Kennedy, John Fitzgerald (1917–63) A charismatic Democratic President of the United States, Kennedy's life and term of office were tragically cut short by an assassin's bullet in Dallas, Texas. He served in the navy between 1941 and 1945 and was severely wounded. Scion of a Boston Catholic Irish family he could rely on family connections to promote a political career. He was elected to Congress, 1947–53 and then became a senator for Massachusetts. He was elected President in 1961, narrowly beating Vice-President Richard Nixon. He thus became the first Catholic president of the USA. From the outset he devoted much attention to foreign affairs. His first foray was a disaster. He had inherited from the Eisenhower administration a plan for exiles to invade Cuba. He was assured that after landing, the expedition would spark a general uprising in the island against Castro's rule. This led him to mistrust military self-confidence and this was to serve him well in

October 1962. He met Nikita Khrushchev in Vienna in June 1961 and the Soviet leader thought that he could browbeat him in the future. The result was the Cuban Missile Crisis when Khrushchev discovered that he had underestimated the young American President. Khrushchev did extract a promise that the USA would not invade Cuba and would withdraw its missiles from Turkey.

Khrushchev, Nikita Sergeevich (1894–1971)   An intelligent, cunning, rumbustious Soviet leader who broke the Stalinist mould but was eventually removed by the *nomenklatura*. Khrushchev became the first Soviet leader to visit the United States and to promise that communism was round the corner in his homeland. Khrushchev was a political officer during the war and in 1944 was appointed Prime Minister and first Party Secretary of Ukraine with the task of rebuilding the shattered republic. In 1946 Khrushchev was replaced by Kaganovich as First Secretary but in 1948 he was back again as Party leader. Stalin brought him back to Moscow in 1949 to head the Moscow Party organisation and he also became a secretary of the Central Committee. This made him a key player after Stalin's death in March 1953 and by June 1957 he had outmanoeuvred Beria, Malenkov and Molotov to become a dominant, national leader. The defeat of the Anti-Party group in June 1957 allowed Khrushchev to stack the Politburo with his appointees and marked the dominance of the Party apparatus over the government. In 1961 Khrushchev launched a new Party programme and expected the foothills of communism (to each according to need) to be reached by 1980. He was later to be the butt of much ridicule for this utopian prediction. In many ways his reform presaged those of Gorbachev. There were considerable differences, however. Khrushchev never questioned the leading role of the Party and would not contemplate any market-oriented reforms. Arguably, in doing so, he doomed himself to failure. In foreign policy Khrushchev was very innovative but a high risk taker. The 20th Party Congress demolition of Stalin infuriated Mao Ze Dong, who felt he should have been consulted beforehand. This contributed to the Hungarian revolution of 1956 and weakened the communist edifice worldwide. The greatest crisis occurred in October 1962 when the superpowers almost began a nuclear war. In agriculture he launched the virgin land programme, a vast expansion of the cultivated area, which increased output – but at great expense. By 1963 he was importing grain from the United States. He was removed by the *nomenklatura* whom he had almost totally alienated by October 1964.

Kissinger, Henry Alfred (1923–)   Born in Fürth, Germany, his family moved to the USA in 1938 to avoid the Nazi persecution of the Jews. He was a major influence in the formation of US foreign policy from 1969 to 1977 under Presidents Nixon and Ford. He served in the US army during the war and in the US military government in Germany. He became a professor of government at the University of Harvard in 1962, specialising in security studies. He was head of the National Security Council, 1969–75, and Secretary of State, 1973–7. An indefatigable negotiator, he was a realist in negotiations with China, the Soviet Union, Vietnam and the Middle East. He was the architect of détente, one result of which was the strategic arms limitations talks in 1969. He supported Pakistan in the Pakistani–Indian war of 1971, helped negotiate the SALT I agreement (signed in 1972), and fostered warmer relations between America and the People's Republic of China in 1972. After long negotiations with the north Vietnamese, a ceasefire agreement was initialled in Paris in January 1973. He shared the Nobel Peace prize for apparently resolving the

Vietnam crisis. After the Arab–Israeli war of 1973 he negotiated a truce between the belligerents. He stayed in office after Nixon's resignation and left office in 1977 and afterwards became a leading commentator and writer on international affairs.

Kosygin, Aleksei Nikolaevich (1904–80) Technically the most competent prime minister the Soviet Union ever had, from 1964–80, but, as he lacked the guts for a political fight, was not very effective. In 1965 he launched reforms geared to increasing the decision-making role of enterprises. These reforms petered out after the Soviet-led invasion of Czechoslovakia in August 1968 led to a recentralisation of decision making. Until 1968 Kosygin took the lead in representing the Soviet Union abroad but afterwards he conceded primacy to Brezhnev. Gorbachev found him cool, if not cold. This may be due to the fact that as a survivor of the purges of the 1930s and 1948 he avoided factional politics like the plague. When informed of the coup against Khrushchev his first question was about the position of the KGB. When told it was for, he said he was also for the coup.

Kryuchkov, Vladimir Aleksandrovich (1924–) One of the many top officials mis-judged by Gorbachev who appointed him Chair of the KGB in 1988. Kryuchkov became the leader of the attempted coup of August 1991. When Gorbachev was able to remove Chebrikov as KGB chief in 1988, he chose Kryuchkov to succeed him. This may have been due to the fact that Kryuchkov had been close to Andropov. Kryuchkov consistently misinformed Gorbachev about domestic and foreign pol-icy. Gorbachev was later shocked to find that Kryuchkov had bugged his office. Gorbachev remains very bitter about being betrayed by Kryuchkov.

Malenkov, Georgy Maksimilianovich (1902–88) The Gorbachev of his era, he pro-moted new political thinking at home and abroad as Prime Minister, 1953–5. He was a member of the group around Stalin who displayed great tactical skill but after Stalin's death was rather easily outmanoeuvred by Khrushchev. When war broke out he became a member of the State Defence Committee (GKO), responsible for technical supplies to the army and air force. He was actively involved in transferring Soviet industry to the east – when about one-third of enterprises were moved to the rear to avoid enemy occupation. In 1946 he was elected a secretary of the Central Committee and Deputy Prime Minister. This underlined his considerable adminis-trative talents and his political skill. He was a member of the Politburo, 1946–57. Stalin came to regard him as his number two during the last years of his life and he was, among other things, responsible for Party organisations. In the cut and thrust of the late Stalin era Malenkov proved ruthless in defending his own position and this earned the undying hatred of Khrushchev. On Stalin's death in March 1953, Malenkov became head of the Party and Prime Minister but was soon forced to give up one of these posts. He chose to remain Prime Minister and thus opened up the way for Khrushchev to challenge him for supremacy, using the Party as his base. Malenkov ushered in a period of détente at home and abroad, promoting a more consumerist approach to economic growth. Khrushchev proved too agile for him and he had to resign in February 1955. He sided with the Anti-Party group (so called because they opposed the Party having a major say in running the economy) in July 1957 and their defeat meant the end of his active political career. He was dispatched to Ust Kamenogorsk, Kazakhstan, to manage the hydroelectric plant there. Malenkov soon returned to Moscow and he lived privately. There were reports that he attended Orthodox services. News of his death took some time to emerge as relatives had asked for the information to be withheld.

Mao Zedong (1893–1976)   The leading Chinese statesman of the twentieth century, Mao is the father of the communist Chinese state, founded on 1 October 1949. He was one of the founders of the Communist Party of China in 1921 and became leader in 1931. He was a leading military figure during the Long March, which began in 1934–5 and resulted in moving from the south east to the north west of China to avoid attacks by the nationalist leader, Chiang Kai-shek. His victory over the Nationalists in Nanjing in April 1949 opened up the road to power. His policy of the Great Leap Forward 1958–60, failed economically and caused many famine deaths. He launched the Cultural Revolution which ran from 1966 to 1976 in an attempt to fashion a China in his own image and undermine interest groups which had formed, especially in industrial regions. The policy failed and damaged China economically and internationally. After his death many of his radical polices were dropped and this paved the way for a quiet revolution which saw China adopt a market-oriented approach to economic growth. Mao revered Stalin but criticised him bitterly after his death. He believed that he was the natural successor to Stalin as the leader of the communist world. This appalled Khrushchev and the Soviets. The two countries gradually went their separate ways. Gorbachev's failed economic reforms were a warning to the Chinese not to attempt political and economic reforms together.

Mikoyan, Anastas Ivanovich (1895–1978)   A master politician who exhibited great tactical skill, he managed always to stay at the top, be it Stalin, Khrushchev or Brezhnev who was in control. An Armenian, after the February Revolution he was a Bolshevik organiser in the Caucasus, doing battle with the nationalists. He formed a close alliance with Stalin early on and later played a key role in developing trade. There were many stories of his astuteness as comrade commerce. He is negotiating with Henry Ford and he is offered one of the new Ford models. He enquires about the price and is told it is 50 cents. He takes one but Ford apologises for not having 50 cents' change. Mikoyan, quick as a flash, replies: 'That's alright, I'll take two!' During the war he was chair of the committee of supply for the Red Army. He chose wisely in allying himself with Khrushchev after Stalin's death and Khrushchev sent him to Cuba where he fell in love with Castro's revolution, saying that it reminded him of his youth. In October 1964 he rang Khrushchev in Pitsunda, Crimea, summoning him to a Politburo meeting to be dismissed. He had changed sides but he remained a friend. Mikoyan proposed Khrushchev be given an honorific Party title which Brezhnev rudely turned down. Khrushchev confided to Mikoyan that he was ready to go and would not put up a fight. After defeat, Mikoyan kissed Khrushchev goodbye and they never met again. His son, Sergo, kept the information about Khrushchev's death from him, but he read about it in *Pravda*. He managed to send a wreath to the funeral. In 1988 Sergo Mikoyan was the first of the children of the old elite to acknowledge openly the responsibility of their parents for the terrible past.

Nixon, Richard Milhous (1913–)   US President from 1969 to 1974 who, facing almost certain impeachment, became the first US president to resign from office. He was Vice-President, 1953–61, under President Eisenhower. His reputation as an anti-communist made him an attractive running mate for Eisenhower in 1952. Nixon retired from politics in 1962 after failing to beat John F. Kennedy in 1960 for the presidency and defeat in a Californian gubernatorial election. He re-entered politics in 1968 and won the presidential election, defeating the Democrat Hubert

H. Humphrey. His policy of reducing US military forces abroad and helping smaller nations to develop and defend themselves through aid became known as the Nixon doctrine. He gradually withdrew US troops from Vietnam in an attempt to cut back the US commitment there. He achieved a breakthrough in US-Sino relations when he paid a state visit to China in 1972. He became the first US president to visit Moscow, in May 1972. At its conclusion the Soviet Union and the US announced the SALT I nuclear arms limitation agreements together with a bilateral trade accord and plans for joint scientific and space programmes. He won a landslide victory over Democrat George McGovern in 1972 and, in January 1973, effectively ended US direct participation in the Vietnam conflict. Nixon and his Secretary of State, Henry Kissinger, adopted a *Realpolitik* approach to US foreign policy and treated the Soviet Union as a normal state with legitimate security needs. The Watergate affair destroyed him and he retired from office. His successor Gerald Ford granted him a pardon. A flawed man, his greatest gifts were in foreign policy.

Pasternak, Boris Leonidovich (1890–1960) World famous for his novel *Dr Zhivago* which was turned into a successful film in the west. Pasternak was born in Moscow into a Jewish family which was very artistic, his father being a painter. He published his first poems in 1913 and proved a fine lyric poet. He wrote prose also but gradually found Stalin's Russia more and more uncongenial. Pasternak turned to translation, including Goethe and Shakespeare. His *Dr Zhivago* (in the Old Church Slavonic orthography; it would be *Dr Zhivogo* in modern Russian) hinted at spiritual values and the search for freedom. It was published in Italy in 1957. Pasternak was awarded the Nobel Prize in 1958. He was treated as a traitor by the Soviet establishment and had to decline the Nobel Prize. One doctor stated that the book was an insult to the medical profession, without having read it. The scandal shortened his life and Khrushchev, in his memoirs, regretted not having read the work himself at the time. *Dr Zhivago* was published in the Soviet Union in 1988, thus completing his rehabilitation as one of the great Russian poets and writers of the twentieth century.

Primakov, Evgeny Maksimovich (1929–) An astute politician who rose to prominence under Gorbachev and then played an even more important role in Yeltsin's Russia. In 1986 he was elected a candidate member of the Party Central Committee and in 1988 became the first head of a department for world economy and international relations in the USSR Academy of Sciences. His progress was very rapid thereafter and in April 1989 he was made a full member of the Central Committee and in September 1989 a candidate member of the Politburo. In 1989 he was elected to the USSR Congress of People's Deputies and the USSR Supreme Soviet and from June 1989–March 1990 he was Chair (speaker) of the Soviet of the Union, one of the two houses of the USSR Supreme Soviet. In March 1990 he was made a member of Gorbachev's Presidential Council. He was a frequent visitor to Iraq and some observers believe he had foreknowledge of Iraq's plan to invade Kuwait. From December 1990–January 1991 he travelled to Baghdad and negotiated with Saddam Hussein in an effort to stave off the Gulf War. He also travelled to Baghdad during the war in an attempt to broker a settlement.

Reagan, Ronald Wilson (1911–) President of the United States between 1981 and 1989, he made his name as an actor in many films before taking up politics. By the early 1960s he had moved from being a liberal Democrat to a conservative Republican. In 1976 he failed to gain the presidential nomination ahead of Jimmy Carter but gained the Republican nomination in 1980. He defeated Carter easily with 51% of the popular vote. In March 1981 he was shot and seriously wounded but made a remarkably fast recovery. Economically, he rapidly increased defence spending and reduced non-defence outlays. Personal taxation was also cut. There was economic growth but the lack of tax revenue saw the national debt double during the years 1981–6. In 1983 he launched the strategic defence initiative (SDI) or Star Wars without consulting many in the scientific and defence establishment. In 1983 the Caribbean island of Granada was invaded to remove a Marxist regime. As a Republican, Reagan treated negotiations with the Soviet Union with great caution but surprised everyone by establishing a working relationship with Mikhail Gorbachev at summits in Geneva, Reykjavik, Moscow and Washington. One of the agreements reached was the INF treaty which limited the number of intermediate-range nuclear missiles.

Ryzhkov, Nikolai Ivanovich (1929–)   An industrial manager, Ryzhkov was Gorbachev's Prime Minister and supported perestroika until it became economically too radical for him. In September 1985 Gorbachev chose him as Chair of the USSR Council of Ministers where he remained until a heart attack forced him to retire in January 1991. He was elected to the USSR Congress of People's Deputies, 1989, as a nominee of the CPSU. In June 1991 he stood against Yeltsin in the Russian presidential elections and polled 16.9% and came second. Ryzhkov was a moderate reformer whose industrial and planning experience gave him insights into the difficulties of moving to a market economy. He was never in favour of moving rapidly and opposed the Shatalin–Yavlinsky 500-day programme, proposing a more moderate variant, called the regulated market approach. He did not support the private ownership of land and did not favour Russia's accepting western credits as this would lead (he suggested) to the west's enslaving Russia.

Sakharov, Andrei Dmitrievich (1921–89)   The father of the Soviet hydrogen bomb, he became the most famous dissident in the Soviet Union until recalled to Moscow by Gorbachev where he devoted his last years to active support of democracy. In the 1960s he became involved in the dissident movement through his second wife, Elena Bonner. He published an article in 1968 in the west advocating close Soviet–American cooperation and a convergence of the two social systems. This resulted in his removal from secret work but he carried on research at the Lebedev Institute on other matters. He actively supported human rights in the 1970s and was awarded the Nobel Peace Prize in 1975. He was a thorn in the flesh of Yury Andropov who could not jail him, since American scientists warned that such action would lead to a curtailment of scientific contacts between the two countries. Andropov came up with the astute solution of exiling Sakharov to Gorky (now Nizhny Novgorod) in January 1980, which, as a closed city, could not be visited by the western media. His wife acted as his conduit with the outside world. Gorbachev needed the intelligentsia on his side against the bureaucrats during glasnost and invited Sakharov back to Moscow in December 1986. Sakharov gave qualified support but wanted more radical reforms. He was elected to the USSR Congress of People's Deputies and became a leading democrat, condemning, for instance, the war in Afghanistan. He enjoyed immense moral authority. His fellow scientists regarded him as often politically naive.

Shevardnadze, Edvard Amvrosievich (1928–)   Gorbachev's Foreign Minister who was responsible for implementing the new political thinking abroad until he resigned in

December 1990, warning about the possibility of a right-wing coup. In March 1985 Shevardnadze was a staunch supporter of Gorbachev and soon became a full member of the Politburo. Gorbachev astonished the world in July 1985 when Shevardnadze replaced Andrei Gromyko as Soviet Foreign Minister. After all Shevardnadze, a Georgian, knew no foreign language other than Russian and had no diplomatic experience. However, he soon proved an excellent advocate for the new political thinking. He was a welcome change from 'grim Grom' Gromyko and added a dash of flair to diplomacy. He became a member of the Presidential Council, March 1990, but left the Politburo, July 1990, when it was reorganised to include only Party officials. He resigned from the Communist Party, June 1991. He remained loyal to President Gorbachev after the failed August 1991 coup and was reapppointed Soviet Foreign Minister in November 1991 but was overtaken by the dissolution of the Soviet Union the following month. He then returned to his native Georgia where he later became head of state.

Stalin, Iosif Vissarionovich (1879–1953)   One of the dominant political actors of the twentieth century who has left an indelible mark on Russia and the world. The system he spawned, Stalinism, lived after him. Short of stature, with a pock-marked face, Stalin did not speak Russian until the age of 11. A Georgian by birth, he came to dominate Soviet Russia in a manner that no communist leader had done before or after him. The Stalin cult presented Stalin as a god. He was very well read, possessed of an elephantine memory and never forgot a slight. He was highly intelligent and had a great facility to grasp an argument, draft memoranda and penetrate to the core of any matter. His Russian prose is clear and fluent. He was a master of intrigue and a shrewd tactician. He was a Hercules Poirot when it came to detecting the human weaknesses of an opponent. Stalin then ruthlessly and mercilessly exploited his advantage. Trotsky, intellectually more gifted, was nevertheless like a rabbit mesmerised by Stalin's stoat. The German invasion of June 1941 stunned him and Molotov made the announcement of the attack to the Soviet people. The wartime conferences with the allies made him very popular in the west. (He was known as 'Uncle Joe' and it had to be explained to him that this was an affectionate sobriquet.) The Russians acquired another empire after 1945, in eastern and south eastern Europe and the rule was that the Party set up shop after the Red Army had finished its work. Stalin did not want Mao Ze Dong and the communists to take power in China until he had established some type of control over them. Stalin failed to develop good relations with the west after 1945 and the Cold War took hold in 1947. This began an arms race which eventually proved a great economic liability for Moscow. Stalin's declining years saw him withdraw from the public gaze and become erratic and indeed paranoid. His death was slow and painful. It was his custom to lock himself in his quarters for the night. He suffered a stroke during the night and was found only in the morning. There was still a record on the gramophone. Stalin had spent his last hours listening to Chopin, played by a Russian pianist.

Suslov, Mikhail Andreevich (1902–82)   A desiccated ideological calculating machine, the *éminence grise* of Soviet ideology, the sea-green incorruptible of the Soviet establishment, all these fit the formidable guardian of Soviet political and moral orthodoxy. He was temperamentally unsuited to coexist with Khrushchev but managed it; he was, however, much more at home with Brezhnev's more orthodox, conservative style. He did not seek the company of westerners and once at a

Kremlin reception placed tables between himself and foreign diplomats. He and Andropov were competitors and Suslov's death permitted Andropov to come back into the Central Committee secretariat and challenge for leadership of the Party. He gave the Czechoslovak communists a dressing down after the August 1968 Warsaw Pact invasion of their country. He protested against the increasing corruption among the Soviet *nomenklatura* but could do little other than berate the perpetrators.

Tereshkova, Valentina Vladimirovna (1937–)   The first woman in space when she made her one and only space flight in Vostok VI in June 1963. As a cosmonaut she was a military officer and continued her education, graduating from the Zhukovsky Aviation Academy in 1969. In 1992 she was appointed Chair of the Presidium of the Russian Association for International Cooperation. She was elected to the USSR Congress of People's Deputies, 1989. In 1963 she married fellow cosmonaut Adrian Nikolaev and she took the name Nikolaeva-Tereshkova. When their daughter was born in 1964 she became the first child in the world whose parents were both cosmonauts. She later divorced him, citing drunkenness. She represented the Soviet Union abroad at many conferences and was known as a formidable, business-like woman. A crater on the reverse side of the moon is named after her.

Thatcher, Margaret Hilda (1925–)   British Conservative politician who was Prime Minister between 1979 and 1990. She was the first woman prime minister in European history and the first to win three consecutive general elections. She studied chemistry at Oxford and after graduation was a research chemist. She qualified as a lawyer and entered parliament in 1959. She favoured less government intervention in the economy and private life and trade union power was one of her targets. In 1982 she led Britain to success in the Falklands defeating the occupying Argentineans. Known as the 'Iron Lady' for her domination of the cabinet and the 'Thatcher revolution' described the policy of strict monetarism, privatisation and a greater role for the private sector in education, social services and housing. She and Gorbachev first met in December 1984 and they immediately took to one another. 'This is a man I can do business with' became a well-known expression. She was an effective link between Gorbachev and Presidents Reagan and Bush. She and Bush tried to save Gorbachev but failed. Her conviction that her policies were correct split the Conservative Party and she was obliged to resign.

Ustinov, Marshal Dmitry Fedorovich (1908–84)   A very influential administrator of the Soviet defence sector, winning for it during the Brezhnev years an unprecedented proportion of the Soviet state budget. When Marshal Grechko died in 1976 he was chosen to succeed him as USSR Minister of Defence. Ustinov, a civilian, broke the tradition that a military man should be defence minister. He was promoted Marshal a few months afterwards because, according to some sources, the top military would not talk to a mere non-professional military general. Ustinov remained in office until he died. In his memoirs, Gorbachev relates that discussion of the military budget and burden to the country was taboo at Politburo meetings.

Vyshinsky, Andrei Yanuarevich (1883–1954)   A merciless, venomous state prosecutor who gained worldwide notoriety for his courtroom behaviour during the great purge trials in the 1930s during which he humiliated some former leading communist leaders. His violent language and behaviour may have been geared to prove to Stalin that he was absolutely loyal to him. He became well known abroad during the Metro–Vickers trial in 1933, when several British engineers were accused of attempting to wreck the construction of Soviet hydroelectric stations. He starred during the three great show trials (1936–8), featuring, among many others, Zinoviev, Kamenev, Bukharin and Rykov. He exhibited great skill in keeping his head at a time when many of his high-profile contemporaries were losing theirs. In 1940, as Deputy Commissar for Foreign Affairs, he supervised the incorporation of Latvia into the USSR and supervised the advent to power of the communists in Romania in 1945. Vyshinsky was Soviet representative on the Allied Mediterranean Commission and attended the Yalta Conference in 1945. In 1949 he became USSR Minister of Foreign Affairs and the permanent Soviet representative at the United Nations where he turned his venom on the United States, especially during the Korean War (1950–3). Like Molotov, Vyshinsky was not an assertive foreign minister. After Stalin's death, Molotov took over again as foreign minister and Vyshinsky dropped to being his first deputy. However, he remained at the United Nations and he died of a heart attack in New York. Had he lived he would most probably have been targeted by Khrushchev for his debasement of Soviet law under Stalin. He died unloved in the west and Leonard Schapiro once described him, memorably, as the nearest thing to a human rat he had ever seen!

Yakovlev, Aleksandr Nikolaevich (1923–)   The father of glasnost, he was a committed reformer who eventually came to realise that Marxism–Leninism was a brake on Soviet society and the country should move forward to social democracy. In 1953 he moved to Moscow to work in the Central Committee apparatus but spent the years 1956–60 studying at the Academy of Social Sciences of the Central Committee. He was one of the first exchange students at Columbia University (1959). Yakovlev was Soviet ambassador to Canada, 1973–83. He accompanied Mikhail Gorbachev on an agricultural tour of Canada and made quite an impression on the future Soviet leader. In July 1985 Gorbachev made him head of the Central Committee propaganda department, a key centre from which to promote perestroika. By 1991 he was Gorbachev's senior adviser. Yakovlev developed a reputation as an anti-American before the Gorbachev era but this was softened in the light of the new political thinking and he fully supported arms control and reduction. In Canada he had studied the impact of television on politics and was able to help Gorbachev to develop his media personality. Yakovlev was pushed aside in the last days of the Soviet Union but after the failed coup of August 1991 he remained loyal to Gorbachev. In 1992 he became Vice-President of the Gorbachev Foundation.

Yazov, Marshal Dmitry Timofeevich (1923–)   One of the ringleaders of the attempted coup in August 1991, something which he came to regret bitterly. He was born into a Russian family in Omsk *oblast* and joined the Red Army (1941), graduated from the Frunze Military Academy (1956) and the Academy of the General Staff (1967). He was engaged in the personnel department, USSR Ministry of Defence, 1974–6, after which he became First Deputy Commander, Far East military district. In 1979 he was appointed Commander of the Central Group of Armies in Czechoslovakia and in 1980 he became Commander of the Central Asian military district. In 1981 he was elected a candidate member of the Central Committee. In 1984 he returned to the Soviet Far East military district as commander. He impressed Gorbachev and the Soviet President made him USSR Minister of Defence in 1987. His promotion was swift as he was viewed as an officer of a new type committed to perestroika in the armed forces. He was elected a full member of the Central Committee in June

1987, a candidate member of the Politburo (September 1989–July 1990), a member of the Presidential Council (March 1990) and a marshal of the Soviet Union in April 1990. His illustrious career came to an ignominious end in August 1991 when he was a member of the Emergency Committee. He was arrested, charged with treason, but was amnestied by the State Duma later.

Yeltsin, Boris Nikolaevich (1931–)   The first democratically elected president of Russia, leader of the opposition to the attempted coup against President Mikhail Gorbachev in August 1991, his star began to wane in the mid-1990s when he was dubbed Tsar Boris, adrift in his Kremlin court. In March 1985 he was one of the first to be summoned to Moscow and when Gorbachev wanted his own man to take over the Moscow Party apparatus, he chose Yeltsin. Yeltsin, an outsider, was no match for the Moscow *nomenklatura* and they orchestrated a vicious campaign against him. In October 1987 Gorbachev sacked him. Yeltsin suffered a heart attack on 9 November 1987. In February 1988, at Gorbachev's suggestion, he lost his seat as a candidate member of the Politburo. This episode led to an unbridgeable gap between Gorbachev and Yeltsin and henceforth the country was too small for both of them; one of them had to destroy the other. Barred from expressing his criticisms of the slowness of perestroika in the official Soviet media, Yeltsin resorted to giving revealing interviews to foreign correspondents in Moscow. Yeltsin was elected a delegate, from Karelia, to the 19th Party Conference in June 1988, despite attempts by the leadership to prevent it. The 19th Party Conference was carried live on TV and, on the last day, Yeltsin asked for the floor and delivered a detailed apologia of his position, requesting that the Party rehabilitate him now, not posthumously. This was a fine piece of cheek by Yeltsin and made him the most popular politician in the country. President Gorbachev held a referendum on 17 March 1991, seeking support for a new Union of Sovereign States. Republics added their own questions and Yeltsin asked Russian voters if they were in favour of a directly elected Russian president, which they were. Yeltsin became President of Russia in June 1991. His hour of glory came in August 1991 when he became the people's champion by leading the opposition to victory over the Emergency Committee. He drove home the point that the episode was aimed at Russia and reducing its sovereignty. Skilfully, he had demanded that President Gorbachev be restored to power, but, when he did return to Moscow, Yeltsin was the victor. He banned the activities of the Communist Party, with Gorbachev protesting in vain, and the Party itself in November 1991. When Gorbachev stepped down in December 1991, Yeltsin and Russia were there to take over from him and the Soviet Union. His leadership of Russia avoided civil war but his years in office left a dreadful legacy of corruption and failure.

Zhukov, Marshal Georgy Konstantinovich (1896–1974)   The most prominent and successful Red Army commander during the Great Fatherland War. He came to international notice as Commander of Red Army forces at Khalkin Gol, Mongolia, 1939, against the Japanese. This was one of the two decisive battles which led to the Japanese deciding not to press on with their attack into the Soviet Union. Zhukov was made Chief of the General Staff and Deputy Commissar for Defence, January–July 1941. In October 1941 he replaced Voroshilov as commander of the northern sector and was personally responsible for the defence of Leningrad. He was then moved to Moscow and made Commander-in-Chief of the entire Western Front and successfully repelled two German offensives against the capital. He counterattacked in December 1941, drove the Wehrmacht back and reached a standstill by February 1942. He was responsible for the defence of Stalingrad and took part in the planning of the offensive in November 1942 which broke through the German lines and eventually encircled Paulus' 6th Army. In June 1944 he drove through the German Army Group Centre and eventually halted outside Warsaw in August 1944. The offensive was resumed in January 1945 and by April his troops crossed the River Oder and launched the final assault on Berlin. He was the Soviet representative at the signing of the surrender of the German armed forces. He then became the First Commander of the Soviet Occupation Forces in Germany. Zhukov emerged as a brilliant and decisive commander, very cautious in the beginning but very daring at the end of the war. He was enormously popular with his troops and struck up a close relationship with General Eisenhower, the US Commander-in-Chief. He could be rude, abrasive and ruthless. Stalin demoted him to commander of the Odessa military district after the war. One of the things held against him was that he was greedy. Instead of taking a few things he filled a whole train with German booty and sent it to Moscow. Stalin gave him a dressing down for this. After Stalin's death he was part of the conspiracy against Beria and played a leading role in his arrest. Zhukov was most valuable to Khrushchev during the struggle for power in June–July 1957. He ensured that Khrushchev's supporters in the Central Committee got to town to take part in the crucial Central Committee meeting which saved Khrushchev. Khrushchev rewarded Zhukov by making him USSR Minister of Defence but dismissed him in October 1957. He was much too ambitious for Khrushchev.

REFERENCES AND FURTHER READING

REFERENCES

Beschloss, M. R. (1991) *Kennedy v. Khrushchev, The Crisis Years 1960–63*. London: Faber & Faber.

Beschloss, M. and Talbott, S. (1993) *The Inside Story of the End of the Cold War*. London: Little Brown.

Bialer, S. (1989) *Politics, Society, and Nationality Inside Gorbachev's Russia*. Boulder, CO: Westview.

Borg, D. and Heinrichs, W. (1980) *Uncertain Years: Chinese–American Relations, 1947–1950*. New York: Columbia University Press.

Boukovsky, V. (1995) *Jugement à Moscou. Un Dissident dans les Archives du Kremlin*. Paris: Robert Laffont.

Cohen, W. (1980) *Dean Rusk*. Totowa, NJ: Cooper Square.

Cohen, W. I. (1993) *America in the Age of Soviet Power, 1945–1991*. Cambridge: Cambridge University Press.

Cohen, W. I. and Iriye, A. (eds) (1990) *The Great Powers in East Asia, 1953–1960*. New York: Columbia University Press.

Dashichev, V. L. (1997) in *Jahrbuch für Historische Kommunismusforschung*. Berlin: Akademie Verlag.

Dobrynin, A. (1995) *In Confidence: Moscow's Ambassador to America's Six Cold War Presidents*. New York: Random House.

Duggan, C. and Wagstaff, C. (eds) (1995) *Italy in the Cold War: Politics, Culture and Society 1948–58*. Oxford: Berg.

Ekedahl, C. McGiffert and Goodman, M. A. (1997) *The Wars of Eduard Shevardnadze*. London: Hurst.

Gaddis, J. L. (1987) *The Long Peace: Inquiries into the History of the Cold War*. Oxford: Oxford University Press.

Gaddis, J. L. (1990) *Russia, the Soviet Union and the United States*, 2nd edn. New York: McGraw-Hill.

Gaddis, J. L. (1998) *We Now Know: Rethinking Cold War History*. Oxford: Oxford University Press.

Garthoff, R. (1989) *Reflections on the Cuban Missile Crisis*, rev. edn. Washington, DC: The Brookings Institution.

Garthoff, R. L. (1994) *Détente and Confrontation, American–Soviet Relations from Nixon to Reagan*, rev. edn. Washington, DC: The Brookings Institution.

Garver, J. W. (1982) *China's Decision for Rapprochement with the United States, 1968–1971*. Boulder, CO: Westview.

Gelman, H. (1984) *The Brezhnev Politburo and the Decline of Détente*. Ithaca: Cornell University Press.

Gorbachev, M. (1987) *Perestroika: New Thinking for Our Country and the World*. London: Collins.

Gorbachev, M. (1996) *Memoirs*. London: Doubleday.

Graham, B. (1997) *Just as I Am*. San Francisco: Harper.

Halliday, F. (1983) *The Making of the Second Cold War*. London: Verso.

Hamilton, Nora et al. (1988) *Crisis in Central America*. Boulder, CO: Westview.

Harding, H. (1992) *A Fragile Relationship: The United States and China since 1972*. Washington, DC: The Brookings Institution.

Harrison, H. M. (1993) 'Ulbricht and the concrete "rose". New archival evidence on the dynamics of Soviet–East German relations and the Berlin Crisis, 1958–1961', *Cold War International History Project*. Woodrow Wilson Center, Washington, DC, no. 5, May.

Harrison, H. M. (1994) 'New evidence on Khrushchev's 1958 Berlin Ultimatum', *Cold War International History Project Bulletin*. Woodrow Wilson Center, Washington, DC, no. 4, autumn.

Herring, G. (1986) *America's Longest War*, 2nd edn. New York: McGraw-Hill.

Holloway, D. (1984) *The Soviet Union and the Arms Race*, 2nd edn. New Haven: Yale University Press.

Hough, J. (1986) *The Struggle for the Third World*. Washington, DC: The Brookings Institution.

Kaplan, L. (1994) *NATO and the United States*, updated edn. Boston: Twayne.

Kennedy, P. (1989) *The Rise and Fall of the Great Powers*. London: Fontana.

Khrushchev, N. (1970) *Khrushchev Remembers*, vol. 1, trans. and ed. by Strobe Talbott. Boston: Little Brown.

Khrushchev, N. (1971) *Khrushchev Remembers*, with an introduction, commentary and notes by Edward Chankshaw, trans. by Strobe Talbott. London: Sphere Books.

Khrushchev, N. (1974) *Khrushchev Remembers: The Glasnost Tapes*, with a foreword by Strobe Talbott, trans. and ed. by Jerrold L. Schecter and Vyacheslav V. Luchkov. Boston: Little Brown.

Khrushchev, N. (1974) *Khrushchev Remembers: The Last Testament*, vol. 2, trans. and ed. by Strobe Talbott. Boston: Little Brown.

Kissinger, H. (1979) *The White House Years*. London: Weidenfeld & Nicolson.

Kissinger, H. (1982) *Years of Upheaval*. London: Weidenfeld & Nicolson.

LaFeber, W. (1993) *America, Russia, and the Cold War 1945–1992*, 7th edn. New York: McGraw-Hill.

Leffler, M. (1992) *A Preponderance of Power: National Security, The Truman Administration, and the Cold War*. Stanford: Stanford University Press.

Lenczowski, G. (1990) *American Presidents and the Middle East*. Durham, NC: Duke University Press.

Litwak, R. S. (1984) *Détente and the Nixon Doctrine*. Cambridge: Cambridge University Press.

McCauley, M. (2003) *The Origins of the Cold War 1941–1949*, 3rd edn. Harlow: Longman.

Matlock, J. F. Jr. (1995) *Autopsy on an Empire*. New York: Random House.

Menon, R. (1986) *Soviet Power and the Third World*. New Haven: Yale University Press.

Nogee, J. L. and Donaldson, R. H. (1992) *Soviet Foreign Policy since World War II*, 4th edn. New York: Pergamon.

Oberdorfer, D. (1992) *The Turn: From Cold War to the New Era: The United States and the Soviet Union, 1983–1990*. London: Cape.

Paterson, T. (ed.) (1989) *Kennedy's Quest for Victory*. New York: Oxford University Press.

Porter, B. D. (1984) *The USSR in Third World Conflicts*. Cambridge: Cambridge University Press.

Shambaugh, D. (1991) *Beautiful Imperialist*. Princeton, NJ: Princeton University Press.

Shultz, G. P. (1993) *Turmoil and Tragedy: My Years as Secretary of State*. New York: Charles Scribner's.

Smith, G. (1986) *Morality, Reason and Power*. New York: Hill and Wang.

Stueck, W. (1995) *The Korean War: An International History*. Princeton, NJ: Princeton University Press.

Taubman, W. (1982) *Stalin's American Policy*. New York: Norton.

Taubman, W. (2003) *Khrushchev: The Man and His Era*. New York: Norton.

Ulam, A. (1974) *Expansion and Coexistence, Soviet Foreign Policy 1917–1973*, 2nd edn. New York: Holt, Rinehart & Winston.

Vance, C. (1983) *Hard Choices*. New York: Simon & Schuster.

Westad, O. A. (2000) *Reviewing the Cold War: Approaches, Interpretations, Theory*. London and Portland, OR: Frank Cass.

Young, J. W. (1993) *The Longman Companion to the Cold War and Détente*. Harlow: Longman.

Zelikow, P. and Rice, C. (1995) *Germany Unified and Europe Transformed: A Study in Statecraft*. Cambridge, MA: Harvard University Press.

Zimmerman, W. (1969) *Soviet Perspectives on International Relations, 1956–1967*. Princeton, NJ: Princeton University Press.

Zubok, V. and Pleshakov, C. (1996) *Inside the Kremlin's Cold War: From Stalin to Khrushchev*. Cambridge, MA: Harvard University Press.

FURTHER READING

The best survey to start with is Odd Arne Westad, *Reviewing the Cold War Approaches, Interpretations, Theory* (London, Portland, OR: Frank Cass 2000). The founding father of post-revisionism, John Lewis Gaddis has rethought his position and the result is *We Now Know: Rethinking Cold War History* (Oxford: Oxford University Press, 1998). He concludes that ideology is the central theme. This is an indispensable source.

Among the best reviews of the Cold War are: Richard Crockatt, *The Fifty Years War: The United States and the Soviet Union in World Politics, 1941–1991* (New York: Routledge, 1995); J. P. D. Dunbabin, *The Cold War: The Great Powers and Their Allies* (Harlow: Longman, 1994) (2 vols); Ralph B. Levering, *The Cold War: A Post-Cold War History* (Arlington Heights, IL: Harlan Davidson, 1994); Ronald E. Powaski, *The Cold War: The United States and the Soviet Union, 1917–1991* (New York: Oxford University Press, 1998); Martin Walker, *The Cold War: A History* (New York: Henry Holt, 1993). See also: Douglas Brinkley, *Dean Acheson: The Cold War Years, 1953–71* (New Haven: Yale University Press, 1992); Gabriel Gorodetsky (ed.) *Soviet Foreign Policy 1917–1991: A Retrospective* (London: Frank Cass, 1994); John W. Young, *Cold War Europe, 1945–1989: A Political History* (London: Edward Arnold, 1991). A good selection of articles is Klaus Larres and Ann Lane (eds) *The Cold War: The Essential Readings* (Oxford: Blackwell, 2001).

The most stimulating account of Soviet policy is Vladislav Zubok and Constantine Pleshakov, *Inside the Kremlin's Cold War: From Stalin to Khrushchev* (Cambridge, MA: Harvard University Press, 1996). See also Vojtech Mastny, *The Cold War and*

Soviet Insecurity: The Stalin Years (New York: Oxford University Press, 1996). Hannes Adomeit, *Soviet Risk-Taking and Crisis Behavior: A Theoretical and Empirical Analysis* (London: Allen & Unwin, 1982) is a thought-provoking and stimulating study.

On nuclear weapons, see John Lewis Gaddis, Philip Gordon, Ernest R. May and Jonathan Rosenberg, *Cold War Statesmen Confront the Bomb: Nuclear Diplomacy since 1945* (New York: Oxford University Press, 1999).

On western Europe, see the stimulating book by Geir Lundestad, *'Empire' by Integration: The United States and European Integration, 1945–1997* (Oxford: Oxford University Press, 1998). On détente, see: Richard Davy, *European Détente: A Reappraisal* (London: Sage, 1992); John van Oudenaren, *Détente in Europe: The Soviet Union and the West since 1953* (Durham, NC: Duke University Press, 1991); Odd Arne Westad (ed.) *The Fall of Détente: Soviet-American Relations during the Carter Years* (Oslo: Scandinavian University Press, 1997).

On eastern Europe, see Odd Arne Westad, Sven Holtsmark and Ivor B. Neumann (eds) *The Soviet Union in Eastern Europe, 1945–89* (New York: St Martin's Press, 1994).

On Britain, see Sean Greenwood, *Britain and the Cold War 1945–1991* (Basingstoke: Macmillan, 2000).

The troubled Sino-Soviet alliance is covered in Odd Arne Westad (ed.) *Brothers in Arms: The Rise and Fall of the Sino-Soviet Alliance, 1945–1963* (Stanford, CA: Stanford University Press 1998). On Sino-American relations, see: Chen Jian, *China's Road to the Korean War: The Making of the Sino-American Confrontation* (New York: Columbia University Press, 1994); Shu Guang Zhang, *Mao's Military Romanticism: China and the Korean War, 1950–1953* (Lawrence, KS: University Press of Kansas, 1995); ibid., *Deterrence and Strategic Culture: Chinese-American Confrontations, 1949–1958* (Ithaca, NY: Cornell University Press, 1991).

On the Middle East, see Galia Golan, *Soviet Policies in the Middle East from World War Two to Gorbachev* (Cambridge: Cambridge University Press, 1990).

On Japan, see: Walter LaFeber, *A History of US–Japan Relations* (New York: Norton, 1997); William R. Nester, *Power Across the Pacific: A Diplomatic History of American Relations with Japan* (Basingstoke: Macmillan 1996); Michael Schaller, *Altered States: The United States and Japan since the Occupation* (Oxford: Oxford University Press, 1998).

The standard biography of Khrushchev is William Taubman, *Khrushchev: The Man and His Era* (London: Free Press, 2003). This is a monumental study which provides an enormous amount of information on Khrushchev as a person and his relationship with the United States and the west, among other things. See also Sergei N. Khrushchev, *Nikita Khrushchev and the Creation of a Superpower* (University Park, PA: Pennsylvania State University Press, 2000). His son reveals much about the private life and thinking of his father.

On Eisenhower, see Stephen E. Ambrose, *Eisenhower: The President* (New York: Simon & Schuster, 1984).

On the Cuban Missile Crisis, the most illuminating books are: Aleksandr Fursenko and Timothy Naftali, *'One Hell of a Gamble': Khrushchev, Castro & Kennedy, 1958–1964* (New York: Norton, 1997); Michael R. Beschloss, *The Crisis Years: Kennedy and Khrushchev, 1960–1963* (New York: HarperCollins, 1991).

On the end of the Cold War, see: Beth A. Fischer, *The Regan Reversal: Foreign Policy and the End of the Cold War* (Columbia, MO: University of Missouri Press, 1997); Raymond L. Garthoff, *The Great Transformation: American–Soviet Relations and the End of the Cold War* (Washington, DC: Brookings Institution, 1994).

On espionage, see the very revealing Christopher Andrew and Oleg Gordievsky, *KGB: The Inside Story of its Foreign Operations from Lenin to Gorbachev* (New York: HarperCollins, 1990). See also Richard J. Aldrich, *The Hidden Hand: Britain, America and Cold War Secret Intelligence* (London: John Murray, 2001), which reads, at times, like a James Bond novel.

INDEX

Abalkin, L. 96
ABM treaty (1972) 63–4, 66, 88, 153–4
Acheson, D. 37
Adenauer, K. 47
Afghanistan 6, 9, 24, 27, 29–30, 51, 58, 61, 71, 75–6, 78, 83, 85, 87, 117, 136–8, 140
Africa 4, 6, 67–9, 73, 131
Akhromeev, Marshal S. 87, 89, 162
Albania 69, 73
Algeria 78, 74
Allison, G. 98
Andropov, Yu. V. 28, 78–9, 82, 132, 135–6, 139
Angola 29 58, 67–69, 83, 115–16, 118
Arab-Israeli war 26
Arbatov, G. A. 162
Argentina 131–2
Arkhipov, Captain V. A. 57
Attempted Coup of 18–21 August 1991 100–1
Australia 41, 48
Austria 26, 46
  Peace Treaty, May 1955 154

Baghdad Pact 50
Baker, James 88, 92, 96–7
Baltic States (and republics) 89
Bangladesh 115
Bandung conference 51, 149
Beijing Summit 149
Belarus, or Belorussia 100–1, 139
Belgium 106
Belovezh agreement 100–1
Beria, L. 43, 45
Berlin,
  agreement 57
  blockade 8, 25, 29, 34–5, 111
  crises (1958–63) 9, 26, 52–6
  Wall 26
Bevin, E. 25
Bolsheviks 24
Brandt, W. 64
Brazil, 114
Brezhnev, L. I. 9, 19, 21, 27, 66, 71–2, 75, 77, 93, 126–8, 136, 138–40, 162–3
  Brezhnev doctrine 9
  and Africa 70–2
  and Nixon 64–8

Brinkmanship 25–6, 52–8
Brzezinski, Z. 70–6
Bulganin, N. A. 15, 51–2
Burma 48, 51
Bush, Barbara 99
Bush, President George, Sr. 6, 18, 29, 113, 117, 163
  and Gorbachev 18, 29, 87–101
  and Yeltsin 99
Bush, President George, Jr. 6

Cambodia (Kampuchea) 48, 66, 81, 83, 118, 137
Camp David Summit 149
Carter, President, J. 18, 27, 70–6, 78, 81, 163–4
  doctrine 75, 117
Castro, F. 56–8, 80, 90
Ceaucescu, N. 94
Central Committee (of the Communist Party) 121, 130–8, 140, 147–8
Chernenko, K. U. 80–1, 93, 136, 164
Chernyaev, A. 134
Chiang, Kai-shek 35–6, 48–9, 81
Chile 148
China 4–5, 9–10, 16, 25, 31, 35–6, 40–1, 44–5, 48–9, 68, 74–5, 94, 101, 106, 108, 114, 116–17, 128, 141
  and US 10, 62–3, 67, 70–2, 81
  and USSR 5, 9–10, 16–17, 60, 121–2, 140–1
Chuikov, V. I. 164
Churchill, Sir Winston 48
CIA 51, 56, 77, 83, 85
Cold War 22–3, 27–31
  theories for 31–3
Comecon 154
Cominform 154–5
Commonwealth of Independent States (CIS) 100, 156
Communist Party of the Soviet Union (CPSU) 37
  19th Congress 43
  22nd Congress 56
  27th Congress 47
Conference on Security and Co-operation in Europe (CSCE) 27–8, 70
Conventional Forces in Europe (CFE) Treaty 29, 89, 97, 99, 155–6

Corvalan, Luis 148
Council of Europe 93
Cuba 27, 30, 62, 68, 73–4, 78, 80, 83,
    89–90, 107, 115, 134, 137
  missile crisis 9, 17–18, 26, 56–8, 72,
    123–6, 156
Czechoslovakia 25, 34, 60, 87, 93, 111
  Warsaw Pact invasion, 1968 26–7, 60–1

Daniloff, N. 85
Dashichev, V. 140–4
De Gaulle, General C. 107
Deng Xiaoping 72, 94, 106
Détente 24, 27, 29–30, 60–73, 126–30, 143
Dewey, T. E. 35
Dobrynin, A. 57–8, 80
Dubcek, A. 61
Dulles, John Foster 48–51, 164–5

East Germany *see* German Domocratic
    Republic
Egypt 26, 64–5, 71
Eisenhower, President D. D. 12, 26, 41,
    48–51, 53–4, 58–9, 116, 165
  and military-industrial complex 12
  doctrine 117
El Salvador 74, 115, 118, 131–4
Enlightenment, European 20–1
Estonia 94
Ethiopia 30, 58, 67–8, 78, 83
Eurocommunism 61, 73
European Union 106–7

Fitzwater, M. 88
Ford, President G. 66–70, 73, 165
Ford, Henry 105
France 6, 25–6, 34–5, 38, 47–8, 73, 86, 92,
    106–7
Franco, General F. 6, 56, 73

Gagarin, Yu. 54
Geddis, J. L. 33
Geneva Conference 149–50
Geneva Summit, July 1955 150
Geneva Summit, 19–21 November 1985 28,
    83–5, 150
Gerasimov, G. 84, 165–6
German Democratic Republic (DDR/GDR)
    14, 16, 23, 25–6, 29–30, 34–5, 44,
    52–6, 87, 89, 91–3, 111, 138
  and Berlin Wall 92–3
Germany, Federal Republic (West) 5,
    14–15, 23, 26–7, 34–5, 69, 106,
    111–12
  unification 23, 89, 91–3
Glassboro' 60, 150
Gomulka, W. 47
Gorbachev, M. S. 5, 9, 14, 19, 23–4, 28,
    61, 70, 81–101, 108, 113, 132–3, 166

and attempted coup 100–1
and Bush 87–101
and China 94
and Cold War 9, 24, 27
and eastern Europe 93–4
and Europe 90–1
and foreign policy 24
and German unification 91–3
and Mrs Thatcher 90–1, 146–7
and new political thinking 82–3, 144–5
and Reagan 77, 83–7, 145–6
and Yeltsin 94–6, 99–101
Gordievsky, O. A. 166
Graham, B. 123
Great Britain 20, 25, 34–5, 48, 56, 86, 92,
    106, 111
Greece 23, 25, 41, 73, 111, 117
Grenada 71, 90
Grishin, V. V. 136
Gromyko, A. A. 55, 79–81, 136, 138–9,
    166–7
Grosz, K. 93
Group of Seven (G7) 98
Guatemala 71, 115, 118
Guevara, Che 57–8
Gulf War, 1991 96–9

Halliday, F. 33
Helsinki 91, 96
  Final Act 9, 69–70, 73, 156–7
  Summit, 9 September 1990 150–1
Hitler, A. 14, 109
Ho Chi Minh 47–8
Honecker, E. 93
Hong Kong 106, 108, 117
Howe, G. 90–1
Human rights 27
Hungary 26, 87, 93
  revolution (1956) 47

ICBMs 54, 74, 85
IMF 25, 98
India 25, 48, 114, 116–17
Indo-China 26–7, 38, 47–8, 58–9, 116
Indonesia 25, 48, 106, 114, 117
INF Treaty, 1987 28, 77, 79, 81, 86–7, 90,
    157
Iran 7, 50, 71
Iraq 7, 50–1, 74, 117
Islam 23
Israel 50–1, 60, 64–7, 71, 122–3
Italy 73, 91, 106, 134–5

Japan 3–5, 8, 14, 32, 35, 38–9, 41, 106–8,
    114–15, 117
Jaruzelski, W. 139–40
Jews 35
Johnson, President L. B. 27, 58–60, 67,
    113, 116, 167

KA007 shot down (September 1983) 79
Kazakhstan 7, 99
Kennan, G. 33, 37
Kennedy, President, John F. 26, 54–6,
   58–9, 116, 123–6, 167–8
   Cuban missile crisis 26, 56–8
Kennedy, Robert 57–8
KGB 75, 83–5, 95, 97, 130–6
Khasbulatov, R. 95
Khomeni, A. 71–2
Khrushchev, N. S. 8, 15–16, 19–21, 24, 26,
   30, 44–60, 121, 138, 168
   and Berlin crises (1958–63) 16, 52–6, 111
   and China 10, 121–2
   and Cuban missile crisis 56–8, 123–6
   and Germany 15–16
Kiev 99–101
Kim Il-sung 10, 14, 39
Kirilenko, A. P. 133, 136
Kissinger, H. 6, 18, 61–3, 65–6, 68, 71,
   73–4, 126–30, 168–9
Kohl, H. 91–2
Komsomol 43
Korea 3
   North 7, 10, 80, 107
   South 23, 25–6, 38–42, 44, 48, 74, 106,
   115, 117
Kosygin, A. N. 60, 62, 169
Kravchuk, L. 100
Krenz, E. 91
Kryuchkov, V. 97, 169
Kuwait 96–7, 117

Laos 48, 58, 118, 123
Latin America 4, 11
Latvia 94, 96
Lebanon 80
Lenin, V. I. 3, 19
Leningrad (St Petersburg), affair 7
Leninism 22, 26
Libya 27, 68, 85, 147–8
Ligachev, E. K. 00
Lippmann, W. 23
Lithuania 94, 96, 99
Locke, John 5
Lukyanov, A. I. 98
Lumumba, Patrice 51–2

MacArthur, General D. 30
Macmillan, H. (Lord Stockton) 16, 54
McNamara, R. 56–8
Malaya 48
Malaysia 106, 117
Malenkov, G. M. 7, 43–4, 168
Malinovsky, Marshal R. 56
Malta Summit, 2–3 December 1989 89, 151
Mao Zedong 9, 16, 35–6, 40–1, 49, 60,
   106, 121–3, 170
Marshall Plan 3–4, 20, 23, 33, 35–6, 111

Marx, Karl 4, 6, 18–19
Marxism-Leninism 7–8, 19, 21, 112–13
Matlock, J. F. Jr. 94, 97, 100
Middle East 30, 41–2, 49–51, 60, 64–6, 72,
   75, 110, 112, 117
Mikoyan, A. 57–8, 170
Minsk 100
Mitterrand, F. 90
Moiseev, General M. 97
Molotov, V. M. 8, 14, 43–4
Moscow Summit, 22–26 May 1972 151
Moscow Summit, 27 June–3 July 1974 151
Moscow Summit, 29 May–2 June 1988 28,
   151
Moscow Summit, 30 July–1 August 1991
   151
Moscow Treaty, 12 August 1970 157–8
Mozambique 29, 58, 67, 83
Mutual and Balanced Force Reductions
   (MBFR) 28

Nagy, I. 47
Nasser, President, A. 50–1, 65–6
NATO 8, 25, 35, 41, 52–3, 64, 69, 73–4,
   85, 92, 107, 111–12, 137, 141
Nazarbaev, N. A. 99–101
Netherlands 106
New Political Thinking 82–3
New York Summit, December 1988 151–2
New Zealand 41, 48
Nicaragua 27, 74, 83, 86, 90
Nigeria 115
Nixon, President R. M. 27, 36, 59, 61, 63,
   67, 71, 113, 126, 170–1
   and Brezhnev 61–2, 64–8
   doctrine 117
NSC-68 37–8, 40, 112
Nuclear Non-Proliferation Treaty, 1 July
   1968 158
Ogarkov, Marshal N. 79
Ostpolitik 5, 64

Pakistan 48, 115
Palestine 135–6
Panama 131–2
Paris Summit, May 1960 152
Pasternak, B. L. 171
Pavlov, V. 98
Pelshe, A. 136
Perestroika 87, 91
Persian Gulf 75, 117
Philippines 48
Ponomarev, B. 131–2, 136
Poland 9, 20, 47, 77, 93, 138–9
Pope John Paul II 28
Popov, G. Kh. 98
Portugal 68, 73, 106
Powers, G. 54
Primakov, E. M. 98, 171

Quadaffi, Colonel 85, 147–8

Reagan, President R. 6, 13, 75–81, 113,
    171–2
    and Gorbachev 18, 83–8, 145–6
Reykjavik Summit, 11–12 October 1986
    85–6, 89, 145, 152
Romania 75, 94
Roosevelt, F. D. 109–10
Russia, or Russian Federation 8, 94,
    114
Russian Orthodox Church 87
Ryzhkov, N. I. 96, 172

Sadat, A. 71
Sakharov, A. D. 172
Saudi Arabia 67, 86, 101
Schmidt, H. 64, 74
SDI, strategic defence initiative 13, 79, 84,
    86, 145–6
Second World War (1939–45, for Russia
    and American 1941–5) 24
Shcherbakov, V. I. 98
Shevardnadze, E. A. 82, 86–9, 92–3, 96–9,
    172–3
Shmelev, N. 88
Shultz, G. 80–1, 85–6, 88
Singapore 106, 117
Sino-Soviet Treaty, February 1950 158
Solzhenitsyn, A. 7–8
Somalia 58, 68, 74, 118
South East Asia Treaty Organisation
    (SEATO) 48–9
Spain 73, 106
Sputnik 13, 52
St Petersburg *see* Leningrad
Stakhanovite movement 30, 90–1
Stalin, I. V. 3, 19–20, 24–5, 36, 37–46,
    108, 173
Strategic Arms Limitation Treaty (SALT I),
    1972 27, 63–4, 66, 73, 158
Strategic Arms Limitation Treaty (SALT II),
    1979 70–2, 74–5, 85, 158–9
Strategic Arms Treaty (START), 1991 29,
    77, 81, 88–9, 99, 159–60
Strategic Defence Initiative (Star Wars, SDI)
    28–9, 90
Suslov, M. 136, 173–4
Synman Rhee 39
Syria 64–5

Taiwan 10, 48, 63, 67, 81, 106, 117
Tanzania 115
TASS 36
Tereshkova, V. V. 174
Test Ban Treaty, August 1963 160
Thailand 48, 106, 117
Thatcher, Mrs M. 90–1, 98, 137, 146–7,
    174
Tito, Marshal J. B. 43

Truman, President H. 3–4, 23, 34–42,
    110–11
    doctrine 25, 111, 117
Turkey 8, 23, 41, 50–1, 111, 117

Ukraine 99–101
Ulbricht, W. 14, 53–6
Union of Sovereign States 160
United Nations 47, 51–2, 79, 87, 117
United States,
    and China 10–11, 62–3, 71–2
    and German unification 00
    and security 11–17
U2 incident (1960) 26, 54
Uruguay 131–2
USSR
    and China 5, 10–11
    and culture 17–18
    and security 11–17

Ustinov, Marshal D. 132, 136, 174

Vance, C. 70–4
Vatican 91
Vienna Summit, 3–4 June 1961 152
Vienna Summit, 15–18 June 1979 152
Vietnam 6, 23, 25–6, 48, 58–60, 62, 74–5,
    78, 83, 108, 116, 118, 123, 128, 134,
    137
Vilnius 96
Vladivostok summit, 23–24 November 1974
    152–3
Voznesensky, N. 7
Vyshinsky, A. Ya. 174–5

Warsaw Pact 26–7, 47, 54, 61, 69, 89, 93,
    139, 160–1
Washington Summit, 16–24 June 1974 153
Washington Summit, 7–10 December 1987
    29–32, 87, 153
Washington Summit, 30 May–4 June 1990
    153
Watergate 59, 66
Weizsacker, von R. 91
West Germany *see* Germany, Federal
    Republic
World Bank 24, 25, 107

Yakovlev, A. N. 175
Yavlinsky, G. 95, 98
Yazov, Marshal D. 98, 175–6
Yeltsin, B. N. 87, 176
    and Bush 94
    and Gorbachev 94, 97, 99–101
Yugoslavia 44–6, 52, 117

Zaikov, L. 84
Zakharov, G. 85
Zhou, Enlai 62–3
Zhukov, G. K. 176–7

SEMINAR STUDIES IN HISTORY

General Editors: Clive Emsley & Gordon Martel

The series was founded by Patrick Richardson in 1966. Between 1980 and 1996 Roger Lockyer edited the series before handing over to Clive Emsley (Professor of History at the Open University) and Gordon Martel (Professor of International History at the University of Northern British Columbia, Canada and Senior Research Fellow at De Montfort University).

MEDIEVAL ENGLAND

The Pre-Reformation Church in England 1400–1530 (Second edition)
Christopher Harper-Bill   0 582 28989 0

Lancastrians and Yorkists: The Wars of the Roses
David R. Cook   0 582 35384 X

Family and Kinship in England 1450–1800
Will Coster   0 582 35717 9

TUDOR ENGLAND

Henry VII (Third edition)
Roger Lockyer & Andrew Thrush   0 582 20912 9

Henry VIII (Second edition)
M. D. Palmer   0 582 35437 4

Tudor Rebellions (Fifth edition)
Anthony Fletcher & Diarmaid MacCulloch   0 582 77285 0

The Reign of Mary I (Second edition)
Robert Tittler   0 582 06107 5

Early Tudor Parliaments 1485–1558
Michael A. R. Graves   0 582 03497 3

The English Reformation 1530–1570
W. J. Sheils   0 582 35398 X

Elizabethan Parliaments 1559–1601 (Second edition)
Michael A. R. Graves   0 582 29196 8

England and Europe 1485–1603 (Second edition)
Susan Doran   0 582 28991 2

The Church of England 1570–1640
Andrew Foster   0 582 35574 5

STUART BRITAIN

Social Change and Continuity: England 1550–1750 (Second edition)
Barry Coward   0 582 29442 8

James I (Second edition)
S. J. Houston   0 582 20911 0

The English Civil War 1640–1649
Martyn Bennett   0 582 35392 0

Charles I, 1625–1640
Brian Quintrell   0 582 00354 7

The English Republic 1649–1660 (Second edition)
Toby Barnard   0 582 08003 7

Radical Puritans in England 1550–1660
R. J. Acheson   0 582 35515 X

The Restoration and the England of Charles II (Second edition)
John Miller   0 582 29223 9

The Glorious Revolution (Second edition)
John Miller   0 582 29222 0

EARLY MODERN EUROPE

The Renaissance (Second edition)
Alison Brown   0 582 30781 3

The Emperor Charles V
Martyn Rady   0 582 35475 7

French Renaissance Monarchy: Francis I and Henry II (Second edition)
Robert Knecht   0 582 28707 3

The Protestant Reformation in Europe
Andrew Johnston   0 582 07020 1

The French Wars of Religion 1559–1598 (Second edition)
Robert Knecht   0 582 28533 X

Philip II
Geoffrey Woodward   0 582 07232 8

The Thirty Years' War
Peter Limm   0 582 35373 4

Louis XIV
Peter Campbell   0 582 01770 X

Spain in the Seventeenth Century
Graham Darby   0 582 07234 4

Peter the Great
William Marshall   0 582 00355 5

EUROPE 1789–1918

Britain and the French Revolution
Clive Emsley   0 582 36961 4

Revolution and Terror in France 1789–1795 (Second edition)
D. G. Wright   0 582 00379 2

Napoleon and Europe
D. G. Wright   0 582 35457 9

The Abolition of Serfdom in Russia 1762–1907
David Moon   0 582 29486 X

Nineteenth-Century Russia: Opposition to Autocracy
Derek Offord   0 582 35767 5

The Constitutional Monarchy in France 1814–48
Pamela Pilbeam   0 582 31210 8

The 1848 Revolutions (Second edition)
Peter Jones   0 582 06106 7

The Italian Risorgimento
M. Clark   0 582 00353 9

Bismarck & Germany 1862–1890 (Second edition)
D. G. Williamson   0 582 29321 9

Imperial Germany 1890–1918
Ian Porter, Ian Armour and Roger Lockyer   0 582 03496 5

The Dissolution of the Austro-Hungarian Empire 1867–1918 (Second edition)
John W. Mason   0 582 29466 5

Second Empire and Commune: France 1848–1871 (Second edition)
William H. C. Smith   0 582 28705 7

France 1870–1914 (Second edition)
Robert Gildea   0 582 29221 2

The Scramble for Africa (Second edition)
M. E. Chamberlain   0 582 36881 2

Late Imperial Russia 1890–1917
John F. Hutchinson   0 582 32721 0

The First World War
Stuart Robson   0 582 31556 5

Austria, Prussia and Germany 1806–1871
John Breuilly   0 582 43739 3

Napoleon: Conquest, Reform and Reorganisation
Clive Emsley   0 582 43795 4

The French Revolution 1787–1804
Peter Jones   0 582 77289 3

The Origins of the First World War (Third edition)
Gordon Martel   0 582 43804 7

The Birth of Industrial Britain
Kenneth Morgan   0 582 30270 6

EUROPE SINCE 1918

The Russian Revolution (Second edition)
Anthony Wood   0 582 35559 1

Lenin's Revolution: Russia 1917–1921
David Marples   0 582 31917 X

Stalin and Stalinism (Third edition)
Martin McCauley   0 582 50587 9

The Weimar Republic (Second edition)
John Hiden   0 582 28706 5

The Inter-War Crisis 1919–1939
Richard Overy   0 582 35379 3

Fascism and the Right in Europe 1919–1945
Martin Blinkhorn   0 582 07021 X

Spain's Civil War (Second edition)
Harry Browne   0 582 28988 2

The Third Reich (Third edition)
D. G. Williamson   0 582 20914 5

The Origins of the Second World War (Second edition)
R. J. Overy   0 582 29085 6

The Second World War in Europe
Paul MacKenzie   0 582 32692 3

The French at War 1934–1944
Nicholas Atkin   0 582 36899 5

Anti-Semitism before the Holocaust
Albert S. Lindemann   0 582 36964 9

The Holocaust: The Third Reich and the Jews
David Engel   0 582 32720 2

Germany from Defeat to Partition 1945–1963
D. G. Williamson   0 582 29218 2

Britain and Europe since 1945
Alex May   0 582 30778 3

Eastern Europe 1945–1969: From Stalinism to Stagnation
Ben Fowkes   0 582 32693 1

Eastern Europe since 1970
Bülent Gökay   0 582 32858 6

The Khrushchev Era 1953–1964
Martin McCauley   0 582 27776 0

Hitler and the Rise of the Nazi Party
Frank McDonough   0 582 50606 9

The Soviet Union Under Brezhnev
William Tompson   0 582 32719 9

NINETEENTH-CENTURY BRITAIN

Britain before the Reform Acts: Politics and Society 1815–1832
Eric J. Evans   0 582 00265 6

Parliamentary Reform in Britain c. 1770–1918
Eric J. Evans   0 582 29467 3

Democracy and Reform 1815–1885
D. G. Wright   0 582 31400 3

Poverty and Poor Law Reform in Nineteenth-Century Britain
1834–1914: From Chadwick to Booth
David Englander   0 582 31554 9

The Birth of Industrial Britain: Economic Change 1750–1850
Kenneth Morgan   0 582 29833 4

Chartism (Third edition)
Edward Royle   0 582 29080 5

Peel and the Conservative Party 1830–1850
Paul Adelman   0 582 35557 5

Gladstone, Disraeli and later Victorian Politics (Third edition)
Paul Adelman   0 582 29322 7

Britain and Ireland: From Home Rule to Independence
Jeremy Smith   0 582 30193 9

TWENTIETH-CENTURY BRITAIN

The Rise of the Labour Party 1880–1945 (Third edition)
Paul Adelman   0 582 29210 7

The Conservative Party and British Politics 1902–1951
Stuart Ball   0 582 08002 9

The Decline of the Liberal Party 1910–1931 (Second edition)
Paul Adelman   0 582 27733 7

The British Women's Suffrage Campaign 1866–1928
Harold L. Smith   0 582 29811 3

War & Society in Britain 1899–1948
Rex Pope   0 582 03531 7

The British Economy since 1914: A Study in Decline?
Rex Pope   0 582 30194 7

Unemployment in Britain between the Wars
Stephen Constantine   0 582 35232 0

The Attlee Governments 1945–1951
Kevin Jefferys   0 582 06105 9

The Conservative Governments 1951–1964
Andrew Boxer   0 582 20913 7

Britain under Thatcher
Anthony Seldon and Daniel Collings   0 582 31714 2

Britain and Empire 1880–1945
Dane Kennedy   0 582 41493 8

INTERNATIONAL HISTORY

The Eastern Question 1774–1923 (Second edition)
A. L. Macfie   0 582 29195 X

India 1885–1947: The Unmaking of an Empire
Ian Copland   0 582 38173 8

The United States and the First World War
Jennifer D. Keene   0 582 35620 2

Women and the First World War
Susan R. Grayzel   0 582 41876 3

Anti-Semitism before the Holocaust
Albert S. Lindemann   0 582 36964 9

The Origins of the Cold War 1941–1949 (Third edition)
Martin McCauley   0 582 77284 2

Russia, America and the Cold War 1949–1991 (Second edition)
Martin McCauley   0 582 78482 4

The Arab–Israeli Conflict
Kirsten E. Schulze   0 582 31646 4

The United Nations since 1945: Peacekeeping and the Cold War
Norrie MacQueen   0 582 35673 3

Decolonisation: The British Experience since 1945
Nicholas J. White   0 582 29087 2

The Collapse of the Soviet Union
David R. Marples   0 582 50599 2

WORLD HISTORY

China in Transformation 1900–1949
Colin Mackerras   0 582 31209 4

Japan Faces the World 1925–1952
Mary L. Hanneman   0 582 36898 7

Japan in Transformation 1952–2000
Jeff Kingston   0 582 41875 5

China since 1949
Linda Benson   0 582 35722 5

South Africa: The Rise and Fall of Apartheid
Nancy L. Clark and William H. Worger   0 582 41437 7

US HISTORY

American Abolitionists
Stanley Harrold   0 582 35738 1

The American Civil War 1861–1865
Reid Mitchell   0 582 31973 0

America in the Progressive Era 1890–1914
Lewis L. Gould   0 582 35671 7

The United States and the First World War
Jennifer D. Keene   0 582 35620 2

The Truman Years 1945–1953
Mark S. Byrnes   0 582 32904 3

The Korean War
Steven Hugh Lee   0 582 31988 9

The Origins of the Vietnam War
Fredrik Logevall   0 582 31918 8

The Vietnam War
Mitchell Hall   0 582 32859 4

American Expansionism 1783–1860
Mark S. Joy   0 582 36965 7

The United States and Europe in the Twentieth Century
David Ryan   0 582 30864 X

The Civil Rights Movement
Bruce J. Dierenfield   0 582 35737 3